Foreword

Since the dust settled after the Battle of the Little Bighorn on June 25 and 26, 1876, controversy has been rife. There have been accusations and counter accusations about the role played by Lieutenant Colonel George Armstrong Custer in the battle in which he and 268 of his 7th Cavalry Regiment were killed. Partisanship has been the order of the day, deliberate falsehoods have been told and there have been cover-ups to deflect attention away from mistakes made by other officers, especially Brigadier General Alfred H. Terry, who commanded all the troops, including Custer's Regiment, involved in the theatre of war that led to the Little Bighorn disaster.

Most of the articles included in this book were written as a response to books and articles in which have appeared distortions by some authors intent on pursuing their own agendas, particularly those who seem determined to find any reason, whether supported by facts, to castigate Custer, especially noticeable on the internet in recent times. Other articles will hopefully clarify often asked questions about some of the leading Indian participants, and one will show how even after the passage of time, just how dangerous it is to take at face value, the stories of some of the soldiers involved. Because some of the articles covered different looks at similar subjects, the reader will note that it was necessary to use repetitive areas of evidence. This was unavoidable when ensuring that the contrary points of view were thoroughly disproved.

Finally, as a counterpoint, I have written about the last fight of Custer and his five companies. A view entirely of my own, based on painstaking research, which led me to look at that action in a fresh way. Hopefully it will help to place many of the articles in perspective.

IN CUSTER'S BOOTS

Dedicated to Diane Davis Merkel, who first persuaded me that
I could write about this subject.

IN CUSTER'S BOOTS

The Little Bighorn Campaign:
Revelations, Reconstructions, and Reviews

GORDON RICHARD

CASEMATE

Pennsylvania & Yorkshire

Published in the United States of America and Great Britain in 2026 by
CASEMATE PUBLISHERS
1950 Lawrence Road, Havertown, PA 19083, USA
and
47 Church Street, Barnsley, S70 2AS, UK

Paperback Edition: ISBN 978-1-63624-627-7
Digital Edition: ISBN 978-1-63624-628-4

A CIP record for this book is available from the British Library

The views expressed in this publication are those of the author and do not necessarily reflect the official policy or position of the Department of Defense or the U.S. government. The public release clearance of this publication by the Department of Defense does not imply Department of Defense endorsement or factual accuracy of the material.

Printed and bound in the United Kingdom by CPI Group (UK) Ltd, Croydon, CR0 4YY
Typeset in India by DiTech Publishing Services

For a complete list of Casemate titles, please contact:

CASEMATE PUBLISHERS (US)
Telephone (610) 853-9131
Fax (610) 853-9146
Email: casemate@casematepublishers.com
www.casematepublishers.com

CASEMATE PUBLISHERS (UK)
Telephone (0)1226 734350
Email: casemate@casemateuk.com
www.casemateuk.com

Cover images: (front) George Armstrong Custer astride a horse, circa 1870. (National Park Service, Little Bighorn Battlefield National Monument); (back) Marker where Lieutenant Colonel George Armstrong Custer fell at the Battle of the Little Bighorn, June 25, 1876. (Bobbyv71/Wikimedia Commons, CC BY-SA 4.0)

The Publisher's authorised representative in the EU for product safety is Authorised Rep Compliance Ltd., Ground Floor, 71 Lower Baggot Street, Dublin D02 P593, Ireland.
www.arccompliance.com

Contents

CHAPTER I

An Alternative View of the Fight of the Custer Battalions

From the late nineteenth and early twentieth centuries, a standard version of the Battle of the Little Bighorn began to appear, fueled by the research of Walter Camp who, using comments made by Lieutenant Edward Maguire at the Reno Court of Inquiry of 1879, firmly believed that Lieutenant Colonel Custer and his immediate command had been driven back from Ford B (Medicine Tail Coulee) to where it had been annihilated. My research led to this chapter, which demonstrates that it makes no sense for Custer not to go south to rejoin the other elements of his regiment, but instead, if under attack at Ford B, to turn further north, away from help. This chapter offers readers the opportunity to reconsider what happened at the battle.

> I guess we'll get through with them in one day.
> LIEUTENANT COLONEL GEORGE ARMSTRONG CUSTER, MORNING OF JUNE 25, 1876

The Battle of the Little Bighorn or Custer's Last Stand, an engagement between Lakota Sioux and Cheyenne warriors with the U.S. Army 7th Cavalry Regiment commanded by Lieutenant Colonel George Armstrong Custer, was fought on June 25–26, 1876, on land in Montana, which would become the Crow Indian Agency.

The outcome has fascinated people for almost 150 years, because Custer and the 209 men in his immediate command were all killed by the Indian warriors. That outcome shocked America at the time and has had historians and others seeking the answer as to why ever since. The many books about the subject have analyzed every aspect of that 1876 military campaign ad nauseam but the focus has naturally been on how did five companies of an elite cavalry regiment perish at the hands of half-naked, comparatively poorly armed native warriors?

For the purposes of my following analysis, I will focus solely on the actions involving Custer's command, using a scenario not hitherto considered. The journey preceding it, the discovery of the Indian camp on the morning of June 25 from a promontory called The Crow's Nest, the disposition of the pack train and the other two battalions of three companies each, commanded by Major Marcus A. Reno and Captain Frederick Benteen respectively, I will not recount, though certain elements will be referenced.

Very often, the focus of attention on what happened to the Custer battalions after they reached Medicine Tail Coulee overlooks the equally important question of what their objective was in being there in the first place.

Much criticism is leveled at Lieutenant Colonel Custer for splitting his forces in the face of the warrior numbers that were present, but I do not believe such criticism is justified.

It would be justified in only two circumstances. First, if he had not expected the Indian village to flee and scatter as Indians usually did when faced with a military force. This fear had been the major concern of the army command during the 1876 summer campaign. That the Indians had recently fought Brigadier General George Crook's Wyoming Column to a standstill eight days earlier at the Battle of the Rosebud, causing Crook to retreat, was not known to Custer and would not be known to his Commanding Officer Brigadier General Alfred H. Terry until July. Custer therefore had no inkling that his opponents had an entirely different mindset than usual and could not have discovered it in any other way than when his command was attacked. Criticism, in this respect, can only be with hindsight wisdom.

Second, criticism would be acceptable if the deployments he made were haphazard and devoid of any known military strategy. If that had been the case, separating his command could only be seen as impulsive, because then he would have been reckless in exposing the separated elements to unnecessary risk.

But on June 25, 1876, Custer had been a successful cavalry commander for over ten years and did not abruptly forget what he had learned during that time. He once said, "It requires no extensive knowledge to inform me what is my duty to my country, my command … First be sure you're right, then go ahead! I ask myself, 'Is it right?' Satisfied that it is so, I let nothing swerve me from my purpose."[1] It is unlikely then that Custer would have dispersed his forces other than with what he thought were sound military reasons at the time.

Yet at the Reno Court of Inquiry at Chicago in January 1879, both his second-in-command, Major Marcus A. Reno and Senior Captain Frederick W. Benteen denied that any strategy at all existed. Captain Benteen testified: a) "There was no plan at all" and b) "If there had been any plan of battle, enough of that plan would have been communicated to me so that I would have known what to do under certain circumstances. Not having done that I do not believe there was any plan."[2] Whilst Major Reno said: a) "There was no plan communicated to us if one existed. The subordinate commanders did not know of it," and b) "I might say there that I do not think there was any plan."[3] I believe Custer's subordinates were self-serving, as the suggested lack of a plan deflected attention away from their own shortcomings on the day of the battle.

When Custer looked out over the Little Bighorn valley for a second time from either the Crow's Nest or Varnum's Lookout that morning, those with him included the frontiersman and Crow interpreter Mitch Boyer plus some Crow scouts, who were not only looking into a valley that was part of their homeland, but who had also camped in the area where the great Indian village was sited. Being made aware of that, Custer would not have spurned the chance to obtain all the information he could from them about the terrain from there to the Indian camps in preparation for his initial plan to approach the village at dawn the next morning. Returning to the command however, he was informed that Indians, rifling a lost hard-tack box, had seen the command. Believing that the village would scatter once warned, he decided on an immediate offensive. First Lieutenant Edward S. Godfrey confirms this, reporting Custer as saying, "At all events our presence has been discovered ... that we would march at once to attack the village ..."[4] Also, Second Lieutenant Winfield S. Edgerly, "... as our presence had been discovered it would be necessary to attack at once ...,"[5] and courier George Herendeen when Custer tells him, "... besides they have discovered us ... The only thing to do is to push ahead and attack the camp as soon as possible,"[6] and finally, Major Reno, "... we could not surprise them and it was determined to move at once to the attack."[7]

Custer was therefore primed to move aggressively against the camps and his subordinates were fully aware of that, so what tactics did he have in mind? The possibilities open to him would be dictated by what the Indians did. Whilst they were expected to flee and scatter, their sheer numbers could well mean that much of the village could be intact when he reached it and the warriors would then be forced to put up some resistance to enable their families to escape. That the latter scenario was probable had been given substance by the Crow Scout, Hairy Moccasin. In June 1916, in an interview he said, "I was sent ahead [from the Crow's Nest]. Custer said, 'You go and find that village.' I went to a butte at the head of Reno Creek, from where I could see the village. I reported the camp to Custer. He asked if any were running about away from the camp. I said 'No.' We then came on down to the forks of Reno Creek. When we stopped there to divide up I could hear the Indians in camp shouting and whooping."[8]

The usual tactic against a standing village was envelopment, whereby a holding force would engage the enemy while other parts of the command swung to the left or right to hit him in the rear or on the flank. The late Major Jay D. Smith described such tactics in two articles he authored. In one, citing military strategist Carl Von Clausewitz as his basis, he says, "Custer used an envelopment while employing the principles of offense, maneuver, and surprise,"[9] and in the other, "These were some of the best professional soldiers in the world. A few words or gestures were all that were needed to provide all the information required for a complete battle. Objectives and unit tactics were understood by all. Often a complete battle plan consisted only of stating which units would go where."[10] Viewed in this light, the deployment of the battalions commanded by Reno and Benteen can be seen to fit the requirements of an envelopment plan which had, of course, been used at the Washita and the

Powder River fights, so it was widely known. There are corroborations that it was also to be used at the Little Big Horn from testimony and elsewhere.

At the Inquiry, Sergeant Edward Davern, Reno's orderly at the battle, testified that First Lieutenant William W. Cooke, Custer's Adjutant, said to Reno, "Girard comes back and reports the Indian village three miles ahead and moving. The General directs you to take your three companies and drive everything before you."[11] In answer to the question, "Was anything else said?" Davern replied, "Yes, sir; Colonel Benteen will be on your left and will have the same instructions."[12] Second Lieutenant Edgerly, in his papers, says, "Major Reno was ordered to 'march straight to the village, attack any Indians you may meet, and you will be supported.' Captain Benteen was ordered to 'move to the left at an angle of about forty-five degrees from Reno's direction, attack any Indians he might meet, and he would be supported.'"[13] Plus we have an officer with Brigadier General George Crook's Wyoming Column in 1876, Major Henry R. Lemly, asserting that Second Lieutenant George D. Wallace, Custer's Engineering Officer, told him that when Custer separated from Reno his plan was to march to the lower end of the village, crossing at one of the lower fords, and to make his attack there. His attack was to be the signal for Reno, just as soon as the latter saw or heard him, to press forward in the reasonable expectation that the combined pressure would stampede the Indians out of their villages.[14]

Perhaps the most significant evidence in terms of Benteen's intended role, is Second Lieutenant Charles A. Varnum's letter of August 1876 to his parents saying, "Just then Colonel Benteen and three companies came in from a trip they had endeavored to make to the rear of the of the village …"[15] which was endorsed by part of Captain Myles Moylan's testimony when he was questioned regarding support for Reno:

> Q. But at the time you were moving down this bottom and engaged in the timber and in going back to the top of the hill, was there any belief as to where the balance of the command was? What was your opinion?
> A. My opinion was that it was on the rear of our trail and was coming to our assistance.
> Q. And Captain Benteen's command?
> A. That I do not know so much about. It passed away to the left and I thought might come in through the foothills.[16]

It is possible then that Benteen was meant to come to the village up the west bank of the river, possibly via the South Fork of Reno Creek, as the entry to the Little Bighorn River valley course was almost certainly too far for Custer to have wanted him separated from the rest of the command.

Testimony which promotes the lack of an attack strategy is therefore false, contradicted by the weight of evidence demonstrating that Custer had planned the envelopment, but were the orders given by Custer to his senior subordinates as senseless as Benteen claimed? The only order Reno received was to attack the village and he would be supported by the whole outfit. His command was supposed to be Custer's holding force, but it didn't hold for long. Benteen's column was ordered to the left to eventually find its way to the west of the river, probably via the South Fork of Reno Creek initially, to block anyone from the camps fleeing that way and with the ultimate task of attacking the village from the south wherever he saw fit. By his own admission, Benteen disobeyed his orders by returning to the main trail instead of crossing one more hill into the valley of the South Fork. Both officers therefore had ample reason to avoid the truth at the Court of Inquiry and we need to look at what Custer was trying to achieve with his immediate command in the light of what he expected his subordinates to be doing.

In his testimony at the Court of Inquiry Major Reno stated, "I moved forward in accordance with the orders received from Lieutenant Cooke to the head of the column. Soon after that Lieutenant Cooke came to me and said, 'General Custer directs you to take as rapid a gait as you think prudent, and charge the village afterwards, and you will be supported by the whole outfit.'" Reno also said, "From the manner I received the order I could not conceive of any other manner of being supported except from the rear." Yet in his report of July 5, 1876, he wrote, "After traveling over his trail, it is evident to me that Custer intended to support me by moving further down the stream and attacking the village in the flank ..."[17] The latter comment being made of course, in all rationality, without any idea that he would have to justify his actions at a Court of Inquiry. The inference he made in his testimony is that Custer was expected to follow him across the Little Bighorn but changed his mind and turned to the north. His report, however, accurately describes Custer's adherence to the envelopment plan, a plan that would have been known to both Reno and Benteen.

Custer's turn to the north was therefore pre-determined by the tactics Reno describes in his report and not for any other reason. Sergeant Daniel A. Knipe suggested that the move was because he personally saw some Indians on the bluffs, but Trumpeter John Martin, who was also close to Custer, did not see them, so Knipe's tendency to embroider his own role appears to have come into play here. Some writers have suggested that Ree Interpreter Fred Gerard's news that the Indians were coming out to meet Reno prompted Custer to change his mind and move north instead of following Reno to attack the village. That theory is based on the idea that the warriors would stall the attack until their families had safely fled to the north then flee themselves, the very scenario that was the biggest worry of all the military commanders. That might hold true if Custer had not expected such a move from the warriors, but in fact it was their standard behavior in such circumstances, as First Lieutenant Edward S. Godfrey described, "If the advance to the attack be made in daylight it is next to impossible that a near approach can be made without discovery. In all our previous experiences, when the immediate presence of the troops was once known to them, the warriors swarmed to the attack, and resorted to all kinds of ruses to mislead the troops, to delay the advance toward their camp or village, while the squaws and children secured what personal effects

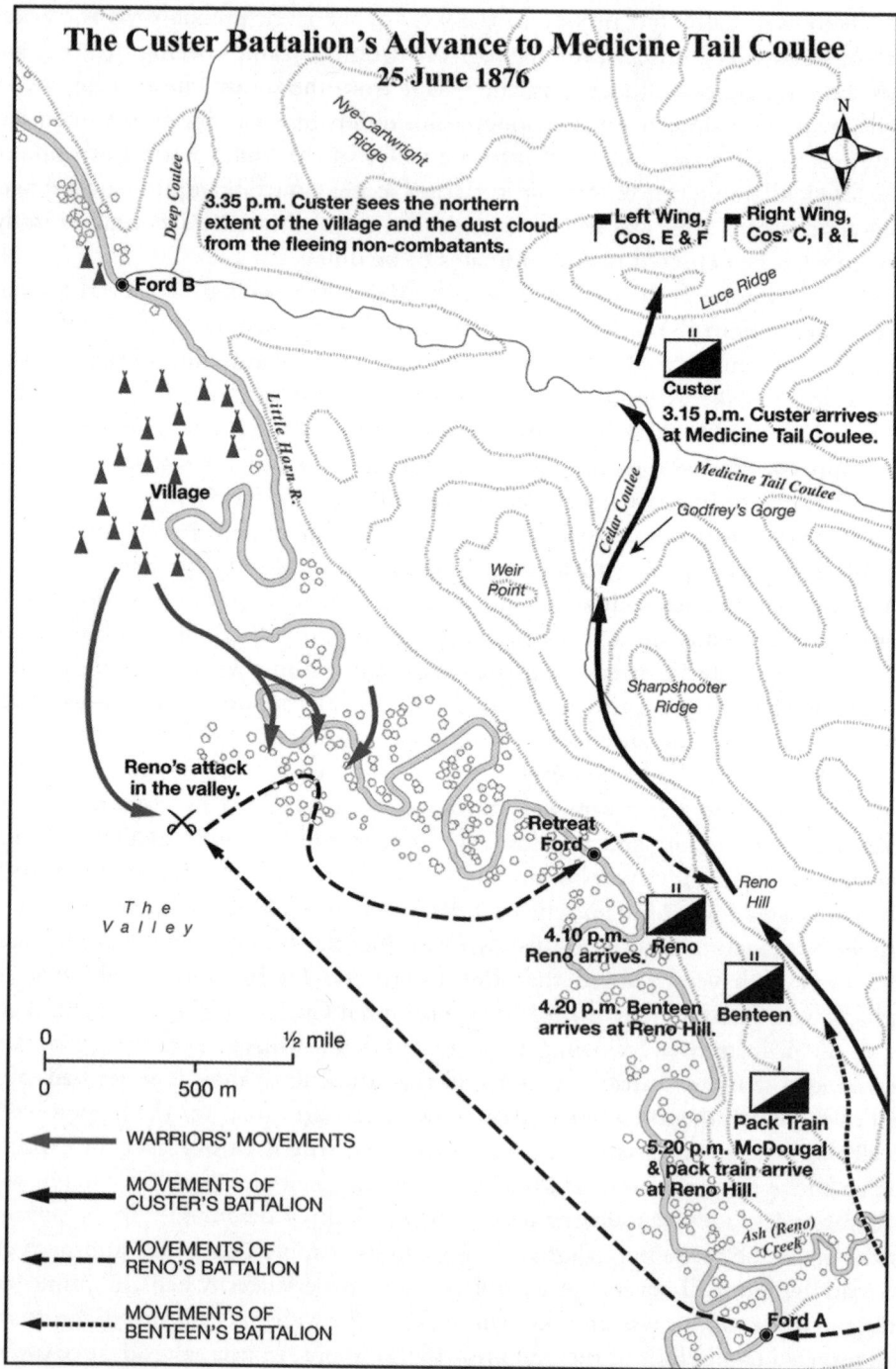

The Custer Battalion's Advance to Medicine Tail Coulee
25 June 1876

3.35 p.m. Custer sees the northern extent of the village and the dust cloud from the fleeing non-combatants.

Ford B

Nye-Cartwright Ridge

Deep Coulee

Little Horn R.

Village

Left Wing, Cos. E & F

Right Wing, Cos. C, I & L

Luce Ridge

Custer

3.15 p.m. Custer arrives at Medicine Tail Coulee.

Cedar Coulee

Medicine Tail Coulee

Godfrey's Gorge

Weir Point

Sharpshooter Ridge

Reno's attack in the valley.

The Valley

Retreat Ford

Reno Hill

4.10 p.m. Reno arrives.

Reno

4.20 p.m. Benteen arrives at Reno Hill.

Benteen

Pack Train

5.20 p.m. McDougal & pack train arrive at Reno Hill.

Ash (Reno) Creek

Ford A

0 — ½ mile
0 — 500 m

→ WARRIORS' MOVEMENTS

← MOVEMENTS OF CUSTER'S BATTALION

←--- MOVEMENTS OF RENO'S BATTALION

←····· MOVEMENTS OF BENTEEN'S BATTALION

The Custer battalions advance to Medicine Tail Coulee. (Gordon Harper, *Fights on the Little Horn*, 2014) they could, drove off the pony herd, and by flight put themselves beyond danger, and then scattering made successful pursuit next to impossible."[18]

Being aware of this meant Custer was not only unsurprised by Gerard's news, but also delighted, because at that point the Indians were behaving as he expected them to. His turn to the north was therefore in response to what he had anticipated would happen and he wanted to get to the northern end of the village to attack and crush the warriors between his battalions and those of Reno and Benteen. Initially, of course, his movement was in the order of a reconnaissance-in-force, or probably more accurately, a movement-to-contact, much like what would nowadays be called a "search and destroy" mission.

There is a great deal of argument about the route he took to get to Medicine Tail Coulee, but the details of that move are not that germane to the outcome of the battle, except for those interested in timings and where Custer was seen on the bluffs by some of Reno's men. For my purposes it suffices to say that after watering his horses for ten minutes in a small creek just off the North Fork of Reno Creek, as testified to by Trumpeter Martini,[19] Custer took his five companies north along the bluffs that led past a hill, now known as Reno Hill, where the commands of both Reno and Benteen became entrenched sometime later, to a rise called Sharpshooter's Ridge, stopping on or more likely near the latter feature to view Reno's force in the valley. Having seen that the Major had deployed a skirmish line and being satisfied that his holding force was in place, Custer moved on, but not before sending Knipe off to the pack train and to go to Benteen, if he saw that officer. It was about 3 p.m. and looking down into the valley, Custer could not only see Reno's skirmish line, but also that there were no Indians fleeing south or coming up from the south behind the Major. That told Custer that Benteen had not run into any Indians on his left oblique and as he could see no sign of Benteen's command in the valley. It also told him that Benteen, against his orders, must have swung back to the main trail. In fact, Benteen was nearing a feature called the Lone Tepee at that time. As Knipe left on his mission, Custer headed for Medicine Tail Coulee, entering it either by Cedar Coulee or by what came to be known as Godfrey's Gorge.[20]

One of the constant questions in this sequence of events is what happened to the Crow scouts and Boyer. Two of the Crows followed Reno into the valley by misunderstanding what Custer, via Boyer, asked them to do. The four others went with Boyer to the ridges above the river while Custer took a different route to the bluffs and arrived there ahead of the scouts, as confirmed by Goes Ahead.[21] The scouts kept moving however, passing Custer's command as he looked into the valley and, at his behest,[22] they rode up a promontory known later as Weir Point, after Captain Thomas B. Weir of D company, who went there to try and locate Custer's command. At that juncture, Hairy Moccasin claimed that the young Crow scout Curley was no longer with them.[23] From evidence supplied by Crow interpreter Russell White Bear to archaeologist and author Fred Dustin, it is likely that Curley remained with

Custer's men.[24] While the Crows were on Weir Point the five companies, apparently without Curley, went with Custer west of Sharpshooters Ridge and east of Weir Point, heading toward Medicine Tail Coulee via Godfrey's Gorge. This is where the Crow scouts and Boyer played a definitive role in the events of that day. In 1909, Goes Ahead told Walter Camp that he and two fellow Crows did not see Custer "after he turned down the coulee to the right."[25] As they were on Weir Point, the Custer battalions would have been in clear sight if they had used Cedar Coulee, but as Boyer and the three Crows had passed Custer near Sharpshooter's Ridge, Boyer would have pointed out that Godfrey's Gorge was the easiest route into Medicine Tail Coulee, not steep, narrow and shrub lined like Cedar Coulee. Goes Ahead also told author and historical researcher Walter Mason Camp:

> As to whether Curley left us and went back, I decline to answer. I prefer that White Man [Runs Him] or Hairy Moccasin answer this question …. We saw Reno's battle and went back south along bluff and met Benteen's command. We three Crows did not see Custer after he turned down the coulee to right. Did not see Custer fight. Did not see beginning of it or any part of it. Does not know whether Custer went to river. We turned back too early to see where Custer went north of Dry Creek (Medicine Tail Coulee).[26]

This statement by Goes Ahead makes it clear that he, Hairy Moccasin and White Man Runs Him left Weir Point, moved a short distance north, where they fired on the Indian village before returning south, probably on the advice of Boyer. What they saw on the way is best summed up in the interview that White Man Runs Him had with Major General Hugh L. Scott at the mouth of Custer Creek or Medicine Tail Creek, four miles from Reno's 1876 entrenchment:

> Q. How far down did Custer go?
> A. Right down to the river.
> Q. How far did they come?
> A. They came down the ravine to the river here and started back.
> Q. What did the scouts do then? Where was Mitch Boyer?
> A. He was on that point there.
> Q. Where was Curley?
> A. He was back on the ridge.
> Q. Where did you go then?
> A. I went back.
> Q. Why?
> A. Mitch Boyer said, "You go back; I am going down to Custer."
> Q. Did you see Reno go to the bluffs then?
> A. No. I saw him fighting across the river but didn't know he had retreated back to the bluffs.
> Q. When Custer came down here could he hear the shooting over there?
> A. Didn't pay much attention; everybody around us was shooting and no one could tell the place where most of the firing was done.[27]

As Boyer was near them when they returned south, it makes it clear that he too could not have seen Reno's retreat, so Custer could not have learned of it from him. We know that on their way south the three Crows met Benteen, as stated by

Goes Ahead. They then spent some time on Reno Hill with the rest of the regiment, before making their way to safety during the evening of June 26, and a fortuitous meeting with Colonel John Gibbon's column. First Lieutenant James H. Bradley, Gibbon's Chief of Scouts, described that meeting in his journal:

> I took the trail of the four supposed Sioux in the hope of catching them in the Big Horn valley, toward which the trail led and where we thought they might have camped, as there was no convenient way of leaving the valley into which they had gone except that by which they had entered it. At the distance of less than two miles the trail struck the river, and we found that they had there crossed, leaving behind a horse and several articles of personal equipment, indicating that they had fled in great haste. An examination of the articles disclosed to our great surprise that they belonged to some of the Crows whom I had furnished to General Custer at the mouth of the Rosebud, which rendered it probable that the supposed Sioux were some of our own scouts who had for some reason left Custer's command and were returning to the Crow agency.[28]

What happened to Curley is not so clear because of the differing stories he told during the years following the battle, but there are some acceptable verifications, as author Dr. Thomas B. Marquis showed in his 1934 booklet, *Curly, The Crow* in which Marquis used quotes by Scout Thomas LeForge from the Marquis book, *Memoirs of a White Crow Indian.*

In that book, LeForge tells of the interview wherein he interpreted while First Lieutenant Bradley made notes of Curley's story. During the narrative, the young Crow repeatedly corrected an apparent impression that he had been in the fight. He declared clearly that he had not been in it. He was not present when the Custer engagement opened, but was on a hill in the background and saw its beginning. After a short time, he went farther away, to another hill, and watched the struggle for a while. He saw some loose horses running away over the hills, and he captured two of them. He started then to go entirely away from the scene. But the captive horses impeded his movements, so he let them loose and took himself on his own pony completely out of probabilities of any of the hostile Indians catching him.[29]

Marquis also quoted from *The Arikara Narrative* in which Red Star, an Arikara Indian who was one of the scouts under Varnum, says he saw "Curly and Black Fox, an Arikara, with Custer at the time Custer looked from the bluffs bordering the east bank of the river just as the Reno men were going into their charge toward the Indian camps."[30] Goes Ahead also saw them:

> Curley and Black Fox remained together, or they got together soon afterward up the river, where Reno's soldiers had crossed for their first approach to the camps. Then Curley proposed that he would take Black Fox on the back trail of the soldiers to a place where he knew they had left some hardtack. The two went toward the present Busby. Curley then said he was going to his home agency and he left the company of the Arikara. Darkness had come and the parting was 10 to 12 miles east of the battle scene.[31]

When Black Fox reached the mouth of the Rosebud, he met the older scouts already there. They came out to meet him; he came on slowly. In answer to their queries, he said he and Curley got together near Reno ford. Curley told Black Fox he would take him back to show him where the soldiers left some hard tack. So, Curley took Black Fox to the flat below the hills overlooking the present town of Busby north side. Curley told Black Fox that for his part he was going home.[32]

That is as near as we can get to the truth about Curley's participation, for he was a 17-year-old youth at the time of the battle and it would be surprising if he had not been affected by the amount of attention he received, from newspapermen wanting to hear his story. Loaded questions and distorted answers did not help his cause, but it is likely he began to believe his own publicity and embellish it rather than stick to the simple facts.

Boyer appears to have ridden north from Weir Point, advised Curley to go home, and from there found his way into Medicine Tail Coulee via a different route to Custer. He met up with the command as they halted briefly in the coulee, a halt verified by the Miniconjou Standing Bear.[33] Not having seen Reno's retreat, Boyer had nothing negative to report to Custer, which left the latter free to follow his original envelopment plan.

That he was expecting Benteen to join in the attack at the earliest opportunity is evidenced by the two messages he sent to that officer. Knipe, if indeed he was a messenger, carried the first and said in his 1903 interview, "Custer and his troops were within about one-half mile to the east side of the Indian camps when I received the following messages from Captain Thomas Custer, brother of the General: 'Go to Captain McDougall. Tell him to bring pack train straight across the country. If any packs come loose, cut them [off] and come on quick—a big Indian camp. If [italics mine] you see Captain Benteen, tell him to come quick—a big Indian camp.'"[34]

When he sent Trumpeter Martin to Benteen from the top of Medicine Tail Coulee, Lieutenant Colonel Custer already knew from his young brother Boston, who had passed Benteen on his way back to his brother, that Benteen's command had not reached the west bank of the river, so the famous "Come on" message was surely exhorting Benteen to hurry and join in the action at the closest point possible. Custer believed Reno was still engaged as the holding force and, as Benteen was over an hour away—too long a time for Custer to wait around for him—Custer needed to find a point from which he could launch an attack at the north of the village while Reno and Benteen engaged warriors to the south.

At the core of most theories is a fascination with what, if anything, happened at Medicine Tail Ford or Ford B. The trouble is, that fascination soon morphed into an obsession and so much attention has been focused on the "ifs," "buts" and "maybes" of Ford B that almost every piece of evidence about Custer being near the river has been taken as a reference to that ford. Unfortunately, Walter Camp reinforced that idea by his insistence that there had been action at that ford. He got that notion from the testimony of Colonel Gibbon's Engineering Officer, First Lieutenant Edward Maguire commenting on his map at the Reno Court of Inquiry:

"The ground was all cut up by hoofs. My theory was that General Custer went to the ford and was met there and driven back and they separated into two bodies to concentrate on the hill at 'E' and I put those lines in as my idea of the route they took."[35] Both Maguire and Camp were wrong.

There is no concrete evidence to support any action at that ford, but the last person to see the command might have provided some helpful information. That was Trumpeter Martin, and although he told differing stories over the years, in his 1908 account to Camp he stated that on his way to deliver Custer's message to Benteen, when he got to the top of the ridge, he saw "Indians charging like a swarm of bees towards the ford waving buffalo hides. At the same time, he saw Custer retreating up the open country in the direction of the battlefield."[36] If true, by putting those two comments together we can surmise that the Indians in question were not armed with guns or there would have been no need for the buffalo hides to deter the soldiers and that being the case, if Custer fell back, it was not because he was driven away by a superior force. There is a simple explanation for his actions, and it has to do with what Custer could see, or rather what he could not see, as he paused in Medicine Tail Coulee. If he was looking to attack across Ford B he would have needed to be sure that it represented the northern extent of the village so that he would not find warriors behind him if he did so. What could he see?

The camp across from that ford is generally assumed to be that of the Cheyenne but Wooden Leg describes their location on the day of the battle thus, "We were near the mouth of a small creek flowing from the southwestward into the river. Across the river east of us and a little upstream from us was a broad coulee, or little valley, having now the name Medicine Tail coulee."[37] The small creek Wooden Leg mentions is probably Onion Creek, which does come in from the southwest to join the river, so the northern limit of the Cheyenne camp was about one mile downstream of Ford B, and it is possible that the entire Cheyenne camp was hidden from Custer by the timber along the river bank. To try to see more, Custer rode a short distance north to the height of Luce Ridge. The movement across Medicine Tail Coulee is described by some Indian accounts. The Oglala He Dog said, "Custer was coming from the north, across the dry creek"[38] and "... saw other soldiers coming on the big hill right over east. They kept right on down the river and crossed Medicine Tail Coulee and onto a little rise."[39] Young Little Wolf, a Northern Cheyenne, stated that, "When Custer was first seen he was opposite Ford B in Medicine Tail Coulee, traveling parallel with river, soldiers deployed and seemingly trying to circle the camp. After he passed Medicine Tail Coulee, Indians followed him."[40]

From Luce Ridge, Custer could see to the north a huge dust cloud and people running, which he deduced must be the noncombatants trying to escape. Still unable to see the full extent of the village but alerted by Boyer to fords further north, Custer took the Left Wing comprising Companies E and F with his Headquarters Group, in that direction. The Right Wing formed by I, L and C Companies and commanded by Captain Myles W. Keogh, was left deployed on Luce, and possibly Butler Ridges, menacing Ford B. It had been agreed that if anything was to go wrong, the best military option would be for both wings to reunite on the high ground along what would come to be known as Battle Ridge, where their combined longer-range firepower, used in a disciplined way, would keep the warriors at a distance and enable Custer to move south to organize a junction with Reno and Benteen.

It is my opinion that, at about 3:50 p.m. as he came down towards the river from Last Stand Hill, Custer's plan was to attack across the nearest available northern ford from which he could see the end of the village, then sweep south, driving before him the little resistance he anticipated meeting, being joined by Keogh as Ford B was reached, and with their combined forces subsequently routing an enemy caught between them and the Reno/Benteen commands. The idea that he would attack with only two companies and his Headquarters Group has been decried by many as militarily rash in the light of the Indian numbers, but what seems to get forgotten is that Custer believed that the main warrior force had gone to meet Reno, so he was not expecting much resistance. In any event, his part of the plan failed and there are various Indian accounts that perhaps explain why, although it is necessary to understand that Indian accounts do not allow for the time lapse between one event and the next and their orientation depends on where they were actually standing. Using a combination of the accounts however, proves beyond doubt that Custer went to the northern fords.

The Cheyenne warrior Wooden Leg saw:

> The soldiers had come along a high ridge about two miles east from the Cheyenne camp. They had gone on past us and then swerved off the high ridge to the lower ridge where most of them afterward were killed."[41] Cheyenne sub chief Two Moon said, "Custer marched up from behind the ridge on which his monument now stands, and deployed his soldiers along the entire line of the ridge. They rode over beyond where the monument stands down into the valley until we could not see them."[42]

The Cheyenne tribal historian, John Stands In Timber, related that, knowing soldiers could be in the area, Cheyenne warriors Wolf Tooth and Big Foot, plus about fifty other young men, succeeded in slipping through the camp police and crossing the river under cover. They got together below Custer Creek north of the village and were about halfway up a wooded hill there when they heard someone shouting. When they drew near, the rider began talking in Sioux. Big Foot could understand it. "The soldiers had already ridden down toward the village. Then Wolf Tooth's party raced back up Custer Creek again to where they could follow one of the ridges to the top, and when they got there, they saw the last few soldiers going down out of sight toward the river."[43] In view of John Stands In Timber's statements that follow,

I believe that this was Custer's five companies beginning their short journey down Medicine Tail Coulee.

As the soldiers disappeared, Wolf Tooth's band split up. Some followed the soldiers, and the rest went on around a point to cut them off. They caught up there with some that were still going down and came around them on both sides. "The soldiers started shooting. It was the first skirmish of the battle, and it did not last very long. The Indians said they did not try to go in close. After some shooting both bunches of Indians retreated to the hills, and the soldiers crossed the south end of the ridge where the monument now stands."[44] The soldiers who crossed below the present monument site were, I believe, Custer's Left Wing on its way to the northern fords from Medicine Tail but they were certainly not in that coulee as the monument is quite a bit north of that. "The soldiers followed the ridge down to the present cemetery site. Then this bunch of 40–50 Indians came out by the monument and started shooting down on them again. But they were moving on down toward the river, across from the Cheyenne camp. Some of the warriors there had come across, and they began firing at the soldiers from the brush in the river bottom. This made the soldiers turn north, but they went back in the direction they had come from, and stopped when they got to the cemetery site. And they waited there a long time—twenty minutes or more."[45]

Having moved north, the Left Wing was then across from the Cheyenne camp which, as Wooden Leg's account has shown, was not opposite Ford B. Also, if they went back in the direction they had come from and stopped at the current cemetery site, again, they could not have been in Medicine Tail.

Is there any corroboration that some warriors shot at the soldiers from the river bottom? John Stands In Timber says, "Hanging Wolf was one of the warriors who crossed the river and shot from the brush when Custer came to the bottom. He said they hit one horse down there, and it bucked off a soldier, but the rest took him along when they retreated north."[46] Also, parts of the interviews with some Cheyennes in 1908 by the anthropologist and historian George Bird Grinnell were summarized by Father P. J. Powell in *People of the Sacred Mountain* thus, "Bobtail Horse, Calf, Roan Bear, and two or three other men who had joined them pulled up close to the river. There, under cover of a low ridge, they opened fire on the advancing soldiers."[47] In his interview, the Cheyenne Brave Wolf also told Grinnell that he had first seen these soldiers riding down along the side of a little dry creek.[48] That description does not accord with Wooden Leg's view of Medicine Tail Coulee as a broad coulee, or little valley, so Brave Wolf was describing a different place, almost certainly the route that Wolf Tooth said the soldiers took down to the river. The "little dry creek" mentioned by Brave Wolf and others, could well be Cemetery Ravine.

Grinnell interviewed several Northern Cheyenne warriors between 1892 and 1925 and their accounts, which build on those of Wolf Tooth and Brave Wolf, appear in Richard G. Hardorff's book, *Cheyenne Memories of the Custer Fight.* Their recollections follow.

American Horse:

> … a man calling out that the troops were attacking the lower end of the village. Then they all rushed down below and saw Custer coming down the hill and almost at the river. I was one of the first to meet the troops and the Indians and the soldiers reached the flat about the same time. When Custer saw them coming, he was down on the river bottom at the river's bank. The troops fought in line of battle, and they fought there for some little time. Then the troops gave way and were driven up the hill. The troops fought on horseback all the way up the hill.[49]

This narrative coincides with the Wolf Tooth description in three ways. First, Custer is going downhill and is nearly at the river, second, the troops are fighting and third, the troops are then being driven up hill on horseback.

Brave Wolf:

> Then we heard the shooting below, and all rushed down the river. When I got to the Cheyenne camp, the fighting had been going on for some time. The soldiers were right down close to the stream, but none were on this side. Just as I got there, the soldiers began to retreat up the narrow gulch … They still held their line of battle and kept fighting and falling from their horses … nearly up to where the monument now stands.[50]

Now we have four more points of coincidence with Wolf Tooth and three with American Horse. As with Wolf Tooth, the action is at the Cheyenne camp, then the troops were down close to the river, they then retreated on horseback, agreeing with Wolf Tooth. who did not say they dismounted. Brave Wolf agrees with American Horse that the troops were right near the river that they fought, then retreated to the monument site on horseback. There is also one other very important piece of information, the comment that, "the soldiers began to retreat up the narrow gulch …" because again, compared with Wooden Leg's description of Medicine Tail, it is plain that Brave Wolf was not talking about that place. White Bull (Ice) said, "Then word was brought that Custer was coming, and the Indians all began to go back to fight Custer. Custer rode down to the river bank and formed a line of battle and to charge. But he then stopped and fell back up the hill."[51] White Bull's recollection is basic, but his account agrees with the others.

Soldier Wolf said:

> When these women were crossing the river and some were going to the hills, they discovered more troops coming. This was the Custer party … someone rode to where the men were fighting Reno and told them that more soldiers were coming below. Then all the men rushed down the creek again to where the women were. By this time, Custer had gotten down to the mouth of the dry creek and was on the level flat of the bottom. They began firing and for quite some time fought in the bottom, neither party giving back. There they killed quite a good many horses … and two soldiers were killed and left there. But soon the Indians overpowered the soldiers and they began to give way, retreating slowly, face to the front.[52]

As it is universally accepted that the women from the village had hidden themselves in Chasing, now known as Squaw, Creek, which is on the west side of the river opposite Cemetery Ridge and Custer Hill, this is further evidence that the actions described did not take place in or near Medicine Tail.

Soldier Wolf's account coincides on four points with previous accounts. He described the "dry creek" that Bobtail Horse mentioned; he spoke of the "level flat of the bottom" which agrees with American Horse; then there is the fact that the soldiers were firing as described by Wolf Tooth, American Horse, Brave Wolf and White Bull, plus the troops retreating, which was recorded by the others.

Tall Bull said:

> … news came to the Indians from down the creek that more soldiers were coming, and all turned back. All rushed back on the west side of the camp, down to a small dry run that comes in from the east, and there, down close to the river, were the soldiers. The Indians all crossed and they fought there. For quite a long time the troops stood their ground right there. Then they began to back off, fighting all the time, for quite a distance, working up the hill, until they got pretty close to where the monument now is ….[53]

Tall Bull's "small dry run that comes in from the east" coincides with the little dry creek mentioned by Bobtail Horse and Soldier Wolf. He also agreed that the soldiers were down close to the river, that there was a fight between Indians and soldiers then the soldiers retreated to near the monument.

White Shield said: I looked back and saw soldiers in seven groups. One company could be seen a long way off the horses were pretty white … I went around and came in below, though the company was coming fast making for the Little Bighorn. Near me I could see only Roan Bear, Bobtail Horse and one other man."[54] Then, "When the Gray Horse Company got pretty close to the river, they dismounted, and all the soldiers as far back as far as I could see stopped and dismounted also. When the Gray Horse Company dismounted, the Indians began to fire at them, and the soldiers returned the fire."[55] Finally, "All the soldiers retreated back from the river, but the Gray Horse Company stood their ground."[56]

White Shield's account generally conforms to those cited previously. He confirmed the presence of Roan Bear and Bobtail Horse near the action, also that E Company at least got close to the river and the exchange of fire between Indians and soldiers, and the soldiers retreating from the river.

In an interview in 1956 with author Don Rickey, John Stands In Timber stated that Wolf Tooth gave him the following information:

> The Custer men tried to cross the river at a ford west of the present railroad tracks, on what is now the Willy Bends place. Cheyennes hidden in the brush on the south side of the ford drove the soldiers back and killed a couple of them in the brush by the river. Then the Custer men retreated to the flats below where the superintendent's house is now located. They waited there for about half an hour, while the Indians assembled in the vicinity and fired at the soldiers from the ridges north of the flats.[57]

The western ford mentioned is probably Ford D, as originally shown on the 1877 map of First Lieutenant William Philo Clark. Wolf Tooth again referred to Indians, notably Cheyennes, hidden in the brush by the river, but said that the brush was on the south side of the ford. The ford he mentioned is likely the one used by Colonel Gibbon on June 29, 1876 which is north of Last Stand Hill and below the present National Cemetery. That makes the action described closer to Deep Ravine, but nowhere near as far south as Medicine Tail.

Of course, there may have been an added factor fueling the soldiers' retreat, a factor that could have been the pivotal moment in the battle. Recall that Hanging Wolf said, "… they hit one horse down there, and it bucked off a soldier, but the rest took him along when they retreated north." The only soldiers important enough to be "taken along" during a gun battle were either Custer himself or his brother Tom and if either one was not bucked off but hit and badly wounded, it might also account for the 20-minute wait in the cemetery area while the wounded man was tended to by the doctor.

There is one further piece of corroborating evidence. The body of newspaper correspondent Mark Kellogg, who was with the Headquarters Group, was discovered by Colonel John Gibbon as he crossed the river at the ford already mentioned, on his way to Last Stand Hill. He wrote of his discovery:

> As we proceeded up the valley, now an open grassy slope, we suddenly came upon a body lying in the grass. It was lying on its back, and was in an advanced state of decomposition. It was not stripped, but had evidently been scalped and one ear cut off. The clothing was not that of a soldier, and, with the idea of identifying the remains, I caused one of the boots to be cut off and the stockings and drawers examined for a name, but none could be found. On looking at the boot, however, a curious construction was observed. The heel of the boot was reinforced by a piece of leather which in front terminated in two straps, one of which was furnished with a buckle, evidently for the purpose of tightening the boot. This led to the identification of the remains, for on being carried to camp the boot was recognized as one belonging to Mr. Kellogg …[58]

Then there is the fascinating article *The Fight in Fishing Woman Ravine*, which provided information from a Cheyenne family's oral history. It concerned the parents of Acker Standing Crane, his unnamed father and his mother, Fishing Woman, who were involved in what happened as Custer's Left Wing approached the river near the Cheyenne camp.

Standing Crane's father told him that the soldiers were "riding down the trail … in little groups and had little flags. They were riding fast. They were headed for the creek."[59] When the Blackfeet woman he was helping to safety started screaming, he told her that "the soldiers were heading too far up river, that they were not headed for the women and children."[60] Soon after the woman started screaming again and he looked again. He says:

> The soldiers had broken apart. Some were going on up the river. The rest had turned from the trail and were following a smaller trail toward where were the women. These soldiers were

riding fast. They had two little flags in front of them. One had little white stars and a forked stem. In front of that little flag was another little flag. It had two tails and big white crossed knives … A little yellow bird sat on top of its pole.[61]

Once again, we have soldiers riding down towards the river near the Cheyenne camp and we have confirmation of Soldier Wolf's account of rushing down the creek to where the women were. It is also clear that the Headquarters Group was leading the soldiers coming towards the women as the second flag mentioned is obviously Custer's personal flag. The trail referred to by Standing Crane's father was verified by two maps, one produced by First Lieutenant William Philo Clark, the other by Captain R. E. Johnston during the surrender interview of the Blackfeet Lakota Chief Kill Eagle. These maps are reproduced in *Drawing Battle Lines*.[62] As Bruce Trinque says, on the maps the trail is shown leading from Custer Hill to the river and a ford some distance north of Deep Ravine, which is further corroboration that Medicine Tail was not the place where the Custer battalions fought near the river.

The soldiers observed by Standing Crane's father continuing northwards along the buffalo trail rode horses which "were all pretty white."[63] Obviously that was E Company under First Lieutenant A. E. Smith, and it is likely that they were heading for the far north to check the possibility of crossing there. The group heading for the place where the women were hiding would therefore have been the Headquarters Group and F Company commanded by Captain George Yates.

Standing Crane continues:

> My father turned loose the Blackfeet woman and ran to where he thought the soldiers would strike the creek. It was just across the creek from where the women were. There were other Indians hurrying there. Some on horses, some on foot. There were not very many warriors. They ran to the edge of the creek and got behind a little rise. They started shooting at the soldiers. Five Indians, my father thought they were Cheyenne; they crossed the creek on horses. They charged the soldiers. The soldiers charged them back. The five Indians turned around. They rode for the creek. The Indians at the creek fired and killed some of the soldiers. Some of the soldiers stopped and got off their horses and the Indians and the soldiers shot back and forth across the river at each other. They did this for some time.[64]

This part of the account has the action taking place directly across the river from where the women were hiding, as described by Soldier Wolf. The five Cheyennes who attacked the soldiers compare very closely with those who were interviewed by Grinnell, and two of them were also named by White Shield. The warriors firing from the little rise at the edge of the river agree with the information supplied by Wolf Tooth. The soldiers and the Indians firing at each other is in all accounts, and soldiers being killed appears in the Brave Wolf, Soldier Wolf, and Wolf Tooth accounts. White Shield also talks of soldiers dismounting.

The few Indians who were fighting were then reinforced as others arrived and Standing Crane's father's account continues: "Then an old man chief, he was Southern

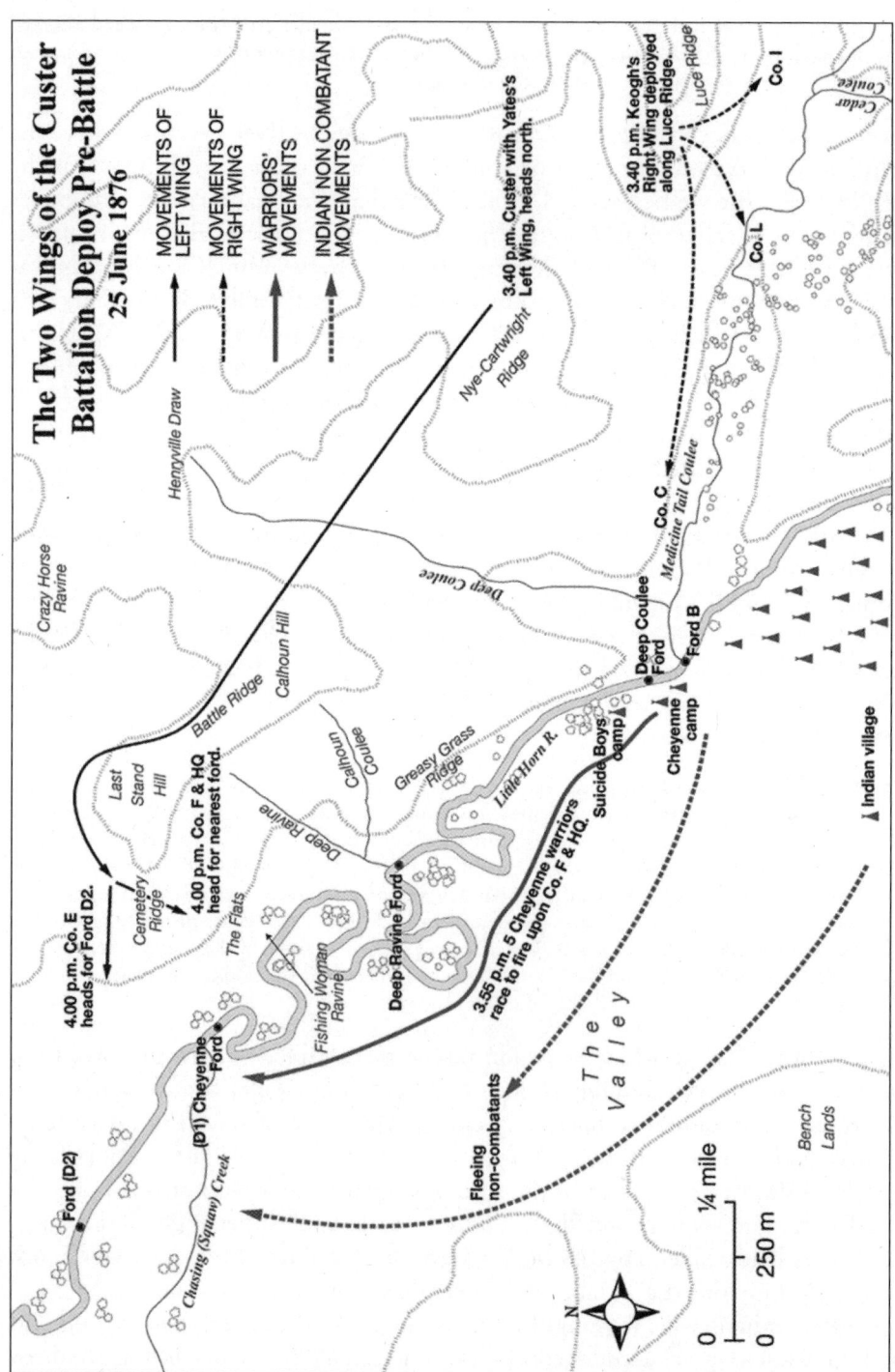

The two wings of the Custer battalions deploy pre-battle. (Gordon Harper, *Fights on the Little Horn*, 2014)

The Two Wings of the Custer Battalion Deploy Pre-Battle
25 June 1876

MOVEMENTS OF LEFT WING

MOVEMENTS OF RIGHT WING

WARRIORS' MOVEMENTS

INDIAN NON COMBATANT MOVEMENTS

3.40 p.m. Custer with Yates's Left Wing, heads north.

3.40 p.m. Keogh's Right Wing deployed along Luce Ridge.

Co. I

Luce Ridge

Cedar Coulee

Co. L

Co. C

Medicine Tail Coulee

Nye-Cartwright Ridge

Henryville Draw

Crazy Horse Ravine

Calhoun Hill

Battle Ridge

Deep Coulee

Deep Coulee Ford

Ford B

Cheyenne camp

Suicide Boys camp

Indian village

Little Horn R.

Greasy Grass Ridge

Calhoun Coulee

Deep Ravine

Last Stand Hill

Cemetery Ridge

4.00 p.m. Co. E heads for Ford D2.

4.00 p.m. Co. F & HQ head for nearest ford.

The Flats

Fishing Woman Ravine

Deep Ravine Ford

3.55 p.m. 5 Cheyenne warriors race to fire upon Co. F & HQ.

3.55 p.m. Fleeing non-combatants

The Valley

(D1) Cheyenne Ford

Ford (D2)

Chasing (Squaw) Creek

Bench Lands

N

¼ mile

250 m

0

0

Cheyenne [Lame White Man], came along. He saw that many Indians were coming up from the Skirt People and the Miniconjou camps. He called to his warriors to follow him. He rode across the creek. Not many Indians had their ponies. The ponies had not yet come into the camps."[65]

That Custer now found his Left Wing repulsed at the northern end of the camps was due to a combination of events that he could not have anticipated. The assumption had been that most warriors would have swiftly moved to the south when Reno's force menaced that end of the village. What Custer did not realize was that at least two-thirds of the Indian fighting strength had been unable to find their horses in time to go and meet Reno. The vast herd seen from the Crow's Nest on the bench lands to the west of the camps was not, in fact, the only one. Wooden Leg told Marquis, "On the bench lands just east of us our horses found plenty of rich grass."[66] Later, he said, "The Cheyenne horses were put out to graze on the valley below our camp. Horses belonging to other tribes were placed at other feeding areas on the valley and on the bench hills just west of the combined Indian camps. The tribal herds were kept separate from each other."[67] There is also confirmation from the Oglala Lakota Foolish Elk, in his interview with Walter Camp: "The Indians were now getting their horses in from the hills and soon came up in large numbers. Some crossed the stream farther down and others crossed the ford and followed on after Custer in overwhelming numbers. They could not see how such a small force of soldiers had any chance to stand against them."[68]

The simplicity of what happened is clear from these Indian accounts, but the time frame is not, because when the Left Wing was baulked at the northern fords it set off a chain reaction that soon involved the Right Wing and took another hour and a half to unfold. As various actions were happening simultaneously, I have broken the time frame down into time segments for the sake of convenience. Those times and segments are not, however, meant to be other than approximate guidelines.

Right Wing, 3:45 p.m.

At about 3:45 p.m., acting on advice from Boyer, Custer left for the northern fords, leaving the Right Wing in position on Luce and Butler Ridges overlooking Medicine Tail Coulee. He had probably told Keogh to allow about twenty minutes for the Left Wing to reach the northern ford crossing point and what to do if things went wrong.

Left Wing, 4:00–4.20 p.m.

At 4 p.m., as Custer, with his Headquarters Group, accompanied by Companies E and F, descended from east of Last Stand Hill and towards the northern fords, they were seen to divide into two parties. E Company on their white, or gray, horses turned further north towards the farthest ford, while the rest moved down closer to the river in the direction of the noncombatants. Some five minutes later, as the Custer group and F Company neared the river, the few Cheyenne warriors who had crossed the river to face the soldiers opened fire.

Whether or not any soldiers were hit is open to question, but nevertheless Custer ordered F Company to dismount and form a skirmish line to return fire. As the few warriors opposing them were hiding in the brush near the river there were no easy targets for the soldiers to aim at, still the skirmish line fired a couple of volleys toward the source of the warrior fire. By now, E Company had ridden fast from the far northern ford to the sound of firing and had dismounted to form a skirmish line.

These events have already been described by American Horse and other Cheyennes in their interviews with Grinnell. They stated, "And there they fought for some little time," "The Indians all crossed and they fought there. For quite a long time the troops stood their ground right there," and "When the Gray Horse Company dismounted, the Indians began to fire at them, and the soldiers returned the fire." The reality of this episode was described by the Cheyenne sub chief Two Moon, "We hurriedly crossed the river, and some went up and some down, to get on each side of where the soldiers were intending to come. They came to the edge and stopped; then, almost in an instant the guns commenced to go, increasing to a roar like thunder. Custer had started his last fight."[69]

The Indian accounts spell out quite clearly that the soldiers and warriors exchanged long-range, inconclusive gunfire for a period. This situation began to change as Custer saw, with some concern, warriors on foot and mounted, racing through what he had believed was a deserted village; warriors he had expected to be engaging Reno's command at the southern end of the camps. Custer now accepted that he had to abort his original plan to get into the village at the northern fords. His force of less than 100 men could not stand against the growing number of warriors he could see coming toward him. Indian accounts again confirm this. The Oglala Eagle Elk, "… noticed that the other Indians were charging from the south end. From that time, others were coming across the creek after the soldiers."[70] The Hunkpapa Iron Hawk said, "… the Indians crossed the river anywhere to confront Custer. The first Indians to reach Custer were about one hundred."[71] Hollow Horn Bear, a Brule, recalled, "They did not appear to want to cross the river after the warriors made their presence felt in such large numbers."[72]

It was now expedient for the Left Wing Group to go back the way it had come, reunite with Keogh's battalion and buy time for Custer to plan again. Orders were therefore given for F Company to move back up toward the higher ground with the Headquarters Group, while E Company would act as rearguard to protect them. The ride down toward the river had been relatively easy. The return journey would be anything but. In temperatures of over ninety degrees, with horses already sweating and dust covered men perspiring heavily into their wool uniforms, that journey needed to be uphill and in the face of enemy fire. It was about 4:20 p.m. when the withdrawal began.

Right Wing, 4:00–4:20 p.m.

Captain Myles W. Keogh, commanding the Right Wing, was eager for the fighting to begin. For one reason or another he had missed the regiment's major engagements at the Washita in 1868 and during the Yellowstone Expedition in 1873. He had served with the Papal Guard and in the Union Army, so he was no stranger to hot action. He had been pleasantly surprised when given command of a battalion at the divide, as Custer had been cool toward him for some time, supposedly after Keogh struck up a close friendship with Custer's wife Libbie. Now the Irishman relished taking his battalion across Ford B and smashing into the flank of any opposition Custer might have run into at that point.

Keogh had deployed his three companies north of Medicine Tail Coulee along Butler and Luce Ridges. From east to west the order was I, L and C. At about 4:10 p.m., waiting to attack across Ford B, Keogh had cause for some unease. He could no longer hear Springfield carbine fire from Reno's command in the valley, only the spasmodic cracks of lighter weapons. But at around the same time he could hear gunshots to his north, including Springfield carbine volley firing. Suddenly warriors started to cross Ford B and move up Medicine Tail Coulee, having, unknown to him, responded to the Left Wing's approach to the northern fords. Keogh quickly appreciated that the situation had changed. The planned joint attack was no longer feasible, so in accordance with orders he began a move to the high ground to try to reunite with the Left Wing Group, as he assumed they were faced with the same problem. Keogh began a disciplined withdrawal from his original position to the Nye/Cartwright Ridge area. I Company provided covering fire to deter the warriors moving up Medicine Tail. The number of cartridges which have been found along this line of retreat indicates that at least part of the Right Wing stayed on the ridges for a while. As C Company exited Butler's Ridge, Corporal John Foley became its first casualty, probably shot by some nimble warrior who had rapidly scaled the gently sloping ridge below the C Company position. The corporal would achieve far more recognition in death than he ever had in his rather undistinguished life.

Tall Bull was one of the warriors who mentioned this action:

> Custer [Keogh] got onto flat near Ford B within easy gunshot of village, and Indians drove him back. By time I got there, had driven the soldiers to the first rise (where Foley lay), and they were going up the ridge to the right of Custer coulee and the Indians driving them. The men who had no horses to go to Reno, first began the attack on Custer, and I did not see the first of it.[73]

That phrase in parentheses "where Foley lay" was inserted by Camp when he transcribed his July 22, 1910, interview with Tall Bull. The location of Foley's body had been quite accurately fixed by several of the 7th Cavalry survivors when, on June 28, 1876, they had helped to bury the bodies of their dead comrades. For example, Sergeant Stanislaus Roy of A Company, who said in his interview with Camp, with references to the map shown to him:

> We then formed a skirmish line and buried the dead. On the way over we followed what we supposed was Custer's trail and at one point it led down pretty close to the river. The first dead body we came to was that of Corpl. John Foley. I heard several say: "there lies Foley of C Company." I saw him and recognized him easily, as he had [a] bald head and black hair. He was of middle age and I knew him well. Foley was at least three-fourths mile in advance of the first group of dead at "C." The next body we came to was that of Sergt. Butler, and from him to first group of dead at "C" the distance was considerable. He lay probably one-half way from Foley to "C." There was no dead horse near either Foley or Butler. I helped to bury the bodies on west slope of ridge, and we wound up with E Troop men over near the gully ... When we went to bury the dead, on June 28, we did not follow Dry Creek to the river but cut straight across to the battlefield, going over the little rise between the two coulees. The first body we saw was that of Corpl. Foley of Co. C on this rise, just over toward the coulee running up to the battlefield. Butler lay 200 or 300 yds. beyond and across the ravine.[74]

In his own records Camp noted, "Ford B is 800 feet from the top of the slope of the little hill on which Foley was found. The edge of the rise of ground on which Foley was found is 800 feet from the river, while Foley's body was found 300 feet farther, he lying about 1,100 feet from the river."[75]

The location of Foley's body is therefore not in dispute, but when he was killed most certainly is. Several of Camp's Indian accounts speak of a mounted man who escaped either from the final moments on Last Stand Hill or the destruction of C Company and fled south before shooting himself in the head. They include the Miniconjou warrior Turtle Rib, in the fighting near Battle Ridge, who "... saw one soldier ride across a hollow and try to get away .... The soldier rode like the wind and appeared to be getting away from them, when he killed himself."[76] The Oglala He Dog said something similar but placed the man's escape from Last Stand Hill: "Says location of Foley is right and he the one who shot himself ... Foley rode out of fight from H [Last Stand Hill.]"[77] The Oglala Red Feather, near Battle Ridge, stated, "One soldier on a sorrel horse tried to get round the Indians ... They saw some smoke and the report of a gun ... (and they concluded) he had shot himself,"[78] and the Cheyenne, Wooden Leg, told Marquis, "A Cheyenne told me that four soldiers from that part of the ridge (near Keogh's stand) had turned their horses and tried to escape .... Three of these men were killed quickly. The fourth one got across a gulch and over a ridge eastward before the pursuing group of Sioux got close to him ... Suddenly his right hand went up to his head. With his revolver he shot himself and fell dead from his horse."[79]

In 1920, in yet another Camp interview, this with Colonel Herbert J. Slocum, who joined the 7th Cavalry as a 2nd lieutenant on July 28, 1876, Camp noted how Slocum told him that during the 1886 10th anniversary trip to the battlefield,

"Corporal Foley: Gall showed them where the lone soldier rode away ... and finally shot himself ... It corroborates my information about Corpl. Foley, as told me by Turtle Rib. Gall told them that this soldier had chevrons on his sleeve."[80]

Two things become clear from these accounts. The first is that at some point in the fighting, either from near Battle Ridge or from Last Stand Hill, one soldier fled southeast on horseback and eventually shot himself in the head. The second is that in his eagerness to corroborate his own ideas, Camp, albeit unwittingly, either directly or via third parties, posed leading questions to the interviewees. There is no other explanation for He Dog apparently mentioning Foley by name, or for Gall stating that "this soldier had chevrons on his sleeve," as He Dog could not possibly have known Foley's name and Gall would not have had the word chevrons in his vocabulary. In both cases the Indian warriors were pointed to their answers by the questions they were asked.

While that does not rule out the possibility that the escapee was Foley, one other thing does. Each of the five warrior accounts cited tells of the escapee shooting himself and one specifically saying in the head. There are at least seven other accounts which state that the man shot himself in the head and it takes little imagination to picture how disfigured his head would have looked after being hit at close range by a bullet from a Colt .45 Single Action revolver. Add to that three days decomposing in blazing heat and the result would not have been pretty. Yet Sergeant Roy, who was with the group that found Foley's body, said several of them immediately knew who the dead man was and Roy "recognized him easily." It is highly unlikely, therefore, that the escapee was Corporal Foley.

The unfortunate corporal's name has also become synonymous with what has become known as the Culbertson Guidon. According to Sergeant Ferdinand Culbertson of A Company, he was a member of the burial party that came across Foley's body and, in turning the corpse over he discovered the bloodstained guidon of Foley's C Company under it. It is odd then, that neither this event nor the presence of Culbertson in the burial party was ever mentioned by Sergeant Roy in his various dealings with Walter Camp, who noted regarding Culbertson, "Found a bloodstained guidon torn from its staff beneath a soldier's body on Custer's battlefield says himself."[81] That Camp added "says himself" is a clear indication that he was skeptical. That Culbertson did not tell him the dead soldier was the clearly identifiable Foley when he later claimed that it was makes that later claim dubious.

As the Culbertson Guidon with authenticating provenance was auctioned in December 2010 for $2.2 million, it has to be accepted that Culbertson did have a guidon of the period, possibly one he recovered at the battlefield. What is very much in dispute is that he found it on, or under, Foley's body. He may even have found the G Company guidon which had been abandoned during Reno's flight from the timber, when Culbertson went to look for Hodgson's body for Reno. However, as A Company was deployed to look for bodies on Custer's Field, it is perhaps more likely that he did find the C Company guidon, except not on Foley. Sergeant Roy, in his letter of March 4, 1909, to Camp revealed, "It was not my troop that covered Foley and Butler"[82] so it casts doubt on the likelihood of Culbertson having the opportunity of turning over Foley's corpse. The bodies of C Company men were scattered all over the battlefield, so it is much more of a probability that if Culbertson did recover their guidon, it was from one of the other dead men.

The provenance for the auction was apparently contained in letters from Roy to Sergeant Samuel Alcott, also of A Company, and from Alcott to Walter Camp, plus an unpublished memoir by Alcott. There is nothing in Camp's work to suggest he took what Alcott had to say seriously, and Camp was like a dog with a bone when he believed in something. The reason for his lack of interest may well have been the fact that Alcott was shown as being on detached service at the Powder River Depot, not at the Little Bighorn, so whatever Alcott was telling him was merely hearsay. Why Roy would confirm Culbertson's story is uncertain, except perhaps he did not witness the finding of the guidon but simply believed what Culbertson told him.

The real impact of Culbertson's story has been to distort the history of the fighting. By placing the torn guidon with Foley, who was also erroneously believed by Camp to have been the escapee who had shot himself, it has been assumed that the corporal was the C Company guidon holder who, in a last desperate bid to escape, rather than let go of his flag, tore it from its staff and thrust it into his tunic before fleeing from the overrunning of his company. That would place him as an escapee late in the fighting rather than as a casualty in the early withdrawal from the ridges above Medicine Tail Coulee. Yet, if, and there is a lot of doubt, Foley was the color bearer for his company, the guidon could just as easily have been torn from its staff by him in the sudden withdrawal from near Butler Ridge because he could not ride up the ridges holding on to the staff with one hand, guiding his horse with the other, and defending himself from attack. Because his body lay in a place relatively isolated from the main warrior surge after the retreating Right Wing, it is not surprising that it was left alone, other than by boys who shot arrows into it, was easily recognizable to Roy and others, and with the guidon, if ever with him, still on it. A reason Foley's body was overlooked by the warriors, and not stripped or mutilated, was because he was the first, or one of the first, casualties of Keogh's command. The remainder of his company would not fare even that well. They would become the catalyst for the collapse of the Right Wing.

Right Wing, 4:20–4:30 p.m.

At roughly the same time as the Left Wing Group began its withdrawal, Keogh's battalion moved to the Nye/Cartwright Ridge area. From there, L Company began firing at warriors moving up to Luce Ridge from Medicine Tail Coulee, as Keogh's other two companies moved the mile to Battle Ridge, past Calhoun Hill via the ravine to the north of Nye/Cartwright and across the Deep Coulee flats. The Oglala,

Respects Nothing, noticed this movement: "The soldiers came up to Calhoun Hill diagonally from the east [south] and the Indians came up diagonally from the river crossing to Calhoun Hill."[83] The Brule warrior, Two Eagles, told Walter Camp that, "There were a few [soldiers who] went from 'E' [The Luce/Nye-Cartwright Ridge complex] to 'D' [Calhoun Hill]."[84] In one interview, the Miniconjou, White Bull, related that he and other warriors rode up Medicine Tail Coulee and joined a "horde of others" in pursuit of L Company, which was bringing up the rear of the fleeing battalions and, "The Indians kept up a constant fire. Two soldiers fell from their horses. The other troopers opened such an intense fire from their saddles that the Indians were forced back."[85] The discovery of Springfield cartridge cases and Indian bullets in this area confirm the action at this location."[86]

Keogh's command was controlling the situation, but it was the calm before the storm. The warriors, who had forced Crook to retreat at the Rosebud, were fired up and ready to do the same for Keogh's force.

Left Wing, 4:20 p.m.

To the north, with E Company acting as skirmishers for protection, the Headquarters Group and F Company started their ascent to a position where they could deploy a skirmish line to cover the withdrawal of E Company. They had not gone far when they suffered their first casualty. Mark Kellogg, the newspaper correspondent, was riding a mule and was about to discover why that species had a reputation for stubbornness. On that hot day his mount was thirsty, it could smell the river, but its rider was moving him away from it. The beast stopped and refused to move, despite the urging of its rider. Then "The old man chief [Lame White Man] hit him on the head with his rifle as he rode by. Then the man on the mule fell off on to the ground. The Indians on foot got him."[87] A few moments later, the Headquarters Group sustained its second casualty as Corporal Henry C. Dose, a trumpeter, was felled by an Indian bullet. His body was described by Lieutenant DeRudio as "... so much disfigured that I did not know who he was, only the marks on his pants showed me he was a trumpeter."[88]

The Cheyenne White Shield confirmed the E Company action saying, "All the soldiers retreated back from the river, but the Gray Horse Company stood their ground."[89] But whooping warriors both mounted and on foot, were moving against them. Individuals were riding up close to the troopers in acts of bravery. Yellow Nose told how "the soldiers soon changed from a stand to a retreat."[90] With bullets whistling past his head, the Cheyenne/Ute warrior circled in front of the soldiers and noticed a pretty flag being held on a long pole by one of the troopers. Yellow Nose decided he wanted that flag.

The warriors rode back and forth in front of E Company as the Headquarters Group and F Company retreated to the northeast. Unfortunately for them, a hunting party of about twenty Cheyenne was coming down from the northwest.[91]

They stopped behind a small ridge north of Last Stand Hill and fired at the Custer group retreating in that direction. Archaeological evidence bears this out.[92]

Left Wing, 4:30 p.m.

Having noted that the rest had retreated while E Company "stood their ground," White Shield observed how pressure grew on Smith's command:

> After they had been shooting for some time, Contrary Big Belly [Cheyenne] made a charge down in front of the Gray Horse Company, and from where the Indians were, they saw that the horses of one other company began to get frightened and started to circle around the men who were holding them. When Contrary Big Belly got back, the companies began shooting fast ...[93]

The Oglala Lakota White Cow Bull saw the troops redeploy too, "Now I saw the soldiers were split into two bands, most of them on foot and shooting as they fell back to higher ground so we made no more mounted charges."[94]

As that pressure started to impact the dismounted E Company skirmishers, their horse-holders found it increasingly difficult to keep control of the mounts in their charge. The Cheyenne sub chief, Two Moon, described what he saw at this point, "Those who were on the hill where the monument now stands and where I am now standing, had gray horses and they were all in the open. The Sioux and Cheyennes came up the valley swarming like ants toward the bunch of gray horses where Long Hair stood."[95]

Prevented from going northeast by the Cheyenne hunters, and being fired at by the Wolf Tooth group from the ridges to the north of Last Stand Hill, the sweat-drenched men of the Custer group struggled to a wide, flat ridge sloping west from Last Stand Hill and dismounted near the present Visitor Centre, known now as Cemetery Ridge. Because they were receiving fire from the northeast, southeast and some from the west, they formed circular skirmish lines with their nervous, excited horses in the center. White Cow Bull boastfully recounted his own exploits during this action, "I found cover and began shooting at the soldiers. I was a good shot and had one of the few repeating rifles carried by any of our warriors. It was up to me to use it the best way I could. I kept firing at the two bands of soldiers, first at one, then at the other. It was hard to see through the smoke and dust, but I saw five soldiers go down when I shot at them."[96]

With the Custer group on Cemetery Ridge and E Company skirmishers both firing as well, there was a cacophony of noise with gun smoke and dust filling the air to add to the confusion. Some of the Custer group soldiers were firing at the warriors who were menacing the stationary skirmishers of E Company. From his position overlooking Last Stand Hill, Wolf Tooth remarked on what was happening to E Company, "When the Gray Horse Company moved south they were confronted by a large number of Indians in and near the big Ravine."[97] The situation was becoming grim for the Left Wing Group, especially for E Company and it was soon to get considerably worse.

Right Wing, 4:30–4:40 p.m.

Approximately a mile to the south, First Lieutenant James Calhoun had moved his L Company to the hill which would bear his name, just south of C Company on Battle Ridge. The two soldier casualties mentioned by White Bull must have only been wounded as no bodies were found on Nye/Cartwright Ridge. The Right Wing deployment is noted by Standing Bear, "Custer [Keogh] came down the ridge across the river—the second or rear ridge from the river. He made no attempt to reach the river to cross. He went right up to Calhoun Hill and his forces along the top of the ridge to Custer Hill [Last Stand Hill]."[98] Dismounting his company, Lieutenant Calhoun placed his horses in the small cleft slightly west of the hill between it and Battle Ridge and deployed his men as skirmishers in the form of a semicircle around the military crest of the hill. Long-range firing kept the outranged warriors at a respectable distance, but individuals began to try to infiltrate closer to the soldier lines. Showers of arcing arrows began to cause problems to both men and horses. Wooden Leg said:

> Most of the Indians were working around the ridge now occupied by the soldiers. We were lying down in gullies and behind sagebrush hillocks. The shooting at first was at a distance, but we kept creeping in closer all around the ridge. Bows and arrows were used much more than guns. From the hiding places of the Indians, the arrows could be shot in a high and long curve, to fall upon the soldiers or their horses.[99]

Other warriors noted the long-distance stalemate and the first Indian attack. The Two Kettle Lakota Runs The Enemy said:

> While Custer [Keogh] was all surrounded, there had been no firing from either side. The Sioux then made a charge from the rear side shooting into the men, and the shooting frightened the horses so that they rushed upon the ridge and many horses were shot. The return fire was so strong that the Sioux had to retreat back over the hill again."[100]

With no clear targets to sight on, the L Company skirmishers caused very few warrior casualties and could not stop the stealthy warriors beginning to surround them and the rest of Keogh's battalion. They were now taking gunfire from Greasy Grass Ridge to their west and upper Deep Coulee, now known as Henryville (because the warriors were using Henry repeating rifles) to their east, as well as taking hits from the arrows falling from the sky. Facing one platoon to the east, Lieutenant Calhoun began to return the fire from Henryville and helped to repulse the first Indian charge described by Runs The Enemy.

Although many hundreds of warriors were already confronting Keogh's command, what the soldiers did not know was that following Reno's retreat, many more warriors were arriving from the south. Foremost among them, and destined to have an important impact on events, was the Oglala Lakota Crazy Horse. Revered by his people as remarkably brave and someone to follow in battle, Crazy Horse had already been very effective in crushing Reno's command. Now he was racing down through the village to help protect the families from the menace of the five Custer companies.

Left Wing, 4:40–4:50 p.m.

For a while, the long-range firing from both E Company and the Yates group on Cemetery Ridge held the warriors back, but the soldiers found there was a big difference between stationary targets on a practice range and the constantly moving warriors. Those on horseback weaved back and for and those on foot used every ridge and hollow to hide behind making targets difficult to hit.

Mounted at the rear of his E Company, First Lieutenant Algernon "Fresh" Smith had organized his men into two lines to face the warriors coming at them from the direction of the river, "some kneeling and some standing" as seen by Two Moon.[101] Now though there was a threat to his rear from the ravine to the east as warriors crept up behind its protective banks. The plight of E Company is recorded in Cheyenne oral history. "But by the time some of them [gray horses] did move toward the big ravine on the battlefield [E Company, Deep Ravine], it was too late and the Indians were all around them in large numbers."[102]

A worried Smith knew it was time to withdraw and unite with the rest of the Left Wing Group on Cemetery Ridge. It was an impossible task. Unable to control their wildly plunging animals the E Company horse-holders could not get them to the troopers as Lieutenant Smith ordered his company to withdraw from their skirmish line positions. The troopers found that the combined tasks of trying to climb the slope to their mounts and reloading their carbines during all the turmoil were beyond them. Eager to mount and ride to a safer position the firing wavered. That was all the encouragement the warriors needed. The bolder spirits among them began to close on the soldiers of E Company.

The Cheyenne White Shield gave a vivid description of what he saw:

> When the Gray Horse Company dismounted, the Indians began to fire at them and the soldiers returned the fire. It was not long before the Indians began to gather in large numbers where I was. After they had been shooting for some time, Contrary Big Belly made a charge down in front of the Gray Horse Company ...[103]

Another version of these events came from the Oglala White Cow Bull:

> Another warrior named Yellow Nose, a Sapawicasa [Ute] who had been captured as a boy by the Shahiyela [Cheyennes] and had grown up with them, was very brave that day. After we chased the soldiers back from the ford, he galloped out in front of us and got very close to them, then raced back to safety.[104]

Yellow Nose was not, however, to be denied his flag. As White Cow Bull explained:

> I kept riding with the Shahiyelas, still hoping that some of them might tell Meotzi [Cheyenne woman a.k.a. Monasetah] later about my courage. We massed for another charge. The Shahiyela chief, Comes-in-Sight, and a warrior named Contrary Belly led us that time. The soldiers' horses were so frightened by all the noise we made that they began to bolt in all directions. The soldiers held their fire while they tried to catch their horses. Just then Yellow Nose rushed in again and grabbed a small flag from where the soldiers had stuck it in the ground. He carried it off and counted coup [struck blows] on a soldier with its sharp end. He was proving his courage more by counting that coup than if he had killed the soldier.[105]

The momentum was now with the warriors and Lieutenant Colonel George Armstrong Custer was going to need every bit of the legendary "Custer's Luck" to extricate the Gray Horse Company from its predicament.

Right Wing, 4:40–4:45 p.m.

After reaching the Oglala camp in the village and checking that the families were safe, Crazy Horse, with a group of between 50 and 100 warriors moved from the west bank of the river via Deep Ravine Ford and up Deep Ravine. Surveying things from the top of the ravine, he quickly realized that he could not go straight across Battle Ridge from there or he would be an easy target for the soldiers on the crest of the ridge, Keogh's I Company. He therefore turned left, toward the basin area then up, passing south around Last Stand Hill's ridge, before moving into the ravine that now bears his name, north of Battle Ridge. Here he paused. The ravine led directly into the guns of the soldiers on the ridge. He needed a different route.

Unsurprisingly, the great Oglala warrior's every move was noted by his people. The Miniconjou Flying By told how, "Crazy Horse and I left the crowd and rode down along the river. We came to a ravine; then we followed up the gulch to a place in the rear of the soldiers that were making the stand on the hill."[106] The Hunkpapa Pretty White Buffalo, the wife of Spotted Horn Bull observed, "I saw Crazy Horse lead the Cheyennes into the water and up the ravine; Crow King and the Hunkpapa went after them."[107] Wherever Crazy Horse went in this fight, he would not go unnoticed.

Once Calhoun's L Company had taken its place south of C Company, Myles Keogh felt confident that his companies could hold their positions until the Yates wing reunited with them. The range of the Springfield carbines was deterring the warriors from getting too close to his command and the longer that lasted the more time it gave for Custer's men to join him. He knew that the Left Wing Group were also under attack but believed they would be able to withdraw safely. Meantime, his battalion would give a good account of themselves.

For a while, after some volley firing from Calhoun's company had made the Indians more cautious, the only action was between his skirmishers and individual warriors trying to infiltrate closer to the soldier lines. Runs The Enemy has already described how the first Indian charge was repulsed, and the Lakota White Bull told his biographer how the warriors went on the offensive but were beaten back by the soldiers' firepower. "The soldiers fired back from the saddle. Their fire was so effective that some of the Indians, including White Bull, fell back to the south."[108]

That situation prevailed only until more warriors arrived on the scene and began to look for ways to surround the Keogh positions. The Oglala Foolish Elk remembered:

> The Indians were now getting their horses in from the hills and soon came up in large numbers. Some crossed the stream farther down and others crossed the ford and followed on after Custer [Keogh] in overwhelming numbers. They could not see how such a small force of soldiers had any chance to stand against them. The Indians were between Custer [Keogh] and the river and all the time coming up and getting around to the east of him passing around both his front and rear. Custer [Keogh] was following the ridges, and the Indians were keeping abreast of him in the hollows and ravines. Personally, he was with the Indians to the east, or on Custer's [Keogh's] right.[109]

For the next ten minutes or so, the status quo prevailed but ominously it was the warriors who were making the positive moves. Crazy Horse and his followers were moving along behind the eastern ridges, others were in Deep Coulee and hiding in the upper part of the coulee, now known as Henryville. The noose was tightening around the Keogh battalion. That was how Wooden Leg saw things:

> The Indians all the time could see where were the soldiers, because the white men were mostly on a ridge and their horses with them. But the soldiers could not see our warriors, as they had left their ponies and were crawling in the gullies through the sagebrush. A warrior would jump up, shoot, jerk himself down quickly, and then crawl forward a little further. All around the soldier ridge our men were doing this. So not many of them got hit by the soldier bullets during this time of fighting.[110]

Captain Keogh watched the Indian movements carefully. He wanted to be sure that the warriors did not get too close to the horses in the gully behind Calhoun Hill or to the L Company skirmishers on their hill, as that would negate the superior range of the Springfield carbines. He sent a messenger to 2nd Lieutenant Henry M. Harrington, acting commander of C Company, to be ready to move quickly with his company if required.

Left Wing, 4:50–5:00 p.m.

From his vantage point on Cemetery Ridge, Lieutenant Colonel Custer could see that E Company was in trouble. He could also see Indians moving up past Last Stand Hill and became concerned that a combination of these facts would seriously compromise his anticipated reunion with Keogh's battalion. Swiftly, Custer made up his mind and gave two orders to Captain George W. M. Yates, the F Company commander. The first was to send a squad of eight mounted F Company men to immediately aid Smith's beleaguered command and the second was to mount up the rest of F Company and charge to drive off the warriors menacing Smith's E Company. At the same time, the Headquarters Group would move to the lower slope of the Hill and Yates was to rejoin them there. Once there Custer believed that a strong defensive position could be established from which an effective field of fire would allow E Company to withdraw and reunite with the rest of the Left Wing.

The Yates group had barely left Cemetery Ridge when Sergeant Major William H. Sharrow was cut down by the firing from the northern ridge. The squad of eight F Company men under the command of Second Lieutenant William Van Wyck Reily, mounted and galloped down to the E Company position, as the Headquarters Group moved as planned. The bulk of F Company charged down the flats at the warriors threatening Smith and his men. The charge had its effect as Wooden Leg described. "After a long time of slow fighting, about forty of the soldiers came galloping from the east part of the ridge down toward the river, toward where most of the Cheyennes and many Oglalas were hiding. The Indians ran back to a deep gulch."[111]

The arrival of the F Company squad was remarked on by the Cheyenne Young Two Moon:

> At the 4th charge, on Yellow Nose's orders, all Indians mounted and Yellow Nose made a charge, and all Indians followed. They crowded the company furthest north and they started to run down the ridge. As they got down part way toward the Gray Horse Company, the latter began to fire and drove the Indians off, and the soldiers reached the Gray Horse Company. Some were killed, however, when they reached the Gray Horse Company. The latter shot at the Indians so fast that they drove the Indians back out of sight over the hill toward the agency.[112]

The bodies of F Company men Corporal John Briody and Private Timothy Donnelly found in the Deep Ravine area, and perhaps Private William Brown, who was found in the village opposite Deep Ravine ford, testify to the observations of Young Two Moon.

Having successfully relieved Smith's command, Yates withdrew to reunite with Custer, who gave the order for F Company to form a skirmish line on lower Last Stand Hill. Custer, with Adjutant Cooke, Dr. Lord, Chief Trumpeter Voss, and Sergeant John Vickory, his color bearer, set up a command post and hospital to the north of the skirmish line. His brother Tom and scout Mitch Boyer joined the skirmish line relishing the action to come. George Custer was ready to cover the withdrawal of E Company.

Right Wing, 4:50–5:00 p.m.

On the crest of Battle Ridge, Myles Keogh had I Company containing the warriors to his east and southeast because they had no cover in that bare terrain. To the north, northwest and west though, the broken ground was ideal for infiltration. With the firing from Henryville obliging Lieutenant Calhoun to face part of his skirmish line in that direction under the command of Second Lieutenant J. J. Crittenden, the shooting at warriors near Greasy Grass Ridge was therefore diminished. Some of the Indians took advantage of this and began to infiltrate from the northwest into Calhoun Coulee just below what became known as Finley Ridge. The Lakota White Bull described what he saw of this situation: "Some Indians went up draw to Custer [Keogh]. White Bull with them—a lot of them. When up in draw, Custer [Keogh] saw them and took shots at them, so they moved back south a way. Custer [Keogh] was at a standstill, and get off horses to shoot, then got back on and made four companies, and one company was shooting at them in the draw."[113] Captain Miles Moylan's testimony at the Reno Court of Inquiry confirmed the White Bull view. "The evidences of fighting were a great many dead men lying about there. I saw Lt. Calhoun's company were killed in regular position of skirmishers. I counted 28 cartridge shells around one man, and between the intervals there were shells scattered."[114]

Though L Company was being kept busy, C Company had been relatively inactive, dismounted and deployed along the southern end of Battle Ridge between Keogh and Lieutenant Calhoun. In the absence of Captain Tom Custer, who was acting as an aide to his brother George, C Company was commanded by 2nd Lieutenant Harrington, a West Point graduate with very little combat experience.

Nevertheless, he had been alerted to be ready to move his company at a moment's notice. Keogh, acutely aware of the constantly increasing warrior numbers and the threat they posed his command and the horses being held in upper Calhoun Coulee, knew he could not afford to be passive. He ordered Harrington to mount his troopers, charge and drive the warriors out of Calhoun Coulee. Harrington was then to hold the Coulee to prevent further infiltration, so taking pressure off L Company.

The lieutenant got his company mounted and led them into a quarter mile charge with revolvers blazing. The warriors in the Coulee hastily retreated, seeking shelter behind Greasy Grass Ridge. The Oglala Eagle Elk remembered the event, "Just at this moment, we noticed that the other Indians were charging from the south end. From that time the others were coming across the creek after the soldiers. The soldiers were shooting a lot, so the Indians were thrown back."[115]

But what neither Harrington nor Keogh knew was that the ridge was hiding a great many more warriors than the ones chased from the coulee. As Pretty White Buffalo revealed:

> To get to the butte Long Hair [Harrington] must cross the ravine; but from where he was marching with his soldiers, he could not see into the ravine nor down to the banks of the river … And I knew that the fighting men of the Sioux, many hundreds in number, were hidden in the ravine behind the hill upon which Long Hair [Harrington] was marching, and he would be attacked from both sides …[116]

Having cleared the coulee, Harrington halted his men just southwest of Finley Ridge and had them dismount. Thus, the dismounted soldiers of C Company lost both their mobility and a quarter of their firepower as the number fours took the horses to the rear. These lost assets would prove to be critical, as would their recently emptied revolvers, because even as the lieutenant followed the manual by dismounting his command to deploy as skirmishers with their carbines, the hidden warriors were primed to counterattack.

Taking some fire from Greasy Grass Ridge, the C Company troopers were just beginning to load their Springfields when a swarm of warriors erupted from behind that ridge. Screaming their war cries and with some firing arrows, the Indians closed rapidly on the startled soldiers. Some of Harrington's men got shots off but that did not stop the warrior force, some of whom were principally interested in capturing the company's horses. The noise and dust had already frightened the cavalry mounts, and now warriors with flapping blankets added to their alarm. The bucking, frenzied animals became unmanageable and broke free from the number fours.

She Walks With Her Shawl, of the Hunkpapa said: "We crossed the Greasy Grass [Little Bighorn] below a beaver dam [where the water is not so deep there] and came upon many horses. One soldier was holding the reins of eight or ten horses. An Indian waved his blanket and scared all the horses. They got away from the men [troopers]."[117] Though horses were always a great prize for the Indians, most of the warriors were hell-bent on attacking the soldiers and swept up Calhoun Coulee into a hand-to-hand fight with the soldiers. At close quarter combat, the warriors held the advantage. Trained from a very young age in that style of fighting, they were in their element. Clubs and axes of stone, hatchets of metal and vicious looking knives began to crunch, cut and stab into the white men who could only try to defend themselves with empty carbines and revolvers. With more raw recruits than any other company, Harrington's command yielded first to fear then to panic. Those not already dead or badly wounded began to flee up the slope to seek the protection of L Company. Harrington and the three company sergeants, Bobo, Finkle and Finley, all still mounted, tried to rally their men in vain. Finley and Finkle fell yards apart on the ridge that bears Finley's name. Bobo whirled his horse around and rode furiously towards his battalion commander with I Company on Battle Ridge. An emotionally distraught Lieutenant Harrington rode straight at the mass of warriors, clubbing at them with his empty revolver until he was engulfed by them and pulled from his mount. His body was never identified, but Reno claimed to have seen through field glasses "the Indians engaged a war dance about three captives, who were tied to the stake, and my impression is that Harrington was among the unfortunates."[118]

The death knell of the Keogh battalion had begun to toll, for Crazy Horse too had not been passive. Moving east he had arrived behind a ridge which sheltered a great many other warriors who had used Deep Coulee. The Miniconjou White Bull met him there.

> I rode around the ridge and dodged the bullets until I met a party of warriors with Crazy Horse. He was a chief of the Oglala and a brave fighter. He wore plain white buckskins and let his

hair hang loose with no feathers in it. He had white spots painted here and there on his face for protection in battle, and it was said he was bulletproof.[119]

Said the Oglala Flying Hawk, "Crazy Horse and I left the crowd and rode down along the river. We came to a ravine; then we followed up the gulch to a place in the rear of the soldiers that were making the stand on the hill. Crazy Horse gave his horse to me to hold along with my horse. He crawled up the ravine to where he could see the soldiers."[120] Crazy Horse led them to the crest of the ridge. From there they could see that they were behind the soldiers on Battle Ridge. Crazy Horse would now show why he was held in such esteem.

Left Wing, 5:00–5:10 p.m.

Even though the warriors had run to hide in Deep Ravine when F Company charged, the men of E Company and the F Company reinforcements were still caught between Cemetery Ravine and Deep Ravine, with the skirmishers facing both west toward the river and southeast toward Deep Ravine. It only needed a spark to ignite the powder keg that menaced them. That spark came in the form of the Southern Cheyenne chief, Lame White Man. After knocking Mark Kellogg from his mule, Lame White Man had watched the action for a while. Seeing the warriors flee from the soldiers' charge, he rode up and "called us to come back and fight. In a few minutes the warriors were all around these soldiers."[121] He then led the charge against Smith's command, calling out, "Come. We can kill them all."[122]

From behind their ridge, Wolf Tooth's band heard a Lakota crier calling out "to get ready and watch for the suicide boys. They said they were getting ready down below to charge …."[123] This group of young men, who had made a pact to die rather than yield to the soldiers, were about to make a significant impact on the fighting. As Wolf Tooth watched, the boys galloped up to Cemetery Ridge, then turned and while "some stampeded the gray horses"[124] the rest "charged right in at the place where the soldiers were making their stand."[125] Already reeling from the charge led by Lame White Man, Lieutenant Smith's command now found itself in a deadly hand-to-hand fight with a vastly superior number of the enemy. Unable to use their carbines and once they had emptied their revolvers, the soldiers used both weapons as clubs, against the war clubs and hatchets of the warriors, an eerie reprise of C Company's demise. As wood, stone and metal crunched into the heads and bodies of the soldiers, desperation tuned to panic and panic to thoughts of flight.

During this wild melee, Lame White Man was killed. Waterman, one of the five Arapahoes present, told Colonel Tim McCoy in 1920: "The soldiers were on the high ground and in one of the first charges we made a Cheyenne Chief named White Man Cripple was killed."[126] The F Company's eight-man squad commander, Second Lieutenant William Van Wyck Reily, was heavily involved in the fighting:

Custer [Reily] shouted loudly to his men and drew nearer to them when he found that they did [not] hear his voice. His appearance attracted the attention of Yellow Nose, who was armed with an old saber, having lost his gun. Custer's [Reily's] men had fallen beside him like grain before a sickle, and he stood alone when Yellow Nose drew his saber and tried to cut him down. The Indian's pony was wild, and when Custer [Reily] fired a pistol at close range the already wounded animal bolted and ran beyond him. Yellow Nose charged the second time, and again Custer [Reily] fired and the pony sprang to one side. Getting his pony firmly in hand for the onslaughts, Yellow Nose rode squarely down upon Custer [Reily], and without danger, as Custer [Reily] had fired his last shot. Custer [Reily] bent his knees as if to ward off the blow of the uplifted sword. He was struck on the back of his head and sank to the ground ....[127]

Utterly routed, E Company was almost completely destroyed but had taken most of the suicide boys with them. Wooden Leg named some of them, "Noisy Walking, Hump Nose, Whirlwind and Limber Bones."[128] Apart from Limber Bones, all these young men were under twenty years old. Many warriors had also suffered a variety of wounds as they charged into the soldiers: "I saw one Sioux walking slowly toward the gulch, going away from where were the soldiers ... As he passed near to where I was I saw that his whole lower jaw was shot away. The sight of him made me sick. I had to vomit."[129] Amidst the heated cauldron of the close-quarter combat, it was almost inevitable that allies were mistaken for enemies. The Miniconjou Standing Bear was involved in such an incident:

Burst Thunder ... came up to us and told us to go down a little ways that there was a dead man here whom we should scalp (a Ree). So we went down and just as they scalped him there were two Cheyennes that came up to us ... One of the Cheyennes got off and turned the body over and found it was a Cheyenne that they had scalped. [This man was identified as Lame White Man].[130]

Left Hand, another of the five Arapahoe present, made a similar mistake:

The soldiers were up on the ridge and the Indians were all around them. There was lots of shooting all around, and the Indians were all yelling ... I saw an Indian on foot, who was wounded in the leg, and, thinking he was one of the Crow or Arikara scouts with the soldiers, I rode at him, striking him with a long lance which I carried. The head of the lance was sharpened like an arrow. It struck him in the chest and went clear through him ... Afterward I found out he was a Sioux ...[131]

More warriors also died in the frantic fight for survival.

The survivors of E Company were few. Three, including "Fresh" Smith managed to escape to the relative safety of the F Company skirmish line on the lower slope of Last Stand Hill. Five others tried to escape to the east but were chased down and killed. Of the eight F Company men who had been sent to support E Company, three were found where the Deep Ravine fighting had taken place and the four others escaped with Smith to the north. Lieutenant Reily, though badly wounded, also managed to stagger to the comparative safety of the F Company skirmish line. Taken to the makeshift hospital further up the hill, his wound proved fatal.

The seriousness of the situation was not lost on Lieutenant Colonel Custer. He immediately sent Trumpeter Voss to Captain Yates with an order to shoot whatever horses remained for use as a defensive barricade. Some of the men wept as they shot the mounts who had been their faithful friends for so long and the horses began to scream as they smelled the blood from those already killed. Higher up the slope, Lieutenant Colonel Custer still sat astride his ex-racehorse, the spirited gelding Vic, watching the warriors beginning to advance toward his remaining force. He could hear firing from the east which gave him one positive to pin some hopes on; there were no warriors attacking him from that direction, which he believed meant that Keogh's battalion was still holding its own and keeping warriors from coming up the eastern slopes. He could only hope now that Myles Keogh would find a way to unite with him.

Right Wing, 5:00–5:20 p.m.

Captain Keogh could only watch in dismay as C Company disintegrated under the warrior onslaught. Some survivors on foot were running towards L Company on Calhoun Hill while Sergeant Bobo was heading straight at the I Company position closely followed by five other C Company men who had managed to mount their sorrel horses. Warrior fire killed Bobo's horse, and he jumped from it as its lifeless body slid down from the crest of the ridge.[132]

Lieutenant Calhoun could see the panic-stricken men from C Company running to his position, though taking casualties all the time. Behind them came a mass of screaming warriors, some firing guns and some using arrows, some wielding their fearsome close-combat weapons, already dripping with blood. To meet this imminent threat Calhoun ordered Crittenden to switch the south facing part of the skirmish line to face west. Waiting until the C Company men had cleared his line of fire, he ordered his skirmishers to fire at the warriors. Some fell but the relentless swarm charged on.

The Oglala Red Hawk described the collapse of C Company and the charge against Calhoun's company:

> The officers tried their utmost to keep the soldiers together at this point, but the horses were unmanageable; they would rear up and fall backward with their riders; some would get away. The Indians force the troopers back to where the first stand was made on Calhoun Hill and the ridge running from there to the river. At this place the soldiers stood in line and made a very good fight. The soldiers delivered volley after volley into the dense ranks of the Indians without any perceptible effect on account of their great numbers.[133]

Red Horse, a Miniconjou, was equally graphic:

> One band of soldiers was right in rear of us; when they charged, we fell back and stood for one moment facing each other. Then the Indians got courage and started for them in a solid body. We went but a little distance, when we spread out and encircled them. All the time I could see their officers riding in front, and hear them shouting to their men. It was in this charge that

most of the Indians were killed. We lost 136 killed and 160 wounded. We finished up this party right there in the ravine.[134]

The casualties did not deter the fired-up warriors and as they got closer to the skirmishers some of the soldiers, already alarmed by seeing the frightened men of C Company running away, began to lose discipline. They began to edge closer to the men next to them instead of keeping their intervals. Their sweating hands fumbled the task of reloading their carbines and the firing at the Indians became ragged. Even as the warrior horde crashed into them, some of Calhoun's men started fleeing towards Keogh's position on Battle Ridge. Calhoun and Crittenden tried desperately to rally their troopers but died in the attempt. Their bodies were found close together behind the line of their dead men. The fate of L Company was related by the Oglala Red Hawk: "The Indians kept coming like an increasing flood which could not be checked. The soldiers were swept off their feet; they could not stay; the Indians were overwhelming. Here the troopers divided and retreated on each side of the ridge, falling back steadily to Custer Hill [Battle Ridge] where another stand was made"[135] Flying Hawk too described the scene: "When they found they were being killed so fast, the ones that were left broke and ran as fast as their horses could go to some other soldiers that were further along the ridge toward Custer."[136]

One soldier who did not take that course of action was the company's first sergeant, James Butler, a 34-year-old veteran of known courage, who raced to the south pursued by several warriors. His badly mutilated body, surrounded by many cartridge shells, was found on the promontory that now bears his name, west of Luce Ridge. Dr. Charles Eastman, the Santee/white physician was told about this by participants, "One company was chased along the ridge to the south, out of which a man got away. A mighty yell went up from the Indians as he cleared the attacking forces, as if they were glad that he succeeded. Away he went toward Reno's position."[137] Said Lieutenant Godfrey, "One of the first bodies I recognized ... was that of Sergeant Butler ... The indications were that he sold his life dearly, for near and under him were found many empty cartridge-shells."[138] That is confirmed by the mutilations. The warriors did not want to face him again in the afterlife.

When Myles Keogh saw the huge numbers of warriors appear from behind Greasy Grass Ridge almost immediately after Harrington's charge had chased away the infiltrators, he expected C Company to withdraw in orderly fashion after stopping the Indians with their firepower. What he saw instead was Harrington's command overrun and cut to pieces, with a few survivors running towards Calhoun, chased by scores of yelling warriors. He probably approved silently when Lieutenant Calhoun swung Crittenden's squad to face the new threat. That confidence swiftly changed to alarm as the warriors kept on coming despite the withering fire from the L Company skirmish line. Now some of the warriors were firing at his own I Company exposed on the western military crest of Battle Ridge. He quickly ordered them to move over to the eastern military crest even though they were exposed to some longer distance firing from the Crazy Horse group behind the eastern ridge. It was there that Sergeant Bobo and the other five C Company men joined him.

Mounted on his horse Comanche, Keogh watched as L Company was in turn overwhelmed so prepared to organize his own company into the best defensive position he could. Before he could do that, events started to move rapidly out of his control. The survivors from his other two companies were running to their horses behind Calhoun Hill, but firing from Crazy Horse killed some of them and the horse-holders. As Flying Hawk recalled, "He shot them as fast as he could load his gun. They fell off their horses as fast as he could shoot. [Here the chief swayed rapidly back and forth to show how fast they fell]."[139]

To assist the Calhoun Hill survivors to reach him safely, Keogh sent a squad from his company forward to fire at the chasing warriors. This distraction presented an opportunity for Crazy Horse to demonstrate just why he had such a highly respected reputation. Seeing the gap open up between the two I Company factions, the Oglala war chief leaped on his pony and executed a bravery run through that gap. Several soldiers fired at him, but none hit. Making a pirouette on his pony, Crazy Horse made a return run and again came through unscathed. His fellow tribesman Red Feather painted a picture of the incident: "While they were lying there, shooting at one another, Crazy Horse came up on horseback—with an eagle horn—and rode between the two parties. The soldiers all fired at once, but didn't hit him."[140] Other warriors too, recalled this pivotal event. Another Oglala, He Dog, stated, "Stretched along the ridge [on which the monument is now], there is a sort of gap in the ridge which Crazy Horse broke through, cutting the line in two"[141] and, "at Keogh is where Crazy Horse charged and broke through and split up soldiers in two bunches."[142]

Myles Keogh instantly recalled his forward squad and the united I Company with the remnants of the rest of the battalion began to slowly retreat towards Last Stand Hill. But the bravery runs of Crazy Horse had fired up his followers even more and he led them in a smashing charge against Keogh's back pedaling force. This was immediately followed by the attack of the warriors coming from Calhoun Hill. Before he could rally his troops, Indian bullets shattered his left leg and knee and penetrated the right shoulder of Comanche. Squealing in pain, the horse bucked wildly, throwing its rider as it galloped off toward the river. The gallant Irishman, crippled, unable to move but still clutching his revolver, died firing at the warriors who killed him. Two of his noncommissioned officers, Sergeant James Bustard and First Sergeant Frank E. Varden tried to protect him but died in the attempt. Trumpeter John Patton fell dead across Keogh's body while Private John Wild was also killed nearby. In fact, nearly all of Keogh's I Company, only moments ago a fighting force, now lay in heaps around their commander. Keogh's second in command, First Lieutenant James E. Porter was not among them, and his remains were never formally identified, but the finding of his bloodstained buckskin coat lining with a bullet hole in the back left no doubt about his fate. Fate also caught up with Sergeant Bobo who had escaped the annihilation of C Company, only to be killed with Keogh.[143] The five C Company men who had followed Bobo did not stop long once they saw the oncoming Indian threat. They spurred their horses toward Last Stand Hill.

Some warrior accounts tell of the last throes of Keogh's panic-stricken command. Having described how Crazy Horse had shot at the horse-holders behind Calhoun Hill, Flying Hawk goes on:

> When they found they were being killed so fast, the ones that were left broke and ran as fast as their horses could go to some other soldiers that were further along the ridge toward Custer. Here they tried to make another stand and fired some shots, but we rushed them on along the ridge to where Custer was. Then they made another stand (the third) and rallied a few minutes. They went on along the ridge and got with Custer's men. Other Indians came to us after we got most of the men at ravine. We all kept after them until they got to where Custer was. There was only a few of them left then.[144]

The Miniconjou warrior Hump observed, "The first charge the Indians made they never slacked up or stopped. They made a finish of it. The Indians and whites were so mixed up that you could hardly tell anything about it. The first dash the Indians made my horse was shot from under me and I was wounded—shot above the knee, and the ball came out at the hip … and I fell and lay right there."[145]

Having seen the Crazy Horse bravery runs, Red Feather said "The Indians got the idea the soldiers' guns were empty and charged immediately on the soldiers. They charged right over the hill. Red Feather, yelling, shot into the soldiers who tried to get away. That made it easier for the Indians, who shot them from behind."[146] The effect of all this on the soldiers was noticed by Red Horse. "When we attacked the other party, we swarmed down on them and drove them in confusion. The soldiers became panic-stricken many of them throwing down their arms and throwing up their hands."[147]

Indian accounts also tell of how some survivors, both on foot and mounted, fled in the direction of Last Stand Hill. Foolish Elk said:

> It did not appear to him that a stand was made by Custer's men anywhere except at the monument. He was in the gully and saw the soldiers killed on the side hill [Keogh] as they "marched" toward the high ground at end of ridge [monument]. They made no stand here, but all were going toward the high ground at end of ridge … The men on horses did not stop to fight … The men on foot, however, were shooting as they passed along.[148]

Turtle Rib too, remarked: "When he got up with the soldiers, there was a running fight with some of the soldiers on foot. Those who kept their horses seemed to be stampeded. Some were going toward the monument, and some were trying to go back the way they came."[149]

However many may have tried to escape to join the Headquarters Group, some did not make it. Only about ten utterly traumatized soldiers reached the Left Wing Group's position on the hill. The escapees must have been overcome with relief at avoiding the fate of their comrades on Battle Ridge but they could not know that their reprieve was only temporary.

Left Wing, 5:10–5:20 p.m.

Whatever hope George Custer entertained of being reunited with Keogh's battalion was even now being destroyed by Crazy Horse and a host of other warriors in the swale to the east of Battle Ridge. Of course, he did not know that, but in any case, he was faced with pressing problems of his own. Warriors were flooding through Deep Ravine and the coulees around his position, as well as using every piece of cover on the terrain leading up from the river.

Having overcome E Company, the warriors' blood was up and they were determined to get to grips with what remained of the Yates group. Following the destruction of the Right Wing, Crazy Horse and his victorious fighters now also swept towards Last Stand Hill from the east. The Hunkpapa Iron Hawk modestly described the menacing storm, "… Crazy Horse at one end, and Iron Hawk was on the side toward the ridge and between the ridge and the river in the attack on Custer. They surrounded Custer."[150]

Even before this new throng of warriors reached him, Custer's hopes of a union with Keogh were totally shattered when the five C Company men galloped into view. They quickly confirmed that the Right Wing had been destroyed by warriors attacking from the eastern slopes of Battle Ridge and Custer instantly knew that he would have to organize a defense against the inevitable attack from that direction against his hill position. He ordered the C Company men to lead their horses to the crest of the hill where they were to shoot them for use as a protective barrier against firing from the east and southeast. As soon as that had been done, Custer deployed a small force to defend the position until Yates could redeploy F Company. Apart from himself there were his brothers Tom and Boston, his nephew Henry Armstrong "Autie" Reed, Adjutant Cooke, Mitch Boyer, Sergeant Robert Hughes, Sergeant John Vickory and Chief Trumpeter Henry Voss, plus the five C Company escapees. They waited for the onslaught as the pounding of Indian ponies' hooves could be heard coming closer.

Lower down the hill, Captain George Yates and his F Company lay behind the barriers of dead horses they had created earlier, already receiving bullets and arrows as the wily warriors used every scrap of cover to creep closer. Runs The Enemy, who had just come from fighting near Battle Ridge told how:

> I left my men there and told them to hold that position and then I rushed around the hills and came up to the north end of the field near where the monument now stands. And I saw hundreds and hundreds of Indians in the coulees all around. The Indians dismounted and tied their horses in a bunch and got down into the coulees, shooting at the soldiers from all sides.[151]

Gall related what he saw of the F Company defense: "They were fighting good. The men were loading and firing, but they could not hit the warriors in the gulley and in the ravine. The dust and smoke was as black evening."[152]

Just below the crest of the hill and behind the five dead horses, George Custer and his small group had now come under fire from the warriors coming from the Right Wing fight. Among them was Crazy Horse. Time was running out for the Boy General of the Civil War.

Left Wing, 5:20–5:30 p.m.

Without horses there were no longer any cavalrymen on Last Stand Hill, and they were ill-prepared to fight an infantry action against a highly mobile foe. The Cheyenne woman Kate Big Head, or Antelope Woman, observed how the warriors were able to avoid being hit. "At that time there must have been hundreds of warriors for every white soldier left alive. The warriors around them were shifting from shelter to shelter, each of them trying to get close enough to strike a coup blow … The remaining soldiers were keeping themselves behind their dead horses." [153] Individual warriors dared to dart forward and kill a soldier with club or axe, but not all escaped unscathed. Kate Big Head saw "one Sioux boy killed by a soldier bullet,"[154] and Wooden Leg described how, "A Sioux wearing a warbonnet was lying down behind a clump of sagebrush on the hillside … The Sioux was peeping up and firing a rifle from time to time. At one of these times a soldier bullet hit him exactly in the middle of the forehead."[155]

With little effective fire coming from the soldiers, it only needed a catalyst to spur the warriors into direct action. A lull in the firing was all the warriors needed. Believing most of the soldiers to be dead they rushed forward only to be met by most of the F Company survivors, who were very much alive. Hand-to-hand fighting followed and what happened made a lasting impression on the warriors who were there. Miniconjou warrior Turtle Rib said, "No stand was made except at the end of the long ridge (where Custer fell), and here the bay and gray horses were all mixed together. There was a big dust, and the Indians were running all around the locality much excited and shooting into the soldiers."[156] The Oglala Red Hawk stated, "Here the troopers divided and retreated on each side of the ridge, falling back steadily to Custer Hill where another stand was made. By this time the Indians were taking the guns and cartridges of the dead soldiers and putting these to use and were more active in the struggle. Here the soldiers made a desperate fight."[157]

Even as that desperate fighting was going on, the Custer group at the top of the hill were coming under increasing pressure. Subjected to rifle fire from the east, southeast, north, and northwest, the ten men did not have enough firepower to hurt the warriors. Having watched the action for a while, Crazy Horse thought it was time he took a hand. There had been ominous rumblings for the white men and now the volcano was about to erupt. He mounted his pony and led a charge over the dead horses atop Last Stand Hill. The result was devastating for the gallant little band of defenders. Brevet Major General George Armstrong Custer suffered a severe chest wound, Cooke, Vickory and Voss were dead or dying, leaving only Tom Custer, brother Boston, Autie Reed, Mitch Boyer, Sergeant Hughes and perhaps some of the C Company men to fight on. The impact of Crazy Horse was recorded by the Arapahoe Waterman: "There was a great deal of noise and confusion. The air was heavy with powder smoke, and the Indians were all yelling. Crazy Horse, the Sioux Chief, was the bravest man I ever saw. He rode closest to the soldiers, yelling to his warriors. All the soldiers were shooting at him, but he was never hit …"[158] It was nearing the end for the five companies that had ridden with Custer.

No Survivors, 5:30 p.m.

The tide of battle that had swept over the Keogh battalion now became a tsunami that destroyed what remained of the Left Wing Group and some others, as the shrieking, whooping warriors swarmed over them. The frenzy of the fighting was graphically depicted by the Miniconjou Beard:

> Hundreds of other warriors joined us as we splashed across the ford near our camp and raced up the hills to charge into the thickest of the fighting. This new battle was a turmoil of dust and warriors and soldiers, with bullets whining and arrows hissing all around. Sometimes a bugle would sound and the shooting would get louder. Some of the soldiers were firing pistols at close range. Our knives and war clubs flashed in the sun. I could hear bullets whiz past my ears. But I kept going and shouting, "It's a good day to die!" so that everyone who heard would know I was not afraid of being killed in battle.[159]

The soldiers' revolvers were only effective for a very short time, for once emptied, there was no time to reload. As clubs they were no match for the lethal close combat weapons of the warriors. Once the high-pitched cracks of the six-shooters fell silent, the troopers received wicked blows to their heads, some from stone headed clubs which caved their skulls in, splattering their brains and further unnerving their comrades. It was a charnel house of death from which no white man survived. Some did try to flee to safety, and several warriors noticed them. Waterman remarked, "The soldiers were entirely surrounded and the whole country was alive with Indians. There were thousands of them. A few soldiers tried to get away and reach the river, but they were all killed."[160] Lone Bear, an Oglala, responded to Camp, "Q: In the last stand at 'G' [Last Stand Hill], did the soldiers all fight to the last, or did some try to break away and escape? A: Soldiers were fighting hard at 'G.' There were a few who tried to get away,"[161] and another Oglala, Respects Nothing, told Eli Ricker:

> At any rate, he said that those were all killed at Custer Hill before those were down along the ravine. These latter, when the others were down, made a break through a narrow gap in the Indian line and ran toward the river trying to escape. They were on foot. The Indians followed

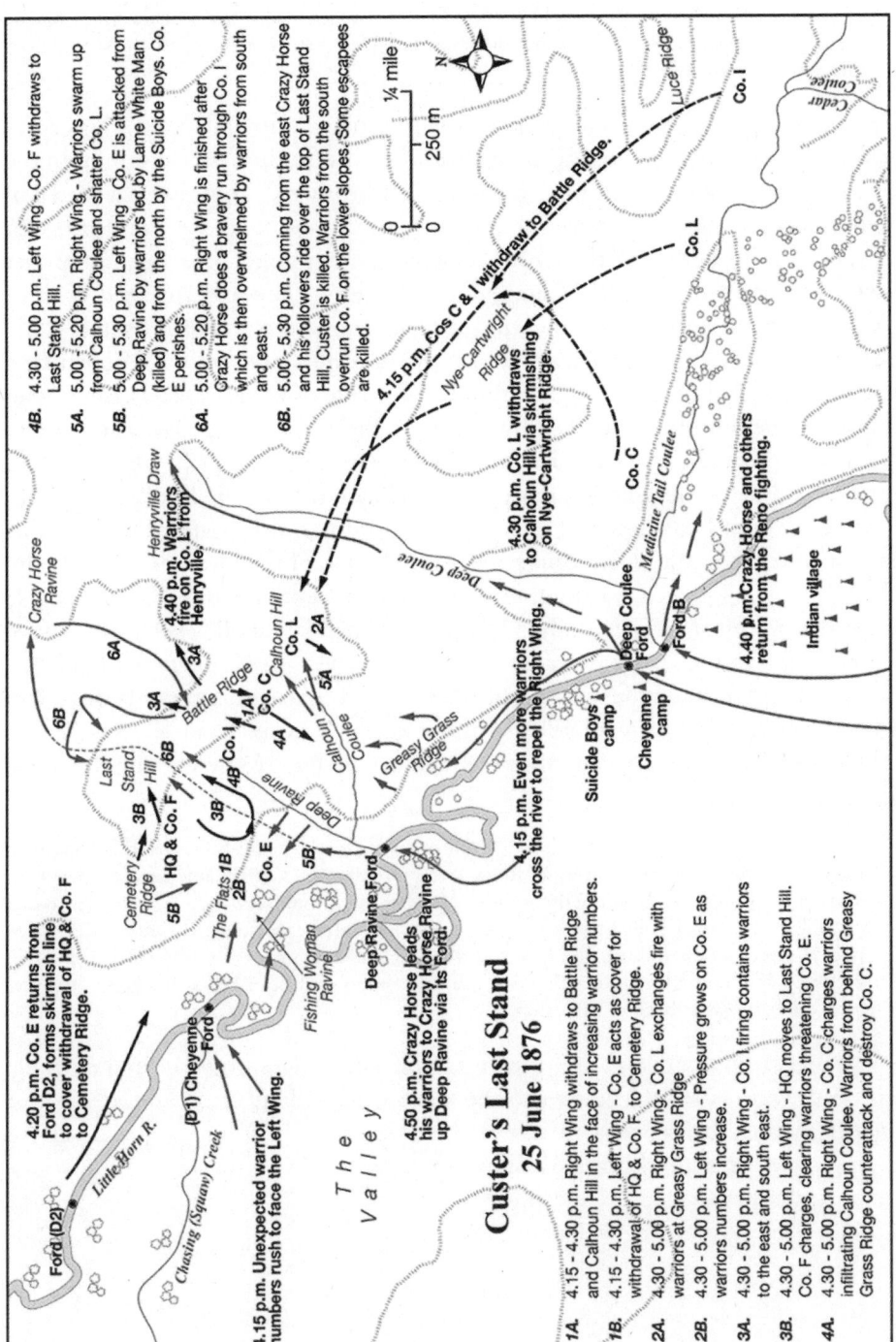

Custer's Last Stand
25 June 1876

4.15 p.m. Unexpected warrior numbers rush to face the Left Wing.

4.20 p.m. Co. E returns from Ford D2, forms skirmish line to cover withdrawal of HQ & Co. F to Cemetery Ridge.

4.40 p.m. Warriors fire on Co. I from Hennyville.

4.50 p.m. Crazy Horse leads his warriors to Crazy Horse Ravine up Deep Ravine via Ford.

4.15 p.m. Even more warriors cross the river to repel the Right Wing.

4.30 p.m. Co. L withdraws to Calhoun Hill via skirmishing on Nye-Cartwright Ridge.

4.15 p.m. Cos C & I withdraw to Battle Ridge.

4.40 p.m. Crazy Horse and others return from the Reno fighting.

1A. 4.15 - 4.30 p.m. Right Wing withdraws to Battle Ridge and Calhoun Hill in the face of increasing warrior numbers.

1B. 4.15 - 4.30 p.m. Left Wing - Co. E acts as cover for withdrawal of HQ & Co. F to Cemetery Ridge.

2A. 4.30 - 5.00 p.m. Right Wing - Co. L exchanges fire with warriors at Greasy Grass Ridge

2B. 4.30 - 5.00 p.m. Left Wing - Pressure grows on Co. E as warriors numbers increase.

3A. 4.30 - 5.00 p.m. Right Wing - Co. I firing contains warriors to the east and south east.

3B. 4.30 - 5.00 p.m. Left Wing - HQ moves to Last Stand Hill. Co. F charges, clearing warriors threatening Co. E.

4A. 4.30 - 5.00 p.m. Right Wing - Co. C charges warriors infiltrating Calhoun Coulee. Warriors from behind Greasy Grass Ridge counterattack and destroy Co. C.

4B. 4.30 - 5.00 p.m. Left Wing - Co. F withdraws to Last Stand Hill.

5A. 5.00 - 5.20 p.m. Right Wing - Warriors swarm up from Calhoun Coulee and shatter Co. L.

5B. 5.00 - 5.30 p.m. Left Wing - Co. E is attacked from Deep Ravine by warriors led by Lame White Man (killed) and from the north by the Suicide Boys. Co. E perishes.

6A. 5.00 - 5.20 p.m. Right Wing is finished after Crazy Horse does a bravery run through Co. I which is then overwhelmed by warriors from south and east.

6B. 5.00 - 5.30 p.m. Coming from the east Crazy Horse and his followers ride over the top of Last Stand Hill. Custer is killed. Warriors from the south overrun Co. F on the lower slopes. Some escapees are killed.

Custer's Last Stand. (Gordon Harper, *Fights on the Little Horn*, 2014) them and killed them with war clubs of stone and wooden clubs, some of the latter having lance spears on them. In this pursuit one Indian stumbled into a low place, among the soldiers, and was killed by them.[162]

The few at the top of the hill fared no better. A badly wounded George Custer was spared the possibility of being captured alive when his brother Tom shot him in the head with a small caliber Colt carried by his elder brother.[163] Tom, twice a Medal of Honor winner in the Civil War and a fierce fighter, took some warriors with him as he died and his body was therefore savagely dealt with later. The Ree interpreter Frederic F. Gerard told Walter Camp, "Tom Custer—they had smashed back of his head in with a stone or hammer and shot an arrow into top of his skull."[164] As to Adjutant Cooke, his Dundreary whiskers were commented on by Wooden Leg: "Here is a new kind of scalp"[165] as he skinned one side of Cooke's face. Others who had been in the hilltop group tried frantically to flee to what they saw as the safety of the river timbered area. They did not make it. Custer's brother Boston and their cousin Autie Reed were killed quite soon after they ran from the knoll. Near them fell Private Weston Harrington of L Company, then lower down, near Deep Ravine, the scout Mitch Boyer and Sergeant Robert H. Hughes of the Headquarters Group, both slain by the frenzied warriors. Private Timothy Donnelly of F Company also made it that far but no further. The Oglala Red Hawk saw it all, "What was left of them retreated to the (what he calls) third stand. These were surrounded and the Indians rushed on the soldiers. Some of the soldiers broke through the Indians and ran for the ravine, but were all killed without getting into it."[166]

These final scenes were etched into the memory of Two Kettle warrior Runs The Enemy:

> The soldiers then gathered in a group, where the monument now stands—I visited the monument today and confirmed my memory of it—and then the soldiers and Indians were all mixed up. You could not tell one from the other. In this final charge I took part and when the last soldier was killed the smoke rolled up like a mountain above our heads, and the soldiers were piled one on top of another, dead, and here and there an Indian among the soldiers. I saw one that had been hit across the head with a war axe, and others had been hit with arrows. After we were done, we went back to the camp.[167]

It would be a camp where many Cheyennes and Lakota lodges would be in mourning. Their dead warriors would be sent to the afterworld with all their honors intoned over their bodies. By contrast, many of the corpses of the white soldiers were so badly mutilated that their initial shallow gravesites would be marked with just one word—"Unknown."

CHAPTER 2

In Custer's Boots

This article was written in response to specious criticisms of Custer being published on the specialist message boards on the Internet. As the criticisms were in the public arena, I thought a more accurate interpretation should be available. It was accepted for publication because looking at the subject matter from Custer's point of view had not been written about previously.

June 25, 1876, the Battle of the Little Big Horn is fought. Overwhelming numbers of Sioux and Cheyenne warriors annihilate the 7th U.S. Cavalry. Lieutenant Colonel George Armstrong Custer is killed along with over 260 of his men. Custer, the Civil War hero, is now cast as the villain. As a soldier with a penchant for taking calculated risks and not averse to being insubordinate, he is now accused of displaying both traits prior to the battle and is blamed for the disaster.

His accuser is Brigadier General Alfred Terry, his commanding officer, who wants to distance himself from any responsibility for the tragedy which represents a distinct threat to his military career. Terry traveled with the Montana Column, a sister command, which followed a different route to the Little Big Horn. He was guilty of some poor decisions that delayed Gibbon's Montana Column, which arrived late, after the battle was over.

Lieutenant Colonel George A. Custer. (Wikimedia Commons)

In the wake of the shocking news about the battle, a chorus of self-serving voices endorses Terry's condemnation of the lieutenant colonel. He had, said Terry, followed the Indian trail into the Little Big Horn valley against orders, attacked a day early thus preventing Gibbon's column from participating in the action as planned, failed to check out upper Tullock's Creek as ordered and failed to send courier George Herendeen through to Gibbon as required. The limited scope of this article prevents an in-depth analysis of all these points, but we can perhaps discover what prompted Custer to apparently overlook the last two matters.

Terry's criticisms imply that Custer, on his journey up the Rosebud, knew that the Montana Column would be in Tullock's Creek from June 24 to 25. But is that true and if not, what did Custer believe?

If the Montana Column had been meant to march up Tullock's Creek, there is no mention of that in any pre- or post-battle document or in any of the journals kept by participants. Tullock's only mention is in Custer's orders, "The Department Commander desires that on your way up the Rosebud you should thoroughly examine the upper part of Tullock's Creek and that you should endeavor to send a scout through to Colonel Gibbon's column with information of the result of your examination. The lower part of this creek will be examined by a detachment from Colonel Gibbon's command."[1]

The above extract is significant because it not only omits any reference to the creek being the intended route of the Gibbon's Montana Column but specifically mentions that only a detachment from that command could be expected there. It also gives no date or time for Custer's examination of the upper part of the creek and equally therefore, no date or time at which Gibbon could expect the arrival of Herendeen.

However, there is an abundance of evidence to show that Terry had planned for Gibbon's command to march up the Big Horn River valley. There is Terry's dispatch of June 21 to General Phil Sheridan, "Gibbon's column will move … for the mouth of the Big Horn … whence it will proceed to the mouth of the Little Horn."[2] After the conference on the steamer *Far West* that day, his orders to Custer issued on June 22 stated, "The column of Colonel Gibbon is now in motion for the mouth of the Big Horn … will … move up at least as far as the forks of the Big and Little Horns."[3]

Custer's opinion is included in his dispatch of the previous evening to the *New York Herald*, "Gibbon's command has started for the mouth of the Big Horn. Terry in the *Far West* starts for the same point today when with Gibbon's force … he will push up the Big Horn as far as the navigation of that stream will permit."[4] Clearly Custer did not consider Tullock's important, or he would have taken the opportunity to stress his own role in what made it so.

But perhaps the most compelling source for details of the route for Gibbon's command came from *Bismarck Tribune* reporter Mark Kellogg. He had not been present at the *Far West* conference, but had quarters on the steamer, was friendly with the entire Headquarters Group and by talking to them had an intimate knowledge of what had been planned. He died in the battle, but in his final dispatch of June 21 says that Custer will "… move on that trail with all rapidity to *overhaul* [italics mine] the Indians" and "in the meantime, General Terry will move on the steamer to the mouth of the Big Horn River, scouting Pumpkin [Tullock's] Creek en route, with General Gibbon … marching toward the Big Horn. This part of the command marches up the Big Horn valley in order to intercept the Indians if they should intend to escape from General Custer down that avenue."[5] The only reference to Tullock's here has it being checked en route to the Big Horn valley.

Now perhaps we have some idea of what was in Custer's mind as he started his command up the Rosebud on June 22. If he was set on ignoring his orders, there is little evidence of it on that march. That pillar of Little Big Horn literature, Dr. John S. Gray, sums it up well, "Custer had arrived at the Busby bend exactly on schedule as worked out at the steamboat conference …. [T]he evidence proves that Custer faithfully observed his orders in both word and spirit."[6] On June 24 too, he had shown his desire to observe Terry's suggestions, when he tried to send the courier George Herendeen through to Tullock's Creek, albeit too early.

By the time his command made camp at 7:45 p.m. on June 24, Custer knew that the Indians were not far ahead but he had ignored Herendeen's earlier approach to leave for the head of Tullock's because there were no trails in that direction. He had some Crow scouts trailing the enemy Indians and they reported back at 9 p.m. with the news that the trail crossed the divide between the Rosebud and the Little Big Horn. Now it was imperative for Custer to establish whether that trail went north or south. Terry's plan was based on finding the Indians to the south, probably near the headwaters of the Little Big Horn. If they had moved north, Terry's planning would need to be modified.

Terry, who had not been on active service for 11 years, created his plan based on guesswork. Educated guesswork perhaps, but the plan held no precise details. For Custer however, guesswork was not good enough. He knew that if there was to be cooperation with Gibbon's command, he had to establish the exact location of the enemy. Without that there could be no fixed target to attack and no explicit intelligence to send to Gibbon on the changed situation. The increasing impracticability of making contact with the other command would also have been exercising Custer's mind because, as we have seen, he believed that they would be moving up the Big Horn valley, further away from him as each hour passed.

We know that Terry was anxious to make contact too, "That evening [June 24] Terry expressed a strong desire to have some communication (as he had anticipated) with General Custer."[7] That desire has invariably been interpreted as meaning Terry needed to know whether he could continue up Tullock's Creek. If he should have been in the Big Horn valley however, is it not more likely that he was anxious for Herendeen's arrival to send him back to Custer with the information that Gibbon was marching up Tullock's? The diversion over Tullock's divide when the courier did not appear rather endorses that possibility.

Early on the morning of June 25, from a promontory on the divide between the Rosebud and Little Bighorn valleys called the Crow's Nest, the Indian village was seen as having turned to the north, thus sited on the lower Little Big Horn. From various incidents, Custer believed the command had been seen and that he had no alternative but to attack with his regiment. But for that I believe Herendeen would have been sent to Gibbon. Herendeen told Walter Camp that on June 25 "I said to Custer, General, the head of Tullock's Creek lies just over those hills yonder. He replied … 'Yes, but there are no Indians in that direction—they are all in our front and beside they have discovered us. It will be of no use to send you down Tullock's Creek.'"[8]

That final comment is often used to show that Custer did not want to share the "glory" with Gibbon's command. I suggest it means that Custer realized the futility of trying to contact Gibbon, believing him to be well up the Big Horn valley by that time, but hoped that he was at least able to act as a blocking force against any Indians who might flee that way. In the circumstances, it was the only way the Montana Column could be involved.

There is a saying, purported to be of Native American origin, which is presented in English as "O Great Spirit, Grant that I may not criticize my neighbor, until I have walked a mile in his moccasins."[9] It would maybe be prudent for all of us to ask the Great Spirit to let us ride up the Rosebud on Dandy on June 24, 1876 wearing Custer's cavalry boots and knowing only what he knew, before we rush to denounce the decisions he took on that and the following day.

CHAPTER 3

Custer's Luck Runs Out

Most books and articles about the battle concentrate on the actions of the 7th Cavalry. This article also includes some insights into the mindset of the Indians prior to the battle and how it affected the outcome, which will give much needed perspective to what took place.

"Porter, there is a large camp of Indians ahead, and we are going to have a great killing,"[1] so Lieutenant Colonel George Armstrong Custer is reported to have said to Dr. Henry R. Porter, Acting Assistant Surgeon with the 7th Cavalry, on the morning of June 25, 1876 as the 7th Cavalry was preparing to attack those same Indians. There was indeed a "great killing" but the victims were Custer himself and over 250 of his men.

Custer has since been heavily criticized by some for his perceived misjudgments or disobedience and his decision to attack has received its fair share of that criticism. Ill advised, it is argued, because he did not heed his scouts' concerns over the enormous number of people in the camp and therefore did not take time for a more studied reconnaissance to seek additional intelligence before he decided on the best course of action to follow.

So, when he stood in the divide between Rosebud Creek and the Little Big Horn River believing enemy scouts had seen the regiment, what information did he have? He knew that Indians did not stand and fight against a large military force but fled and scattered. This view was based on the U.S. Army's experience in Indian warfare and Custer himself had suffered such embarrassment on the Southern Plains in 1867. His own report on his August 4, 1873 engagement with the Sioux on the Yellowstone River stated: "No sooner did the Indians discern our intentions than, despite their superiority in numbers, they cowardly prepared for flight ..."[2]

That last phrase shows that Custer, like most of Terry's subordinate officers, had little belief that the Indians would fight. He was aware that no U.S. force greater than Captain William Fetterman's 81 men in 1866, had suffered any major defeat by Indians who were therefore held in contempt for running away from fights.

The fact that they could not afford to lose seasoned warriors by taking on superior numbers and arms was never considered.

Then too, there was the prime mission of the campaign—to locate the Indians and force them onto reservations. Three different army columns had been searching for them for weeks without success and now they were in large numbers some 15 miles away in the Little Big Horn valley, expected to scatter. The size of the Indian village was not unique, but the situation was. Once before, at Killdeer Mountain in 1864, General Alfred Sully had reported facing as many, if not more, yet the comparison stops there. Sully had four times Custer's force, combined with infantry with longer range rifles and decisive artillery against a foe drawn up in battle lines. However, it was not a situation Custer could turn away from. Yet Custer's accusers seem to think that he should have jettisoned all his previous knowledge of Indian warfare and dreamed up a new strategy on the spot even though urgency was paramount.

Finally, Custer considered his regiment the finest cavalry on the plains, a match for any number of Indians they encountered. Was this just Custer's ego? Not, if measured against the comments of other officers on the campaign. Colonel John Gibbon, who had only 400 men, advised Brigadier General Terry in his April 21 letter, "… moved my camp alongside Fort Pease, where I am strong enough to defy the whole Sioux nation, should they feel inclined to come this way"[3] and Terry, in his May 16 dispatch to General Philip Sheridan, "I have no doubt of the ability of my column to whip all the Sioux whom we can find."[4] He had expressed such confidence about the same time that interpreter Fred Gerard had told the general that there could be as many as 4,000 enemy warriors to face.

Critics have claimed that the "fog of war" misled Custer, that he was thus unwilling to take a realistic view of his own force, that he was overly optimistic about its capabilities and that he let inaccurate intelligence about the enemy lull him into a false sense of superiority. Regardless, his decision-making was compromised being based on faulty assumptions.

Did Custer, therefore, overestimate the capabilities of his regiment? Yes, but only because he was not clairvoyant. Did he misunderstand some factors concerning the Indians, factors that he could have gleaned by further reconnaissance?

The short answer is "No."

There were three elements that affected the mood of his quarry, but no amount of reconnaissance could have discovered two of them. Although he was aware of the third, its significance to the Indians was not something any white military officer of that time would have considered relevant.

The first thing affecting the Indians' attitude stemmed from the fact that when the "hostiles" had been told to go into the agencies by January 31, 1876, the bad winter weather had prevented those who were so inclined from complying. Old Bear's Northern Cheyenne band was on its way to their agency when attacked on the Powder River by General George Crook's cavalry under Colonel J. J. Reynolds on March 17 and so it took refuge with Crazy Horse. That Powder River attack confirmed to the tribes that the whites were determined to end the Indian way of life, so they had nothing to lose by resisting.

Though chronologically not second, the Battle of the Rosebud on June 17 increased the Indians' self-confidence when Crook retreated. Being able to claim a victory against a large—in fact larger—military force than Custer's made them unafraid to face any of the army columns trying to find them. Crook made no attempt to send messengers to Terry or any other field command they might find, so Custer was totally unaware that the "hostiles" were ready to fight.

Even before the Rosebud fight, the tribesmen were already in a confident frame of mind. When the winter roamers began to merge for protection, they looked to Sitting Bull for spiritual as well as political leadership. He did not fail them. During the first week of June, he organized and participated in the annual Lakota Sun Dance, sacrificing 50 pieces of skin from each arm in order to be receive a vision. That vision from the Great Spirit (*Wakan Tanka*) forecast a great victory over the soldiers. On June 24, Custer's Arikara scouts interpreted the signs at the sun dance circle as an omen that the enemy was certain of victory. Custer, however, attributed these concerns to the scouts' long-standing fear of the Sioux as any of the other commanders on that campaign would have assumed. Soldiers could not deal seriously with what they regarded as "superstition."

Custer, therefore, had to make urgent decisions without knowing, or having any way of knowing, that the Indians in the large camp were going to be a far different proposition from any he had ever faced. He could not have foreseen that exceptional situation, but his detractors argue that not only should he have realized it but also, in the blink of an eye, he should have been able to change his ingrained military mindset, abandon the usual tactics against Indians, think up new ones, then advance slowly toward the camp picking up intelligence as he went.

However, as already shown, the only intelligence that might have

Sitting Bull, Hunkpapa Lakota. (Wikimedia Commons)

Sioux Sun Dance ceremony. (Wood engraving by Jules Tavernier and Paul Frenzeny in *Harper's Weekly*, January 2, 1875)

caused him to pause would not be evident on the way to the village. He believed from the start that only two scenarios were possible: either the camp would still be relatively intact when it was reached, or it would already have scattered. It was a case of either or and he would not know which until he neared the location of the village.

The strategic imperative was to stop the Indians scattering. Custer's scouts had apparently located them, but should he heed their warning that there were too many to defeat? If he listened to them, and the mission failed, that decision would be the end of his military career. In any case, he probably knew that intertribal warfare never considered prudent an attack on superior numbers, so the scouts would naturally caution against such action. He realized the risk inherent in attacking the camp, but war after all, is about risk. It is the nature of such conflict.

Believing that the village would be warned of his presence, Custer had no other option other than a rapid approach, as he could not let the enemy simply melt away. Their numbers did not matter. Twice on the Yellowstone in August 1873 he had overcome Indian forces that outnumbered him. His August 11 report had stated: "The number of Indians opposed to us has been estimated by the various officers engaged as from eight hundred to a thousand. My command numbered four hundred and fifty ... Sitting Bull ... for once has been taught a lesson he will not soon forget."[5]

Custer must have known, however, that his 600-plus soldiers could not possibly capture a village of 7,000 people, so what did he hope to achieve?

It could only have been to drive away the warriors, destroy as many of their possessions as possible, capture or disperse as many of their ponies as he could, then corral some noncombatants between the 7th Cavalry and Gibbon's Montana Column. This plan would leave the Indians with little alternative but to go to the agencies and the mission would thus be accomplished.

Whatever his plan, it clearly failed. He did nothing "wrong" but sometimes it is just not your day. "Custer's Luck" lost to Sitting Bull's vision. The Indians' scorned "medicine" was too strong, and George Armstrong Custer suffered, if not the slings, then certainly the arrows, of outrageous fortune.

CHAPTER 4

Custer and the Reconnaissance Question

Prompted by a well-known author's interview criticizing Custer for not carrying out proper reconnaissance (a constant argument), my in-depth research produced the following article, which indicates quite clearly that such was not the case. It will give readers a more balanced look at how Custer deployed his scouts.

Because Lieutenant Colonel George Armstrong Custer, and with him, 209 men of his 7th U.S. Cavalry command, died nearly 150 years ago fighting Sioux, Cheyenne and other Indian warriors near the Little Big Horn River in Montana, a myriad of questions exist as to what happened, and, more importantly, why.

A well-known author was asked, "What was the 7th U.S. Cavalry's [Custer's] biggest blunder?" That question presupposes that there was a blunder and the reply, "a lack of proper reconnaissance, resulting in not knowing the size and exact location of the village, and the terrain, which proved to be a major factor" shows that author's opinion to be that proper reconnaissance had not been performed.

While this answer offers up a valid reason why a seasoned cavalry officer would lead his troops towards such a large force of enemy warriors, it does not, at least in the opinion of this writer, stand up when compared to details of what happened leading up to and immediately prior to the battle. From that point, everything is conjecture, since there were no survivors.

It is generally accepted that Custer could not be faulted for the way in which he rigorously scouted the Rosebud valley during the two and a half days it took the regiment to reach the Busby bend of the Rosebud River. From that point we can compare the cited author's comments with the records of what did take place, including references to the Letter of Instructions General Alfred H. Terry gave Custer on June 22.

The regiment had camped at the Busby bend at 7:45 p.m. and according to Second Lieutenant George D. Wallace, Crow scouts had gone ahead earlier in the day and about 9 p.m. they returned and "... reported that the Indians had crossed the divide to the Little Big Horn River."[1] The scouts were unclear which direction they had taken after that.

That information was vital as Terry's plan was based on the belief that the Indians would most likely camp on the upper part of the river. Custer's initial reaction was to order the Crows to cross the divide between Rosebud Creek and the Little Big Horn River, to establish just where the Indians had camped while he hid his regiment overnight in the confines of Davis Creek. The Crows suggested an alternative. Rather than go into the valley at that time, at first light the next morning, they would be able to see into the valley from a hill and locate the village by the smoke from its campfires, giving Custer the information he needed.

Custer approved of this idea as it would save time while keeping his options open, so he sent the Crow scouts along with interpreter Mitch Boyer, Chief of Scouts Second Lieutenant Charles A. Varnum, some Rees and others on a reconnaissance mission to the hill we now call the Crow's Nest.

A letter from courier George Herendeen to the *New York Herald* published on January 4, 1878 showed that Custer was mindful to ensure these scouts did not miss any important signs on their way. "About dusk we halted and went into camp on the trail. It was then very fresh and the general sent Varnum, Boyer and some scouts on ahead to examine the trail and adjacent country,"[2] Herendeen wrote. Proper reconnaissance was being done.

At first light on June 25, the Crow scouts saw where the Indian camp was by the smoke from cooking fires and the movements of a large herd of ponies. Custer was advised and twice went forward to try and ascertain for himself what the scouts had seen. Unable to see what they'd reported, but following guidance from the scout Charley Reynolds, he finally accepted that the camps were indeed on the lower reaches of the river.

Short of a modern drone overfly, Custer had the best intelligence unit available, since the Crow scouts and Boyer knew the terrain in detail because it was on Crow land. With their local knowledge, the smoke above the tepees would have allowed them to judge exactly where the Indian camps were and their approximate size.

Groups of Crow often camped along the river, which was a favorite hunting ground. Three or four years earlier, the Crows had camped near where the 1876 "hostile" camps were located, where they were attacked by many Sioux, as referenced by Colonel Rodney G. Thomas in his book *Rubbing Out Longhair*.

Custer would also have been fully apprised by Boyer of what the Crow scouts knew of "the exact size and location of the village" as well as "the terrain" features he would encounter. Indeed, one of the Crows, Hairy Moccasin, had viewed the village from close by earlier that morning. Even prior to the divide crossing Custer had started seeking intelligence, as Hairy Moccasin relates, "At that time I ... was an enlisted scout under Gen. Custer's command ... I was sent ahead. Custer said, 'You go and find that village.' I went to a butte at the head of Reno Creek, from where I could see the village. I reported the camp to Custer. He asked if any were running about away from the camp. I said 'No.'"[3]

Presuming that prior to crossing the divide, Custer had done all the necessary reconnaissance, it would be churlish to assume that once in the Little Big Horn valley that factor was lacking.

After the crossing, there is other evidence of just how thorough Custer was in taking every precaution available to him without losing sight of the pressing need to attack the Indians. Second Lieutenant Charles A. Varnum's narrative contains relevant descriptions, first during the preparations for the crossing:

> ... I reported for orders. Custer asked if I felt able to continue scouting. I said I had to ride anyway, & one place was as good as another ... Lt. Hare reported for duty and I sent him to the right front and I took the left front of the advance. From every hill where I could see the valley, I saw Indians mounted.

He also noted, "We marched down a small tributary of the Little Bighorn River. I reported my observations several times ... Behind the highest part of the bluff was the main Indian village." Finally, he wrote, "The last time I reported, probably two miles from the river, I saw a squadron of three troops passing the head of the column at a trot."[4]

In an interview in 1923, Trumpeter John Martin, Custer's orderly, related what occurred as the Custer/Reno group rode down Ash Creek, "All the time, as we rode, scouts were riding in and out, and the general would listen to them and sometimes gallop away a short distance to look around,"[5] Martin said. No stone had been left unturned.

Four of the Crows and Boyer were also busy observing. Hairy Moccasin in his 1916 narrative stated, "We ... crossed Reno Creek. Mitch Boyer was ahead with [us] right behind. ... Custer yelled to us to stop, then told us to go to the high hill ahead (the high point just north of where Reno later entrenched). From here we could see the village and could see Reno fighting."[6]

Crow scout White Man Runs Him, confirmed this in his 1919 narrative:

> Mitch Boyer ... noticed the scouts whom Custer had sent to look over the ridge, had followed Reno, so he called ... [us] ... and said: "Let us go over to the ridge and look at the lodges." When we reached there, we saw that the lodges were over in the valley quite a ways down the river, so we moved on ahead, Custer following ... Custer moved slowly, taking lots of time and stopping occasionally.[7]

Custer then, did not ride blindly down upon the Indian camps, but had scouts constantly observing and reporting to him. It was only near Medicine Tail Coulee that the Crows were dismissed, but Boyer continued with the five companies, the only source of local information that Custer needed from then on. There is ample evidence here to negate the inference that Custer's performance was somehow lax.

Major General Frank S. Ross remarked in a July 1967 article published in *The Little Big Horn Associates Newsletter* that second-guessing is a favorite American pastime. The truth of his statement is evident here because this part of the cited author's opinion is self-fulfilling. To underestimate the "fighting prowess" of the Indian warriors Custer would have needed to know that they had checked Crook on the Rosebud, which he did not.

The strategy and tactics Custer used to approach and threaten the village were standard operating procedures for the army at that time when attacking Indian villages. The Little Bighorn fight was an extraordinary event in Plains Indian warfare.

Apart from the Killdeer Mountain engagement where only the Indian numbers might have been comparable, there was no precedent to guide Custer, nor anything afterwards to measure against what happened to him. The events of June 25, 1876 must be reconsidered in that light.

CHAPTER 5

Whence The Montana Column?

Rigorous research highlighted just how many misleading statements were made post-battle by General Terry and the Montana Column commanders to cover up why it had been so far off its intended schedule and then blaming Custer for not waiting for them. They claimed that they could have joined in the battle if Custer had waited but failed to mention that they originally expected the fighting to be near the Little Big Horn headwaters, not where it took place, a difference of about 80 miles. This analysis dispels many of the accusations levelled at the dead Custer.

President F. D. Roosevelt once said, "Repetition does not transfer a lie into a truth,"[1] an observation pertinent to any examination of what happened to the Montana Column on its way to the mouth of the Little Big Horn River.

The 7th Cavalry's intended route is well documented, especially in Brigadier General Alfred H. Terry's letter to Lieutenant Colonel George Armstrong Custer, the field commander of the 7th Cavalry. Nothing in writing was given to Colonel John Gibbon, commander of the Montana Column and its route has been the subject of much argument over the years, so what did Terry plan for it and was that plan adhered to?

In 1896, Colonel Robert P. Hughes wrote an article[2] claiming that the disastrous defeat of the 7th Cavalry at the Battle of the Little Big Horn was directly attributable to Custer's disobedience of his "orders." One example given was Custer's failure on June 24, 1876, to send scout George Herendeen through Tullock's Creek to the sister command, which, said Hughes, was expecting to join in any action against the Indians.

Brigadier General Alfred H. Terry. (Wikimedia Commons)

His argument was that because Herendeen did not appear, Gibbon's command was obliged to change its route. He says "Instead of leaving the course of the Tullock and making a most arduous and exhausting march to the Big Horn, Gibbon could then have continued up the Tullock, over a fair route, directly to the Indian village."[3]

That view contradicts Terry's words in July 1876, "The movements proposed by Gen. Gibbon's column were carried out to the letter"[4] Plainly one or other of these claims is inaccurate. In fact, as the object in each case was to distance Terry from any blame for the Little Big Horn catastrophe, it is possible that both claims are false.

When Gibbon's route was considered, was Tullock's Creek an integral part of Terry's plan?

Hughes says that late on June 19, Terry made provisional plans acting on information from Major Marcus Reno's recent scout which had found a large Indian trail going up the Rosebud valley.[5] On the morning of June 20, Terry held a conference with Custer and Reno and with important input from Mitch Boyer he settled upon his final plan. Custer was ordered to march his command to the mouth of Rosebud Creek whilst Terry went to the same venue on the steamer *Far West*. By 6 a.m. on June 21, part of the Montana Column was already on the march. Terry, Custer and Gibbon then had a conference on the steamboat and Terry's plan was revealed to all who were present. Though the exact location of the enemy was not known, the trail found by Reno was believed to continue south to the Rosebud headwaters, or divert west to the Little Big Horn and Big Horn valleys.

Assuming Brigadier General George Crook's Wyoming Column was blocking the southern route, Terry wanted his two separate commands to try, if possible, to enclose between them, an enemy predicted to be camped near the upper Little Big Horn. Terry's mood was urgent and positive, so it was in that frame of mind he sent a dispatch to Lieutenant General Philip H. Sheridan early on June 21.

His strategy, incorporated in that dispatch and in his instructions of June 22 to Custer, gave details of the route to be taken by Gibbon. To Sheridan he says "… Gibbon's column will move this morning on the north side of the Yellowstone for the mouth of the Big Horn, where it will be ferried across by the supply steamer, and whence [from which place] it will proceed to the mouth of the Little Horn and so on [and so onwards in 19th-century English]."[6] Custer's orders were similarly worded, "… The column of Colonel Gibbon is now in motion for the mouth of the Big Horn. As soon as it reaches that point it will cross the Yellowstone and move up at least as far as the forks of the Little and Big Horns."[7] This was the plan that Terry explained to Custer, Gibbon and Major James S. Brisbin at the June 21 conference and which Hughes describes thus, "… the plan came to the conference fully matured in Terry's mind."[8]

Two other pre-battle dispatches reinforce Terry's wording, both made to the *New York Herald*. Custer's (attributed dispatch) of June 22: "Gibbon's command has started for the mouth of the Big Horn. Terry, in the Far West, starts for the same point today, where, with Gibbon's force and the Far West loaded with thirty days' supplies, he will push up the Big Horn,"[9] and significantly Mark Kellogg's of June 21: "… Terry … on the steamer to the mouth of the Big Horn River, scouting Pumpkin [actually Tullock's] Creek en route, with General Gibbon … This part of the command marches up the Big Horn valley to intercept the Indians if they should attempt to escape from General Custer down that avenue."[10] Kellogg's wording is crucial because he was not privy to the conference discussions and could only have obtained his information from the officers who were present. That Kellogg's dispatch uses similar, but more detailed information than Custer, is strong evidence that Custer expected the Montana Column to be moving up the Big Horn Valley on June 24 and 25 and not to be in any force in Tullock's Creek.

Finally, there are the words of Captain E. W. Smith, Terry's adjutant, the man who compiled Custer's orders, someone who was at the center of things and who said in a dispatch dated July 1, 1876, "At noon of the 22nd, General Custer … left camp. At the same time, General Terry, with Colonel Gibbon's command … started to ascend the Big Horn, aiming to assail the enemy in the rear."[11] This dispatch is dated very shortly after the battle when any plan to travel via Tullock's and the divide would have been fresh in his mind, yet there is no mention whatsoever of that creek or the detour.

On June 20, Terry ordered Gibbon to move his command toward Fort Pease on the Yellowstone River near its confluence with the Big Horn River, early the next day. This is confirmed by First Lieutenant James H. Bradley, "We were ordered to march at once to Fort Pease …"[12]; Second Lieutenant Edward J. McClernand concurs, "… orders are given for us to march back at once to F(ort) P(ease)."[13] The Fort Pease order appears to be the only one given to the Montana Column at this stage although it is apparent that they expected the *Far West* to overtake them on the march there as Lieutenant Bradley says on June 22, "We expected the steamboat to pass us today, but it did not appear."[14] It was only at 5:30 p.m. on June 23 as the infantry camped a mile below Fort Pease that the steamboat was sighted a few miles below them.

There is one other significant diary entry, and that is from First Lieutenant Edward S. Godfrey, as on June 21 he records, "… it was decided that our Regt. move at 12 M tomorrow up the Rose Bud—the 2nd Cav. to X the Yellowstone River at Fort Pease and move up the Big Horn 'Little Horn.'"[15] Near Fort Pease then would be the point at which the cavalry units of Gibbon's column, commanded by Major James S. Brisbin, would be ferried across the Yellowstone. It should be noted that Godfrey makes no mention of the infantry or artillery.

The only mention anywhere of Tullock's Creek appears in Terry's letter to Custer. Why Tullock's at all? Lieutenant Bradley gives us the probable reason in his journal entry for June 16. "Today the Crows discovered a heavy smoke across and up the river, apparently on O'Fallon Creek."[16] O'Fallon's was an early name for Tullock's, and as that place was known as a route used by the Indians, it perhaps needed to be checked, though no Indians were likely to be there well over a week later. Nevertheless, Terry wrote to Custer, "The Department Commander desires that on your way up the Rosebud you should thoroughly examine the upper part of Tullock's Creek, and that you endeavor to send a scout through to Colonel Gibbon's column, with information on the result of your examination. The lower part of the creek will be examined by *a detachment* [italics mine] from Colonel Gibbon's command."[17] Those words in italics mean that Custer would only expect a small separate unit from the other command to check the lower part of Tullock's, as if the intention had been for the whole of the Montana Column to use the creek, there would have been no need for Terry to mention a detachment. Using those words confirms that checking the creek was only a precaution to ensure that no Indians were in transit there.

Taking all the information from pre-battle records that we have to this point, we can justifiably surmise what Terry had in mind for Gibbon's command. We know what the timetable was because Gibbon, recalling the June 21 conference stated, "My command having already started, was to be at the mouth of the Big Horn prepared to cross the Yellowstone on the third day [June 23]."[18] His command reached Fort Pease punctually on July 23 so nothing it did merited any need for a change in plan.

If all had gone well, the *Far West* would have reached Fort Pease first and orders would have been given to take all the necessary steps, such as cooking meals, to ensure a very prompt start the next morning. Early on June 24, the Indian scouts and the 2nd Cavalry would have been ferried to the south bank of the Yellowstone whilst the infantry and artillery would march up the north bank to near the mouth of the Big Horn to await the steamboat. Then, the cavalry would march to the same point on the opposite bank, ford the Big Horn, and wait for the other units to be ferried over. The united Montana Column would then take the easy route along the west bank of the Big Horn to their destination at the mouth of the Little Big Horn. Meanwhile, the Indian scouts, the detachment mentioned in Custer's letter, would examine the lower part of Tullock's. I believe that two major factors derailed this anticipated timetable. The first was that the steamboat's rate of progress was slower than expected and the second was the sudden illness that incapacitated Colonel Gibbon to whom Terry had left responsibility for giving further orders to the command when the boat reached Fort Pease.

Author James Willert, referring to June 22 tells us, "The *Far West* steamed upriver … at probably no more rapid a pace than 4.2 miles per hour against the strong current. Terry had been hopeful of making contact with the Montana Column proceeding up the north bank—however, bucking the powerful current of the flooded Yellowstone slowed their progress considerably…. [and] had probably proceeded only about 17 miles."[19] Willert also states, "June 23rd was a long taxing day for the *Far West*, as it continued its difficult push upriver against the strong current of the Yellowstone

Steamboat *Far West*. The Yellowstone River's swift current slowed the progress of the vessel. (Wikimedia Commons)

… since the Montana Column scouts, on this evening of the 23rd, had spotted the vessel moored about 15 miles below 'Fort Pease'… indicated a very long day of not less than thirteen hours on the upriver push."[20] This is confirmed by General Terry's diary entry that the steamer tied up at 8:40 p.m. The entry continued, "Said to be about 15 miles by river from Big Horn."[21] If Tullock's had been the destination it is unlikely that Terry would have thought the Big Horn significant.

Starting off early on June 24, the boat reached the cavalry camp 2 miles above Fort Pease at 6:00 a.m., but now Terry was faced with the consequences of being behind schedule, the absence of Gibbon and the fact that the infantry and the Gatling detachment had not been given any orders about what to do once they reached Fort Pease. The infantry had moved at 6:00 a.m., to reunite the whole command at the cavalry camp at 7:30 a.m., but the logistical tasks which should have been completed the previous evening now had to be done. Whilst they were in progress, Terry needed to review his original timetable and plan to minimize the delay in launching Gibbon's command on its way.

Yet although the *Far West* moored alongside Brisbin's cavalry at 6:00 a.m., it took a further four and a half hours before 12 Crow scouts were ferried across to the south bank of the Yellowstone River and another six hours before the rest of the command crossed that river. The question is, why? If, as Hughes insisted, the plan came to the June 21 conference "fully matured in Terry's mind" and if part of that plan was to march the whole of Gibbon's command through Tullock's Creek, then it is reasonable to suppose that Terry had planned from the start to use the Fort Pease base as the crossing point. That being so, even with Gibbon out of commission, all he had to do to get things moving immediately he arrived was to issue orders via Brisbin commensurate with his plan. Those orders should have been put in motion almost immediately and certainly no later than 7:30 a.m. when the infantry arrived from their camp.

Assuming that Tullock's was the planned route, time pressures should have meant the following sequence of orders: a) get the 12 Crows across first as the detachment to examine the creek as mentioned in Custer's orders, b) get the rest of the command across as quickly as possible and c) once ready, the column must march as far as possible along Tullock's before dark. These were the basic steps Terry needed to take if his original plan was to move the command promptly along its chosen route. The actual timings show no such orders could have been given and those timings must be a strong pointer to the fact that it had become necessary for him to reconsider what his options were. What were those options? Firstly, if the Big Horn was the originally intended route, he could still ferry the 2nd Cavalry over the Yellowstone, march the rest of the command to the Big Horn's mouth and ferry them across there. Secondly, he could cross the whole command from where he was and march them to the Big Horn valley or thirdly cross where he was and use Tullock's Creek as an alternative.

What happened is revealed in Terry's diary entries for June 24, "Landed detachment of Indian Scouts on right bank at 10.35. They have been instructed to scout Tullock's Creek. Return at once for Cavalry … Four trips of boat required to cross Cavalry, Infantry and Artillery."[22] If all this had been pre-planned it would hardly merit such a specific diary entry. I believe that on his return from ferrying the Indian Scouts across, Terry clearly was only expecting to find the cavalry waiting to be crossed as indicated by Godfrey's diary entry of June 21, but was surprised to find that the whole command apparently needed to be ferried across. It seems reasonable to assume that whilst Brisbin had given orders to the cavalry, the absence of Gibbon had led to the rest not knowing that they were meant to march to the mouth of the Big Horn. Whatever else he might have been considering, Terry now opted to ferry the whole command across from where they were waiting. In my opinion, Terry was impelled by two factors. Firstly, he was already behind schedule and secondly, the steamboat and the Montana Column were conveniently placed at an easy embarkation point. He therefore chose to make the crossing there only after a long deliberation that simply compounded the time pressures caused by the steamboat's late arrival.

At this juncture, I am not convinced that he had decided to use Tullock's to reach the Little Big Horn. He probably still had the second option to march to the Big Horn valley in mind because, according to Willert, he gave orders to Captain Marsh before he disembarked to "push up the Big Horn only as far as the Tullock confluence."[23] So even at this late stage, Terry appears to be hedging his bets. We do know that he was a man under stress, as Brisbin says in his 1892 letter to Godfrey commenting on the river crossing, "... and I shall never forget Terry's anxiety and impatience to get on."[24] This is indicative of a man unsure of himself and facing time pressures that obliged him to make decisions he had not planned for.

If Tullock's had been Terry's intended route from the start, it is puzzling that along with the Crows, he sent scouts Bostwick and Taylor so that the white scouts could survey the Creek's mouth to see if crossing it presented any problems. As Captain Ball, Lieutenant McClernand and others had written reports of their April scout in this area, surely Gibbon would have made these known to Terry if Tullock's had been the prime choice? There can be no doubt that on June 24 Terry planned a night camp in Tullock's near its confluence with the Big Horn as there are diary entries to that effect, and we know for sure that the Montana Column did camp there that night, but was this creek his route of choice? Another of his diary entries for June 24 is, I believe, highly significant, and unless an alternative interpretation is possible, perhaps tells us without doubt that Tullock's was a last-minute choice by Terry. After mentioning the wounded buffalo seen by the Crow scouts, Terry writes, "Determined to move up the valley at 5 a.m. tomorrow."[25]

Bearing in mind Terry's reputation for judicious use of wording, in the language style of that time "determined" would be synonymous with "decided" or "resolved" in modern usage. Why then did Terry have to decide anything at this stage? If the route had been pre-determined, his diary entry should have read something like, "Will move up the valley at 5 a.m. tomorrow."

The sequence of events surrounding this diary entry are revealing and give further strength to the argument that Terry did not opt for Tullock's until late on June 24.

Firstly, there is the diary entry immediately following Terry's "Determined to move" wording that says, "Sent orders to Far West to enter Big Horn at noon tomorrow [June 25] & make to mouth of Little Big Horn by noon the day after to-morrow [June 26]."[26] These orders are telling because they not only override those of the previous day for the steamboat to "push up the Big Horn only as far as the Tullock confluence" but were issued immediately after Terry had "Determined to move up the valley." This is a clear indication that whatever other options Terry had been considering, he had now come down in favor of Tullock's.

In fact, the orders concerning the *Far West* are very material when considering whether Tullock's was the original choice in Terry's plan. I have referred earlier to what orders would have complemented an already agreed plan to use the creek and have indicated that to conform as nearly as possible to that plan (and to try and offset the steamboat's late arrival), the command needed to march as far along the creek as they could until nightfall. Nobody, from Terry on down, has ever revealed that anything occurred which would explain why the Montana Column did not achieve this target. If Tullock's was supposed to be the original route, and that evening the command had marched as far along the creek as was both possible and militarily expedient, then the steamboat need only have been given the single order to move up the Big Horn to the Little Big Horn on June 24. By issuing his first order to Captain Marsh and then rescinding it, Terry patently demonstrated that Tullock's was not his original choice. If it had been, there were no options to consider, the command would have marched as far as it could on June 24 and Captain Marsh would not have needed his first order.

Another example of last-minute decision making is the fact that Gibbon's infantry crossed the divide with empty water bottles. If Terry had decided to use Tullock's at the June 20 conference with Custer, where Mitch Bouyer was present, the scout, who knew the area well, would not have overlooked the poor water supply in the creek and could not have failed to caution Terry on this point. If the choice of Tullock's was made on board the *Far West* on June 21, then Gibbon would surely have advised him that Ball's scout had shown that water in the creek was generally alkaline and not in profusion. That being so, good military sense would dictate that the water bottles of the command should be filled with good water before starting up the creek.

We can assume the command had full bottles when they crossed the Yellowstone River because there is no mention of any water shortage at the night camp. It is also reasonable to suppose that most of the water they carried on their march to that camp was used in making coffee etc., for their suppers. The question is why would they be allowed to use up most or all of their supply if it was known that their next day's march would be along a route where water was both scarce and largely unsuitable? The only logical answer can be that when the command marched away from the *Far West* at 5 p.m. on June 24, Terry was still hoping to use the Big Horn valley route where there was a ready supply of fresh water.

By the time he got to the night camp and determined to use the Tullock route, the command had already used their supply. That going up Tullock's without full canteens of fresh water was a big problem can be gauged from the precautions taken by the white scouts, "Scouts Hamilton Taylor and Henry Bostwick had awakened early [June 25] … they could foretell a scorching day in the making—no break from the searing heat. Both made sure their canteens were full with Big Horn River water, fully aware that only alkaline pools would greet them along Tullock."[27] We know from Lieutenant Bradley's journal that the camp was about 1 mile above the confluence of Tullock's with the Big Horn so the scouts would have taken roughly half an hour to get to the Big Horn and back. It is astonishing that a contingent from the command was not sent to the Big Horn for the same purpose. It is obvious that Terry was not thinking things through.

Another indicator of Terry's planning on the fly is provided by Lieutenant McClernand. After the battle he said, "Starting at 5:45 a.m. on the 25th, Terry, with the 'Montana Column,' moved up Tullock's Fork. The General used me as a staff officer and as I had recently passed over the ground directed me to select the trail."[28] What is pertinent here is exactly when McClernand was seconded to Terry's staff? Supposing that Tullock's was the plan, it would have been essential for Gibbon at the June 21 conference to have informed Terry about McClernand's knowledge of that terrain. If he had done so, the lieutenant could easily have been brought into the conference to pass on what he knew even though the Montana Column cavalry had already marched, because Gibbon had instructed the cavalry to go only 5 miles in the first instance. As it was, the cavalry, with McClernand, marched on to Fort Pease.

Let us assume then that by the time the conference discussions were over, it was too late to recall McClernand. Surely if Tullock's was his prime objective, the first thing Terry would have done on his arrival on June 24 near Fort Pease would have been to second the lieutenant to his staff and interrogate him about the creek? Yet Terry did not do this, and from McClernand's writings, it is clear he was with one of the cavalry groups as it was ferried across the Yellowstone on that day. His own journal entry for the day shows that he was in camp on Tullock's Fork by 5:30 p.m., so he was obviously not with Terry and his staff, who only started their march to the night camp at 6 p.m. In fact, the earliest time that McClernand could have been attached to Terry's staff was the evening of June 24. Author Roger Darling states:

> Also, through Major Brisbin this same evening, Terry gained a more complete understanding of the April scout …. In this way, Lt. McClernand was finally brought to Terry's attention, with the young engineering officer able to provide details of the very terrain Terry would encounter …. Terry was so impressed by McClernand's descriptions of the prospective route that he was assigned to the lead troop and to direct the column's movement up Tullock Creek the next day.[29]

As Terry's Diary records the return of the Crow scouts at 8:45 p.m. and notes that he arrived at the camp at about 7:30 p.m., there was just one and a quarter hours during which Terry could have apprised himself of McClernand's expertise and ordered him to select the trail.

But did Brisbin, on a whim, just suddenly decide to make McClernand's talents known to Terry? I think not. It is more probable that Terry, having contemplated using Tullock's as an alternative route, discussed the matter with Brisbin who then described the April scout and recommended McClernand. This "seat of the pants" decision making, simply does not fit with what Hughes described as "A well-matured plan, based on reasonable conclusions from known facts"[30] so in the light of all the foregoing information, my belief that Gibbon's command was originally intended to march up the Big Horn valley, remains unshaken.

Early on June 25, after Terry sent Bradley to scout ahead, McClernand led the command up Tullock's. They had only traveled about 3 miles, when they turned off to cross the divide between Tullock's and the Big Horn Valley. Did Terry have a sound military reason for turning off what Hughes described as a fair route, especially if that route was originally part of his planning? Hughes offered one possibility when he claimed that the non-appearance of Herendeen was the reason for the turn off. He implies that maybe the scout had not shown up because there were hostiles in upper Tullock's Creek and Terry needed to divert to avoid them. Yet, that makes no sense because it was believed that each command could deal with any Indians they came across and, in any case, he was actively looking for them. He told Sheridan as much in his June 21 dispatch, "I only hope that one of the two columns will find the Indians."[31]

It is also totally unbelievable that Terry would have turned off his originally planned route simply because Herendeen had not appeared as there could have been any number of reasons why the scout had not arrived. Without additional intelligence, Terry should not have been making any assumptions but simply adhering to his original plan. If that plan included the use of Tullock's and that was "a fair route, directly to the Indian village,"[32] no experienced military commander would decide to detour from it via a route of unknown merit simply because a messenger had not arrived. As Hughes was Terry's aide-de-camp in 1876 and his brother-in-law, it is not hard to understand why he would mount a passionate defense of the general, to try and justify the sudden change of route over the divide, but the simple truth is that neither Terry nor anyone else ever gave an acceptable reason for the turn off. That is because there was only one viable explanation and after the Custer disaster, neither Terry nor any of his officers wanted to bring it to light.

That explanation is rooted in the pre-battle records, which all indicate that Gibbon's command was expected to reach its destination via the Big Horn valley. Terry knew that and he also realized that his June 21 dispatch had advised Sheridan as much. He also understood that Custer would not be aware there had been a change of plan if the Montana Column continued up Tullock's. Terry, perhaps reluctantly, chose Tullock's at the last minute, but I have little doubt that the General remained uneasy at this change in his plan which caused his mind to continually cast about for a better solution in discussions with his staff.

His orders to Captain Grant to start the *Far West* up the Big Horn River at 12 noon on this day precluded any possibility of going back the 1 mile to cross that stream. So after talking with scout "Muggins" Taylor, Second Lieutenant G. C. Doane and Major Brisbin[33] suggested to Terry that the divide might perhaps provide a good trail in the direction of the Big Horn valley. Terry then rashly jumped at the perceived opportunity to both make up time and to get his original planning back on track by ordering the detour. That decision makes it clear that Terry's July 2 assertion that the Montana Column's movements had been "carried out to the letter" was nothing more than a smokescreen to hide the reality of just how wide of the mark the actuality had been. As it was, the turn off combined with what befell Custer would focus a very intensive spotlight on the performance of Gibbon's command unless a way could be found to deflect attention elsewhere. In fact, two ways were found. The first, and most obvious, was to hint that Custer had disobeyed his orders. The second, and more subtle, was to behave as if the Montana Column had religiously followed the route mapped out for it by Terry in what he had written to Sheridan and in Custer.

The post-battle documents showed that to achieve this end a simple subterfuge was used. Instead of referring to Tulloch's as an alternative route to the Big Horn valley and then having to explain the divide detour, they describe both creek and detour in such a way as to sound as if they were part of the necessary but torturous route to the Big Horn valley. Terry, Lieutenant Edward Maguire and Brisbin in a less subtle way, all followed this pattern.

The first document issued immediately after Custer's defeat was Terry's June 27 official report to Sheridan. In it, he referred to the passage of the Montana Column on June 24 and 25 as follows, "At 5 o'clock [p.m., June 24] the column ... marched out to and *across* (italics mine) Tulloch's creek. Starting soon after 5 o'clock [a.m.] of the 25th, the infantry made a march ... over the most difficult country which I have ever seen ... the cavalry ... was pushed farther."[34] Terry's letter of July 9 to Crook perpetuates the illusion that Gibbon's command had followed its planned route, "It was ferried across the Yellowstone at a point just below the mouth of the Big Horn on the 24th ultimo. On the 25th it advanced through country of extreme difficulty ..."[35]

Maguire wrote a letter and a report that are relevant. His letter dated July 2, 1876, to Brigadier General A. A. Humphreys says, "The next morning, Sunday the 25th, the column crossed the divide between Tulloch's Creek and the Big Horn. The march was over a very rough and broken country with but little vegetation save the ubiquitous sage and cactus."[36] The detailed points about the terrain and flora clearly demonstrate Maguire's observational abilities, so it seems utterly astonishing that he describes the movement from the camp to cross the divide in so few words, as if it was one seamless pre-planned action, when it is evident that such was not the case. In his 1876 report, Maguire follows a similar line, "The night of June 24 we passed camp on Tulloch's [sic] Creek. The next day we crossed the divide between Tulloch's Creek and the Big Horn, and reached the latter stream after a severe march of twenty-two miles. The country was exceedingly rough ..."[37]

Major Brisbin was not required to furnish an official report so his letter of January 1892 to Godfrey contains his only known reference to the subject events. In it he states, "It was the 23d (sic) before we got well up Tulloch, and ready to start ... I pushed and pushed, but the evening of the 25th found us on the Big Horn, twelve miles below the mouth of the Little Big Horn River. I [Terry was in command!] had crossed over from Tulloch, hoping to find smoother ground up the Big Horn to the Little Big Horn, but it was worse."[38]

What is fascinating here is that if Tullock's was the planned route, we have Terry, the overall commander, Brisbin, his then second-in-command, and Maguire, a leading figure on Terry's staff, all knowing what had been planned on June 21, yet making no direct reference to the divide turn-off as a major change in that plan. They all had the opportunity in their reports and letters to make it clear that they were following Tullock's as planned, then circumstances forced them to divert over the divide, but they did not do so. The reason for avoiding that issue is because they could not afford to admit that they should really have been in the Big Horn valley and not Tullock's Creek.

By making that admission, they would have had to acknowledge that they were not where Custer expected them to be, so the post-battle importance placed on Tullock's as a stick to beat Custer with, would not have held any weight. It is therefore safe to say that by glossing over the reality of the Montana Column's movements on June 24 and 25, both Terry and Hughes were less than honest in the claims they made. It should have marched up the Big Horn valley and Custer had no other expectation. That is confirmed by the testimony of some of the officers at the Reno Court of Inquiry in 1879 where Wallace and even Reno stated that they believed that Terry was downstream or north of them, but the most telling comments came from Varnum who stated, "I partly knew what General Terry's intentions were as I had heard him and General Custer talking, and I had an idea that General Terry was on the Big Horn somewhere …"[39] So nearly three years later they are confirming that they were only looking north for Terry.

Gibbon not only confirms that view but spells out exactly what his command was meant to do. He says, "that my command should march to the mouth of the Big Horn … be there ferried across the Yellowstone, and march from there to the valley of the Little Big Horn, and *up that stream* (italics mine) to co-operate with Custer's command."[40] Up that stream can only mean moving south east from the Big Horn/Little Big Horn forks. So, Gibbon clearly verifies that the Big Horn valley was the originally intended route as in no other circumstances could his command have marched "up" the Little Big Horn.

Whence the Montana Column? Gibbon spells out what route they were meant to take, and this article provides the reasons why that route was abandoned. None of those reasons are attributable to Custer. Nothing he did or didn't do affected Terry's change of plan. Certainly, Terry was anxious for Herendeen to appear but probably in the hope that the messenger's news would justify the change of route. There was no justification, so Terry, Hughes and others resorted to distorted post-battle comments to obscure the truth.

For nearly 150 years, those distortions have caused unfair criticism of Custer. To paraphrase Shakespeare, "The evil that men do lives after them, the truth is oft interred with their bones."[41] Now perhaps the bones of those long dead men are giving up their truths and those of the much-maligned Custer can at last rest in peace.

CHAPTER 6

Custer Did Follow Terry's "Orders"

A constant anti-Custer argument is that he disobeyed his orders and when this idea was stridently put forward in a book, I set about testing the validity of that claim. It resulted in this article which clearly demonstrates the claim to be unfounded and how Custer's critics have a tendency to omit facts which weaken their arguments.

"I distinctly stated that General Custer had disobeyed General Terry's orders,"[1] wrote Colonel Robert P. Hughes in 1896, 20 years after George Armstrong Custer was killed at the Little Big Horn.

If Custer had been court-martialed, the court would at least have given him a fair and impartial trial, guaranteed by his Fifth Amendment rights. Hughes and those who echo his views simply present a one-sided picture.

A case in point is an uncompromising condemnation of Custer's alleged disobedience in the book *The Strategy of Defeat at the Little Bighorn* by Frederic C. Wagner III.[2] Custer is cited on his apparent disregard of "orders." "[Terry] ... desires that you should ... thoroughly examine the upper part of Tullock's [*sic*] Creek, and ... endeavor to send a scout [George Herendeen] through to Colonel Gibbon's column, with information of the results of your examination."[3]

Were these orders? The June 22 document Custer received from General Alfred Terry has long been the subject of argument, but Hughes, who was there at the time, says this, "He [Terry] also had, before drawing up his letter of instructions ..."[4]

If Terry's words are called "orders" not instructions, it makes it far easier to accuse Custer of disobedience, but either way, there was no day, or time set for Herendeen to be sent. That Custer neither "examined" nor "endeavored" on June 24 cannot be faulted. At 7:45 p.m. that day, Custer set up camp at the Busby bend of the Rosebud and could have sent Herendeen through to Gibbon/Terry a little earlier. His Crow scouts were following a clear trail, but they had not yet returned. Terry's letter had expressed that Custer should, "... proceed up the Rosebud until you ascertain *definitely* [italics mine] the direction in which the trail above spoken of leads."[5]

That information did not come until the Crows returned at 9 p.m. One of them, White Man Runs Him, told General Hugh L. Scott in 1919, "We knew the trail and the way the Sioux were moving but were not sure which way they went."[6] Custer needed to know that, and Terry needed to know that. Wagner asserts that there is nothing in the letter about this, "We see no requirement to include plans or to have found Indians before sending Terry the information required."[7]

Since this was the whole purpose of the campaign, Terry needed this intelligence as Hughes confirms: "One of the most important of the duties to which Terry directed Custer to apply these [Crow] scouts was to send word by some of them of the location of the Indian encampment immediately after having certainly determined it."[8]

Herendeen wasn't sent because it had not been, "certainly determined" and that intelligence wasn't available until around 10 a.m. on June 25. *The Strategy* author, however, argues a step further. According to him, Tullock Creek had been tactically important since April 24. The campaign mission was to track down hostile Indians and force them to settle on reservations. Their recently discovered trail up the Rosebud suggested they would camp on the upper reaches of the Little Bighorn. Though not a certainty, Terry planned on that basis, with some reservations.

Custer's letter from Terry, sent his 7th Cavalry following the trail and spelled out the route for Gibbon's command, "[Gibbon's] column ... now in motion for the mouth of the Big Horn ... will cross the Yellowstone and move up as far as the forks of the Big and Little Horns."[9]

The only mention of Tullock's Creek is in the extract from Custer's letter, desiring him to examine it. Yet Wagner insists it was tactically important, noting "Tullock's passive role in this affair belied its tactical importance ..."[10]

His reference to it is as far back as April 24. Gibbon was at that time camped near the Bighorn mouth and had, unasked, sent out a scouting party. When they returned on May 1, he wired Terry, "Captain [Edward] Ball just in ... Went out on Phil Kearney Road ... thence over on Little Big Horn and Tullock's Fork and down that ..."[11]

Nothing indicates Tullock had any particular importance but Wagner asserts, "... Gibbon ... then penned the Tullock's complex into Little Big Horn history by sending his telegram to Terry. This also shows the importance of the Tullock's Creek valley in the minds of the commanders ..."[12] Why, bearing in mind that Terry and Custer had not yet entered the field?

It must hinge on what befell Gibbon's command. It never followed the Bighorn valley route as planned. Instead of crossing the Yellowstone River on June 23 at about 5:30 p.m., the command was camped, a day late, a mile up Tullock with Terry in direct command as Gibbon was ill.

This situation persuades Wagner that Tullock was important. In other words, on June 24, Terry had moved his command into it therefore it must be important because Terry must have planned it as an alternative to his original plan. On April 24 then,

Gibbon had ordered that location scouted knowing it would be important two months later and this without knowing Terry's final plan. This is "confirmation bias," the tendency to interpret and recall information in a way that affirms one's prior hypothesis: in April, short of knowing where the Indians would eventually be found, Tullock's could not possibly have been important. Furthermore, if using Tullock was an option, why did Terry's July 2, 1876 report state, "The movements proposed by Gen. Gibbon's column were carried out to the letter?"[13]

It is my opinion that the letter does contain "orders" but some are qualified by the phrases used before them i.e., "… impossible to give you any definite instructions in regard to this movement …" and, "… Commander places too much confidence … to impose upon you precise orders …"[14] English language grammatical rules are quite clear, any words that follow those phrases are qualified by them, therefore they are neither definite instructions nor precise orders.

Wagner has not proved Custer guilty. That part of the Terry letter he takes exception to does not contain precise orders; it is what Terry would have liked to happen—if possible. Not sending Herendeen on the evening of June 24 did not deprive Terry of an alternative tactical route. Tullock was not important.

Wagner omits evidence that does not support his claims. He cites that part of the letter which desires Custer to "examine" upper Tullock but ignores this, "… lower part of the creek will be examined by a *detachment* [italics mine] from … Gibbon's command"[15] and overlooks Mark Kellogg's June 21 letter to the *New York Herald* stating, "… Terry will move … to the mouth of the Big Horn River, scouting Pumpkin [Tullock's] Creek *en route*, [italics mine] … Gibbon['s] … part of the command marches up the Big Horn valley …"[16]

Wagner also dismisses Terry's need to know the Indians' location when the lack of fresh intelligence had bothered Terry throughout the campaign. It was essential for him to know in case he had to re-think his plan.

Chapter 4 of *Strategy* begins with these words, "There are times we need to cherry-pick bits and pieces of information fitting our theories to see if they work. This is a dangerous practice for it allows one to fling around all sorts of wild hypotheses based on little or no evidence, stringing out a sometimes obscure tidbit to outrageous and unsupportable conclusions."[17]

Quite, and it underlines why the claims of disobedience are unsupportable. General Custer was not guilty.

CHAPTER 7

A Reasonable Doubt?

This is a different look at the subject of Custer being accused of disobedience of orders, prompted by two authors, years apart, but using very similar reasons for their claims. By using sound evidence to disprove their claims, especially their omission of key data, I was able to show that the accusation of disobedience and the consequences the two authors stressed would result from it, did not hold true. They also skip over the important fact that General Terry did not know that the Indians had stymied his plan by camping on the lower reaches of the river.

The death of Lieutenant Colonel George Armstrong Custer at the Battle of the Little Big Horn on June 25, 1876, may have saved him the disgrace of a courts-martial, as according to some authors, if he had survived, he would have been charged with disobeying the orders of his commanding general, Brigadier General Alfred H. Terry. Still others defend the decisions he made as commander in the field. That controversy, coupled with the question of whether what he received were in fact orders or something else, has raged for over nearly 150 years, as has speculation about the consequences of the alleged disobedience.

An examination of information from both sides of the argument will determine if those who believe Custer disobeyed his orders are unassailable or merely biased. It is necessary to establish, if possible, if there is evidence which will tip the scales one way or another. It is pointless, for example, to side with either Frederick Whittaker, who wrote the hero-worshipping book, *A Complete Life of General George A. Custer*, or Frederick F. Van de Water, who took the opposite tack in his book, *Glory Hunter: A Life of General Custer*, because the prejudices these authors display make their views unreliable.

Although Terry himself never directly accused Custer of disobeying his orders, he did hint at it in his second post-battle report of July 2, 1876:

> The proposed route was not taken but as soon as the trail was struck it was followed. I cannot learn that any examination of Tullock's Creek was made. I do not tell you this to cast any reflection upon Custer. For whatever errors he may have committed he has paid the penalty and

you cannot regret his loss more than I do, but I feel that our plan must have been successful had it been carried out, and I desire you to know the facts.[1]

Ironically however, it was at his funeral in 1890 that the question of his subordinate's alleged disobedience first aired publicly, when Dr. T. T. Munger in giving his sermon stated:

> Custer's fatal movement was in direct violation of both verbal and written orders. When his rashness and disobedience ended in the total destruction of his command, General Terry withheld the fact of the disobeyed orders ....[2]

He later revealed that his source for the accusation was Colonel Robert P. Hughes, Terry's brother-in-law and former aide, and that set in motion claims and counter claims as accusers and defenders crossed verbal swords.

The focal point of the arguments was the document given to Custer on June 22, 1876: did it contain orders, and if so, did Custer disobey any of them? What happened prior to and at the battle however, must be viewed, not merely by concentrating on the words contained in Terry's instructions to Custer, but also in the light of what the army's mindset was at the time and how the realities of the 1876 Sioux Campaign developed in real time. What then were the thoughts of those men responsible for launching the 1876 summer expedition against the professed hostile Indians, who were to be forced to end their free roaming ways and settle on reservations?

In his report of November 9, 1875, the Indian Inspector E. C. Watkins stated:

> In my judgement, one thousand men under the command of an experienced officer, sent into their country in the winter, when the Indians are nearly always in camp, and at which season of the year they are the most helpless, would be amply sufficient for their capture or punishment ... The true policy in my judgement is to send troops against them in the winter, the sooner the better, and whip them into subjection.[3]

The Secretary of the Interior Zachariah Chandler in his letter of December 3, 1875, to Secretary of War William W. Belknap observed:

> Referring to my letter of transmittal of the 29th ult ... requesting that steps be taken to compel the hostile Sioux to go upon a reservation and cease their depredations ...[4]

Zachariah Chandler, Secretary of the Interior. (Wikimedia Commons)

In a letter dated February 26, 1876, which appeared in the *New York Herald* on March 2, Lieutenant General Philip H. Sheridan commented:

> The Indian question in the Black Hills must now be settled by the establishments of posts ... one at or near the mouth of the Big Horn, the other at or near the mouth of Tongue River ... The Black Hills country will probably be covered with towns and villages during the next five or six years ... Military operations have now been commenced against the hostile bands of Sioux by request of the Indian Department ...[5]

Lieutenant General Philip H. Sheridan. (Wikimedia Commons)

Both Indian Inspector Watkins and Secretary of the Interior Chandler have the subject Indians being easily dealt with by being whipped or compelled respectively and General Sheridan not only has the "Indian question" being settled by the U.S. military, he has the Black Hills heavily populated within five to six years, yet at the date of his interview, that territory remained the property of the Sioux Nation. The common thread is patently obvious. The "hostiles" were not going to be any problem.

Were the commanders of the forces in the field any more circumspect? In a letter of April 21, 1876, Colonel John Gibbon, commander of the Montana Column moving east down the Yellowstone River, sent this to Terry:

> I have in accordance with the directions moved my camp alongside Fort Pease, where I am strong enough to defy the whole Sioux nation, should they feel inclined to come this way ... The position here is so strong that one company can easily hold it and let all the rest loose in case we see a chance to strike.[6]

These comments are from a man with just 450 men at his disposal. Terry himself was no less sanguine in his telegram of May 16 to Sheridan:

> I have no doubt of the ability of my column to whip all the Sioux who we can find. I suggest Crook's immediate movement with the idea that if he moved up he would force them toward us and enable us to get at them more easily.[7]

Sheridan continued the theme in his response of the same day:

> I will hurry up Crook, but you must rely on the ability of your own column for your best success. I believe it to be fully equal to all the Sioux which can be brought against it, and only hope they will hold fast to meet it.[8]

Whilst there was universal confidence then that the Indians would soon be subjugated by the soldiers in the field, the only possible snag would be to find them before they broke up into small bands and scattered as Sheridan pointed out in his letter of May 29 to General of the Army William T. Sherman:

> … As no very accurate information can be obtained as to the location of the hostile Indians, and as there would be no telling how long they would stay at any one place, if it was known …[9]

This concern was addressed by First Lieutenant Edward S. Godfrey of Custer's 7th Cavalry, in his *Century Magazine* article of 1892:

> If the advance to the attack be made in daylight it is next to impossible that a near approach can be made without discovery. In all our previous experiences, when the immediate presence of the troops was once known to them, the warriors swarmed to the attack, and resorted to all kinds of ruses to mislead the troops, to delay the advance toward their camp or village, while the squaws and children secured what personal effects they could, drove off the pony herd, and by flight put themselves beyond danger, and then scattering made successful pursuit next to impossible. In civilized warfare the hostile forces may confront each other for hours, days, or weeks, and the battle may be conducted with a tolerable knowledge of the numbers, position, etc., of each other. A full knowledge of the immediate presence of the enemy does not imply immediate attack. In Indian warfare the rule is "touch and go." These remarks are made because the firebrand nature of Indian warfare is not generally understood. In meditating upon the preliminaries of an Indian battle, old soldiers who have participated only in the battles of the Rebellion are apt to draw upon their own experiences for comparison, when there is no comparison.[10]

In summary: In the minds of the whole army command, a single column was more than sufficient to defeat any conceivable force of hostiles; and the greatest perceived danger was that the Indians would scatter before the expedition could compel them to go to their assigned agencies. Therefore, the purpose of coordinating the movements of the columns was not primarily to ensure greater troop numbers in the event of conflict but to cut off avenues of escape the hostiles could use.

Expecting to find the Indians somewhere between the Little Missouri and Big Horn Rivers, three army columns were in the field by the end of May. From the south, the Wyoming Column commanded by Brigadier General George Crook. From the west, the Montana Column under Colonel John Gibbon and from the east, the Dakota Column commanded by Brigadier General Alfred H. Terry, which included the 7th Cavalry Regiment under the direct field command of Lieutenant Colonel George Armstrong Custer.

Their mission: To find the Indians, to fight them, if necessary, but in any event, to ensure that they reported to their allotted agencies and settled there permanently. Crook never tried to rendezvous with the other two columns, both in overall command of Terry, and Sheridan's concern over finding the Indians soon manifested itself. Intelligence had suggested that the Sioux, under Sitting Bull, were camped on the Little Missouri River in northern Dakota Territory but after an arduous march of over 170 miles, not only did the Dakota Column not find them there but (in an ominous example of how difficult it was to get two army columns many miles apart to effect close cooperation) Gibbon's Montana Column, which had been ordered to coordinate in the intended attack, never even got to the Little Missouri location.

As Gibbon had not seen any camps along the Yellowstone, Terry decided to concentrate the search for the hostiles further south and then west, in a sweep toward the Powder River which was reached on June 7 after yet another exhausting march. With still no sign of the elusive Indians, Terry's anxiety was growing and he no doubt pondered on the additional wording of Sheridan's May 16 telegram to him:

> You know the impossibility of any large numbers of Indians keeping together as a hostile body for even one week.[11]

It was now three weeks since the Dakota Column had left Fort Abraham Lincoln and Terry must have worried that the hostile bands had already split up and scattered. It would take an uncharacteristic gamble by the 7th Cavalry's second in command, Major Marcus Reno, to provide the intelligence Terry needed. On a scouting mission many miles up Rosebud Creek (under orders that forbade him from being there) he found a relatively fresh trail that possibly led toward the Little Horn River.

Based on this information, Terry conceived his famous plan, outlined in his June 21 dispatch to Sheridan:

> No Indians have been met with as yet, but traces of a large and recent village have been discovered 20 or 30 miles up the Rosebud. Gibbon's column will move this morning on the north side of the Yellowstone for the mouth of the Big Horn, where it will be ferried across by the supply steamer, and whence it will proceed to the mouth of the Little Horn and so on. Custer will go up the Rosebud tomorrow with his whole regiment and thence to the Little Horn, thence down the Little Horn. I only hope that one of the two columns will find the Indians. I go personally with Gibbon.[12]

Clearly the Indians were expected to be located somewhere on the Little (Big) Horn River and the document given to Custer on June 22 containing Terry's proposals for how Custer should proceed, made it apparent that the best guess was that they were likely to be found near the upper reaches of that river.

The full text of that document is as follows:

HEADQUARTERS DEPARTMENT OF DAKOTA (In the Field)
Camp at Mouth of Rosebud River,
Montana, June 22nd, 1876.

Lieut. Col. G.A. Custer, 7th Cavalry.
Colonel:
The Brigadier-General Commanding directs that, as soon as your regiment can be made ready for the march, you will proceed up the Rosebud in pursuit of the Indians whose trail was discovered by Major Reno a few days since. It is, of course, impossible to give you any definite instructions in regard to this movement, and were it not impossible to do so, the Department

Commander places too much confidence in your zeal, energy, and ability to wish to impose upon you precise orders which might hamper your action when nearly in contact with the enemy. He will however, indicate to you his own views of what your action should be, and he desires that you should conform to them unless you shall see sufficient reason for departing from them. He thinks that you should proceed up the Rosebud until you ascertain definitely the direction in which the trail above spoken of leads. Should it be found (as it appears almost certain that it will be found) to turn towards the Little Horn, he thinks that you should still proceed southward, perhaps as far as the headwaters of the Tongue, and then turn towards the Little Horn, feeling constantly, however, to your left, so as to preclude the escape of the Indians by passing around your left flank.

The column of Colonel Gibbon is now in motion for the mouth of the Big Horn. As soon as it reaches that point it will cross the Yellowstone and move up as far as the forks of the Big and Little Horns. Of course its future movements must be controlled by circumstances as they arise, but it is hoped that the Indians, if upon the Little Horn, may be so nearly inclosed by the two columns that their escape will be impossible.

The Department Commander desires that on your way up the Rosebud you should thoroughly examine the upper part of Tullock's Creek, and that you should endeavor to send a scout through to Colonel Gibbon's column, with information of the results of your examination. The lower part of the creek will be examined by a detachment from Colonel Gibbon's command.

The supply steamer will be pushed up the Big Horn as far as the forks if the river is found to be navigable for that distance, and the Department Commander, who will accompany the column of Colonel Gibbon, desires you to report to him there not later than the expiration of the time for which your troops are rationed, unless in the meantime you receive further orders.

Very Respectfully
Your Obedient Servant,
ED. W. SMITH, Captain, 18th Infantry
Acting Assistant Adjutant General[13]

Whether or not these were orders has been the subject of disagreement for many years but after the catastrophe of June 25, those who want to condemn Custer for that failure use the justification that however politely phrased, the words of a commanding general must be obeyed. Custer's defenders respond that the wording gives Custer discretion to use his own judgement as commander in the field. Whichever line of reasoning is used there is no doubt in my mind that what occurred must be considered as being influenced by all the background I have set out above. Terry most assuredly did not want a failure on his distinguished military record; Gibbon did not want to be left out of the action having spent two and a half months without seeing any and Custer needed a success to eradicate the memory of the humiliation he had received at the hands of a spiteful President Grant, being stripped of the command of the Dakota Column and initially forbidden to go on the expedition at all, for implicating the President's brother Orville whilst giving evidence in the investigations into the trader post scandal by the Clymer Congressional Committee.

With all that in mind let is now examine just what constituted Custer's alleged disobedience of orders. One of Terry's instructions was:

> The Department Commander desires that on your way up the Rosebud you should thoroughly examine the upper part of Tullock's Creek, and that you should endeavor to send a scout through to Colonel Gibbon's column, with information of the results of your examination. The lower part of the creek will be examined by a detachment from Colonel Gibbon's command.[14]

According to all the pre-battle and post-battle records, these matters were expected to be effected on June 24, and on the face of it, Custer did not "examine" and he most certainly did not send the scout George Herendeen, who had been assigned to him for this very purpose, through to Gibbon. The first person to openly accuse Custer, in writing, of disobeying his orders, was Colonel Robert P. Hughes in his 1896 article in the *Journal of the Military Service Institution of the United States*.[15]

Suggesting that Custer had followed the Indians' trail into Davis Creek with the express purpose of attacking them, Hughes commented:

> Nor could Custer fail to know that by no possibility could Gibbon be in the position Terry's order contemplated by the time he (Custer) should stir up the Indians to flight or fight, unless, indeed, information of the course of action he had determined to pursue had been dispatched to Gibbon instanter (the 24th) and reached Gibbon's camp on Tullock's Creek by midnight.
>
> With such information, and an intimation of urgency, it would have been possible for Gibbon at the head of his veteran 2d and 7th to appear on the field of action by the afternoon of the 25th. Instead of leaving the course of the Tullock and making a most arduous and exhausting march to the Big Horn, Gibbon could then have continued up the Tullock, over a fair route, directly to the Indian village.[16]

Other authors have echoed Hughes's arguments. Indeed, in one of the most recent books on the subject, *The Strategy of Defeat at the Little Big Horn*, the author, Frederic C. Wagner III, makes a further claim:

> By sending Herendeen down the Tullock's Creek valley (he would have reported the valley clear of hostiles), Custer would have doubled Terry's choices. Terry would now have options, a commander's dream. Why would he want to be limited to following one specific route when he could have an alternate? By knowing it was safe, Terry had the option of moving up that valley without fear, still believing Custer was continuing up the Rosebud.[17]

In both cases the accusations appear to have some foundation. The words in Terry's instructions seem clear and the criticisms look to be justified if what they claim would have happened is accurate. Did Custer in fact examine the upper part of the Tullock? In his 1892 narrative, Captain Edward S. Godfrey says this of June 24, 1876:

> We made many long halts so as not to get ahead of the scouts, who seemed to be doing their work thoroughly, giving special attention to the right, toward Tulloch's [*sic*] Creek, the valley of which was in general view from the divide.[18]

Godfrey also wrote:

> … we thought we (I mean some of us) saw smoke in the direction of the Tullock, and finally we spoke to the General at one of the halts. He said it could not be, that he had scouts on that side and they most certainly would have seen any "signs" and report to him, and he reiterated that there were scouts out looking toward Tullock's valley.[19]

That is confirmed by Curley, the young Crow scout who told Joseph Dixon:

> We followed the trail until we saw that they had camped on the Little Horn, and then we noticed that the Sioux had gone toward the Little Horn and we waited at the head of Tallec [Tullock] Creek for the command to come up.[20]

Given that information, coupled with the fact that it was plain to see there were no trails leading towards the Tullock, I believe it is safe to say that some examination had been made of the upper Tullock, however cursory, so the accusations of disobedience in this respect appear ill-founded.

There is no disputing the fact however, that Herendeen was not sent. Hughes claims that if he had been sent, he could have reached Gibbon's camp on the Tullock at midnight, and the Montana Column could have reached the Little Big Horn battlefield on the afternoon of June 25 to support the 7th Cavalry. In his 1892 letter to Godfrey,[21] Major James Brisbin, commander of Gibbon's cavalry, declared that Herendeen had told him he had advised Custer on June 24 that it was the right time to be sent. They were then opposite the gap which led to the Tullock at about 6:30 p.m., so we can plot the messenger's journey from there.

Earlier in the day, Mitch Boyer had confirmed to Custer that it was about a 15-mile ride[22] from that point to the southern end of the Tullock. That ride would likely have been at a cautious rate as he would have needed to rest his horse at times and be wary of any groups of hostiles that might be on their way to meet up with those in the Little Big Horn valley. It is conceivable that he might have run afoul of Little Wolf's band of Cheyennes who unbeknownst were shadowing the regiment, but I will assume that he did not. He would also be travelling in gathering darkness, so I suggest an average 8 mph so he would have reached the Tullock's southern end at approximately 8:30 p.m., time to stop for the night.

Right away, the assertion that he could have reached Gibbon by midnight is seen to be false. At that time, Gibbon's camp on the Tullock was at the northern extremity of that valley, more or less 40 miles from its southern tributaries, which is where Herendeen would have been sleeping under the stars. It seems to me that in his zeal to defend Terry, Hughes prevaricated as he well knew where the camp was and at what time. He also had a fairly accurate idea of how far Herendeen would have to ride before even reaching the Tullock's southern end, so he is being economical with the truth in stating that the scout could have reached Gibbon's camp at midnight on June 24.

Nevertheless, could the scout have reached Terry sometime on June 25? Given a starting time of 4:30 a.m., he would probably have a less than forty-mile ride up the Tullock if the Montana Column was moving toward him. His ride would likely have been at a slightly slower rate than hitherto because the valley stream meandered and had to be crossed repeatedly. Assuming 6 mph with no stops, the first potential contact could have been with the scouting party of Lieutenant James Bradley, which had travelled nine miles up the valley[23] starting at 4:30 a.m., expecting the rest of Gibbon's command to follow. So at about 6:30 a.m., that would have put his party roughly eighteen miles away from Herendeen. At 6 mph, the messenger's timing for that distance would see him reach the Bradley location at 9:30 a.m. At 6:45 a.m. meanwhile, the rest of the Montana Column, having travelled just over three miles up the valley, had turned off Tullock's to cross the divide between it and the valley of the Big Horn River, at which time Herendeen was something like twenty-seven miles away and would never have seen them. A cavalry unit had ridden the 6 miles that separated them from Bradley to advise him of the altered plan. At a steady clip of 6 mph, they would have reached Bradley at approximately 7:15 a.m. The return trip with Bradley's party in tow would see them all hurry to catch up to the rest of the column. In his journal, Bradley wrote, "I soon re-joined, taking a short cut across the hills …,"[24] so Herendeen would have missed them too. As he would have needed to make some stops along the way, if only to rest his horse, it made any meeting with Terry even more unlikely.

Suppose that Herendeen had managed to reach the Montana Column before it turned into Tullock's Divide, which would have been at roughly 6:00 a.m., the infantry, having travelled 3 miles already, would still have a march of 37 miles to the Tullock's south forks. At their usual rate of travel of 3 mph, a non-stop journey to that location would take 12 hours. With the necessary breaks to rest both men and animals, it is logical to add at least an hour. Thus, Gibbon's command would reach that point at 7:00 p.m. on June 25 at the earliest, and would not, "… appear on the field of action by the afternoon of the 25th," as Hughes claimed they could. Custer's fight was over by around 6 p.m. that day, so Hughes was well overstating the marching speed of Gibbon's men.

The foregoing timings also undermine Wagner's contention that Herendeen could have reached Terry and given the latter "options, a commander's dream." He states, "Why would he want to be limited to following one specific route when he could have an alternate?" Clearly the alternate is Tullock's Creek, so what was the original "one specific route"? It could only have been that of the Big Horn valley which appeared in all the pre-battle documents as the route for Gibbon's command. How then did Terry end up in Tullock's Creek and how was Custer to know that he was there? These questions are simply ignored by both authors. Forgetting Herendeen for a moment, Wagner makes another statement, "By knowing it was safe, Terry had the option of moving up that valley without fear …" which is contrary to all the campaign correspondence which maintains that each column could take care of itself. It is apparent then, that Terry should not have needed to know it was safe before proceeding up the Tullock, indeed, even if there were Indians in the upper part of the Creek, he would only have been carrying out the task described in his dispatch to Sheridan of June 21, "I only hope that one of the two columns will find the Indians."[25] He chose not to try, which cannot be blamed on Custer.

The categorical statements of both cited authors that Herendeen was expected to meet up with Terry/Gibbon in Tullock's Creek, regardless of date, are in any case totally negated by none other than Herendeen himself. In a letter written to the *New York Herald* in 1878 about a conversation he had on the steamboat *Far West* on June 21, which directly relates to carrying dispatches to Gibbon, he wrote, "General Brisbin came out of the cabin and I asked him where his cavalry would probably be in the next few days so I could find him and he replied, '… about the mouth of the Little Big Horn.'"[26] As Herendeen's journey was to start via Tullock's Creek, Brisbin's comment leaves little doubt that the scout was expecting to have to reach the mouth of the Little Big Horn presumably via the Big Horn valley to deliver his dispatches. Thus, treating the appearance of Gibbon's command in Tullock's Creek as if it was meant to be there, is therefore obfuscation by Hughes to deflect attention away from Terry's poor decision making on June 24 and shows an apparent inflexible determination by Wagner to cast Custer in a bad light for his alleged disobedience of orders.

Did Custer have "sufficient reason" for departing from the instruction to send a scout to Gibbon's column? I believe that this hinges wholly on the focus of the entire expedition, namely, to subjugate the Indians, but first by locating them before they broke up into small bands and went their separate ways. Terry's frustration in this respect had been growing and now over a month since the Dakota Column had left Fort Abraham Lincoln, this was the closest any army force had got to the elusive enemy. Because he did not know the exact location of the Indians on June 24 it is most likely that, in accordance with Terry's instructions to, "… ascertain *definitely* [italics mine] the direction in which the trail above spoken of leads,"[27] Custer was waiting for that news early on June 25 to send Herendeen with it. Also, probably unaware that Terry was in the Tullock that previous day, he would not have had any sense of urgency. Whilst June 24 was the optimum time to send Herendeen, there is no day fixed in Terry's instructions for that to happen and in the circumstances citing Custer for disobedience in this respect is unjustifiable when he probably had good reasons for his actions.

The other point of contention by the two authors under scrutiny is that Custer ignored Terry's instructions to continue south, even if the trail led to the Little Big Horn valley. Hughes, in his previously mentioned article, stated:

> When Custer followed the trail, he knew beyond cavil that the Indians would either flee or fight when he approached them, and unquestionably he knew that in either case Terry had intended that Gibbon should be in position to take part in any event that might arise. Not only did he deliberately disobey Terry's orders, but beyond dispute he knew that in doing so he was neutralizing, or putting Gibbon's command entirely out of the field of action.[28]

Wagner is of the opinion that Custer had already decided he was going to attack even before he got to the Busby bend and comments:

> … the fact remains Custer was bound and determined to seek out and attack this village, one way or the other, with Terry or without …[29]

These are generally held views by those who accuse Custer of being guilty of disobedience but are they supportable? By extracting relevant wording from Terry's instructions, the case can be made, yet the real time situation faced by Custer in the field suggests a different picture. Around 9 p.m. on June 24, the Crow scouts reported to Custer at the Busby bend bivouac that the hostiles had crossed into the Little Big Horn valley via Davis Creek but appeared to have moved north, not south as expected. As Terry's plan was based on the premise that they would be found on the upper reaches of the river, he needed to know if circumstances had changed and Custer, now nearly in contact with the Indians, needed to make decisions which ensured that he did not lose touch with them. Being advised by Mitch Boyer and the Crows that there was a promontory point on the divide between the Rosebud and Little Bighorn valleys from which they would be able to see the smoke from the camps' cooking fires at first light to establish where the village was located, he ordered a small party under his Chief of Scouts, Second Lieutenant Charles A. Varnum, to go there. With his troops camped in the open and perhaps fearful of discovery, he then decided later that night to move into Davis Creek where he could hide his command until he received news from Varnum. If this was a man hell bent on attacking the Indians as soon as he could, the evidence does not confirm this. What he said at an officers' call at 9:30 p.m. was recorded by three of his subordinates. In his narrative, First Lieutenant Edward S. Godfrey says:

> The General said that the trail led over the divide to the Little Big Horn: the march would be taken up at once, as he was anxious to get as near the divide as possible before daylight, where the command would be concealed during the day, and give ample time for the country to be studied, to locate the village and to make plans for the attack on the 26th.[30]

In his letter of July 4, 1876, to his wife, Second Lieutenant Winfield S. Edgerly wrote of June 24:

> Had Officer's Call at about 9, and were told that there were indications of a village within a day's march of us, and that Custer intended making a night march and hiding in the hills the next day, so as to strike the Indians at about daybreak on the 26th.[31]

Finally, Second Lieutenant George D. Wallace wrote in his report of January 27, 1877:

> About 9 p.m. the scouts returned and reported that the Indians had crossed the divide to the Little Big Horn River. General Custer determined to cross the divide that night, to conceal the command, the next day find out the locality of the village, and attack the following morning at daylight.[32]

Early the following morning, a Ree scout named Red Star galloped into camp with a note from Varnum stating that the village had been located. Riding back to the promontory with the scout, Custer could not see the village from it, but was eventually convinced by the scout Charley Reynolds that it was indeed there on the lower part of the river. Whilst Custer had been riding towards them, the scouts had seen a few hostile Indians moving around and believed they had seen the smoke from the soldiers' cooking fires. In *The Arikara Narrative*, Red Star relates what happened when the scouts tried to convince Custer:

> … one of the Crow scouts, Big Belly, got up and asked Custer through the Crow interpreter what he thought of the Dakota camp he had seen. Custer said: "This camp has not seen our army, none of their scouts have seen us."

Big Belly replied: "You say we have not been seen. These Sioux we have seen at the foot of the hill, two going one way, and four the other, are good scouts, they have seen the smoke of our camp."

Custer said, speaking angrily: "I say again we have not been seen. That camp has not seen us. I am going ahead to carry out what I think. I want to wait until it is dark and then we will march, we will place our army around the Sioux camp."

Big Belly replied: "That plan is bad, it should not be carried out." Custer said: "I have said what I propose to do, I want to wait until it is dark and then go ahead with my plan."[33]

Although he was later convinced that his command had been seen by hostile scouts, his exchange with Big Belly (Hairy Moccasin) shows that if Custer had been primed to attack regardless, these scouts had offered him the perfect excuse to do so, yet he twice rejects their concerns. Does this seem like a man "bound and determined" to attack the village or one who was planning a classic cavalry attack at dawn the following day?

Custer then, apparently ignored Terry's instructions concerning the Indian trail:

> Should it be found (as it appears almost certain that it will be found) to turn towards the Little Horn, he thinks that you should still proceed southward, perhaps as far as the headwaters of the Tongue, and then turn towards the Little Horn.[34]

This leads to explanations by Hughes as to what should have happened if that instruction had been followed to the letter. The purpose is clearly set forth in Terry's report:

> Custer was to keep on southward (after determining where the trail led), for the double purpose of intercepting flight if it should be attempted, but above all to so maneuver his strategic columns as to give time for Gibbon's column to come up. This plan was founded on the belief that the two columns might be brought into cooperating distance of each other.[35]

Wagner is more categorical: Custer's instructions were clear: scout the upper reaches of the Rosebud, then cross to the upper Little Big Horn, move north down that river, and drive the Sioux into the blocking point Terry was to reach on the 26th. This being only the 24th, however, Terry would be a good 30 miles from his objective position.[36] To digress briefly, that last clause is intriguing. Where is the author locating Terry? It can only be near the Fort Pease location which is approximately 30 miles from the junction of the Big Horn and Little Big Horn rivers (the objective position), because the Tullock itself is 40 miles long with another say 20 miles to reach the mouth of the Little Big Horn. The 30 miles can therefore only refer to the original route via the Big Horn valley and somewhat scotches the previous claim about giving Terry and alternate route.

Hairy Moccasin, photographed by Richard Throssel c. 1910. (Museum of Photographic Arts/Gift of Graham and Susan Nash)

Returning to the main theme, once again we have statements indicating that the mere following of Terry's instructions would have made everything else fit together rather like the last piece in a completed jigsaw puzzle. Was it indeed that simple? Did Custer ruin a perfect plan? Take Wagner's comment that by following Terry's instructions on June 26, Custer would have been driving the Sioux into the blocking point Terry was to reach that same day. Note the absence of times and distances. Assuming the optimum dawn attack and that the Indians would obediently run toward the Montana Column near the mouth of the Little Big Horn (the objective position) would they in fact have collided with Gibbon's force? Only if the flight from Custer had taken an unlikely nine hours, because it was not until 2 p.m. that day that Terry, with only Brisbin's cavalry and the Gatling gun battery, arrived in the Little Big Horn valley, about three miles from the river's mouth. If that is one example of deeds not copying words, perhaps there are others?

Given that Custer did not continue southward I can only speculate on what might have happened if he had. The starting point for this speculation is provided by yet another statement by Hughes:

A concise summary of what was explicit and positive in his orders presents: That Custer was to go up the Rosebud, following the Indian trail discovered by Reno a few days before, until he should ascertain definitely the direction in which it led. Should he find ("as it appears almost certain that it will be found") that the trail turned towards the Little Big Horn, he should still proceed southward perhaps as far as the headwaters of the Tongue, and then (and not until then) turn towards the Little Big Horn.[37]

So, Custer had to ascertain definitely the direction in which the trail led. Into the Little Big Horn valley was too vague, as they could have gone anywhere from there. Hughes confirmed this in his article:

> The Indian encampment was believed to lie to the north of the Big Horn Mountains, east of and near the Big Horn River, in the valley of the Little Big Horn River; but it was considered possible that it was located on the Rotten Grass, which was one day's march further up the Big Horn River.[38]

Using Hughes's guideline, what did Custer face on his southward march starting out at 4:30 a.m. on June 25? There was a 20-mile journey in seven hours to the headwaters of the Rosebud where he would discover the signs of the June 17 battle between the Indians and Crook's command. He would need to spend say an hour examining the site establishing that the Indians were in force and that Crook had retreated. He would need to send scouts to try and locate Crook, who featured strongly in Terry's plan, whilst watching out for any trails heading toward the Tongue's headwaters 15 miles to the southeast. There would be no contact with Crook who was 30 miles away and the scouts would report no trails toward the Tongue. Now about 5:30 p.m. he could then start his march towards the upper Little Big Horn ending as darkness was falling around 8 p.m. having covered about ten miles.

A 4:30 a.m. start on June 26 would see Custer's command cover the remaining 5 miles to the upper reaches of the Little Big Horn, reaching his target at about 6:30 a.m. He now ran the risk of being spotted by bands of agency Indians travelling in the same direction to join their fellow tribesmen whose trail Custer had originally been following. From 6:30 a.m. therefore, assuming he remained undetected, with the village not on the upper reaches he had at least 40 miles to go before reaching his objective and he was faced with the ever-increasing problem of tired horses. They had already covered 35 miles since the Busby bend camp and many were jaded. Moving slowly and mindfully therefore, Custer would march the remaining 40 miles or so, including stops, in roughly 14 hours. That would put him at the village site around 8 p.m.—to find the Indians gone. Alerted perhaps by Little Wolf and his band of Cheyennes, who had shadowed the 7th Cavalry up to the Busby bend, the huge gathering had simply slipped away earlier that day and the Sioux Campaign of 1876 had ended in failure, but at least not in disaster. A scapegoat would still have been needed and I have little doubt that Lieutenant Colonel George Armstrong Custer would have been in the frame. General Dwight Eisenhower, during World War II, once declared that the search for a scapegoat is the easiest of all hunting expeditions. Custer dead (or alive) appears to have been the easiest available prey for those seeking someone to blame.

Whilst the foregoing scenarios may be disputed as to precise travel speeds and exact mileage, they are strong indications that the clamor over the sending of Herendeen and the insistence that Custer should have continued south are not matters that can simply be expressed as if undeniable. There will always be some who remain firmly convinced that Custer disobeyed his orders and so to justify their claims will omit certain details and scorn others that weaken their case. For example, they never mention the guide and interpreter, F. F. Girard, who apparently overheard this conversation between Terry and his Adjutant E. W. Smith aboard the steamer *Far West* on June 22, 1876, "General Terry then remarked: 'Custer is happy now, off with a roving command of fifteen days! I told him if he found any Indians not to do as Reno did, but if he thought he could whip them to do so!'"[39]

There is also the famous, or perhaps infamous, Mary Adams affidavit in which she swears to have overheard Terry say to Custer on the evening of June 21, "Custer, I don't know what to say for the last." Custer replied, "Say whatever you want to say." Terry then said, "Use your own judgment and do as you think best if you strike the trail. And whatever you do, Custer, hold on to you're [*sic*] wounded."[40] John S. Manion's masterful work established beyond doubt that there were two sisters named Mary and Maria who both worked for the Custers and that various records showed that Mary had travelled with the regiment from Fort Lincoln. Whether or not she was coerced into swearing to the affidavit we will never know, but Girard had no reason to lie about what he had heard.

I have therefore reached the conclusion that the accusations against Custer, though superficially appearing to carry some weight, tend to be biased. The claims for what positives could have resulted if the alleged disobedience had not occurred are in my opinion, mere equivocation. The evidence in his favor, though not indisputable, is compelling enough to have merit. There is, in my view, a more than reasonable doubt that Custer disobeyed his orders—but this will not sway those who are rigidly determined that he did.

CHAPTER 8

The Reno Court—Custer, the Silent Witness

Having read the exchange of correspondence in The Custer Myth *between Colonel W. A. Graham and Captain R. G. Carter about the doubtful evidence given at the Reno Court of Inquiry in 1879, I examined in depth what other questionable comments had been made by officers on the 1876 campaign. The result was this article, which underlines just how much of a conspiracy there was to put all the blame on Custer for the disaster. Readers will appreciate that in 1879, the public only had newspaper accounts to go by, had no concept of what had taken place and simply believed what they read.*

Obfuscation can be defined as the act or an instance of making something obscure, dark, or difficult to understand.[1]

Obfuscation certainly played a large role in the way General George Armstrong Custer's defeat at the Battle of the Little Bighorn is remembered, starting with the modern theory that some testimony at the 1879 Reno Court of Inquiry obfuscated "the whole truth" of what occurred on June 25–26, 1876. At the very least, the testimony fell under the definition of making things "difficult to understand."

In a March 18, 1925, letter to Captain R. G. Carter, Colonel W. A. Graham, the compiler of *The Custer Myth*, alluded to this revised vision of history:

> You would not say that [Captain George D.] Wallace and [Lt. Luther] Hare and [Lt. Charles] Varnum and [Captain Myles] Moylan and [Lt. Charles] DeRudio were all 'cowardly poltroons,' I feel sure. Yet, to be consistent, you must say either that, or that they willfully and deliberately perjured themselves at Chicago in 1879.[2]

In his reply of March 25, 1925, Captain Carter assessed the testimony thusly: "While they may have felt that they were telling the truth so far as it went, not one of them volunteered to tell the whole truth …"[3] Captain Carter goes on to discredit that testimony, "knowing of their conversations in the Post Trader's store at Fort Lincoln, the ostracizing of [Major Marcus] Reno … and then their going as a body before that Court and testifying just exactly the reverse of what their talk had been."[4] While Carter saw through the cloud of obfuscation, Colonel Graham could not believe that army officers would either not tell the whole truth, or withhold some of it.

It has always been believed that the Reno Court was designed to protect the reputation of the army rather than that of Reno and this wasn't the first instance of this kind. Nearly three years earlier, in the summer of 1876, a similar situation arose to protect the personal reputation and career of Brigadier General Alfred H. Terry, who, in his July 2, 1876 report written after the battle wrote:

> ... it would take [General John] Gibbon's column until the twenty-sixth to reach the mouth of the Little Big Horn and that the wide sweep which I had proposed Custer should make would require so much time that Gibbon would be able to cooperate with him in attacking any Indians that might be found on that stream.[5]

In a January 1896 article, "The Campaign Against the Sioux in 1876" Terry's aide-de-camp (ADC) Colonel Robert P. Hughes also referred to a mutual attack being in Terry's plan which was:

> ... based on reasonable conclusions from known facts, contemplating the cooperative action of two bodies of troops, intending to bring them into joint action at a specific date and place ... is defeated by the failure of one column to carry out its assigned share, and this failure not caused by unforeseen conditions ... but because he followed the trail directly ... and arrived at the point of cooperation thirty-six hours in advance of the appointed time.[6]

Gibbon endorsed this view in his narrative, *Gibbon on the Sioux Campaign of 1876*. Referring to the conference held on the steamer *Far West* on June 21, 1876, he asserted that, "It was therefore arranged that Gen. Custer should start the next day ... take up the trail on the Rosebud, and follow it; that my command should march to the ... valley of the Little Big Horn, and up that stream to cooperate with Custer's command."[7]

Major James Brisbin, Gibbon's cavalry commander, made it clear in his January 1892 letter to General E. S. Godfrey when he wrote, "Terry intended ... that we should be in that battle with you."[8]

The conclusion: Custer had jumped the gun, not waited for the Gibbon to get within cooperating distance and had ruined Terry's plan. However, did Terry's Report, Hughes's article, Gibbon's narrative and Brisbin's letter all contain the germ of obfuscation, bearing in mind that all these words were post-battle when a concerted effort was being made to protect Terry's career and reputation?

Terry's July 2 report is at odds with one of June 27, 1876, where he made no reference to any coordinated attack on the Indian village or that June 26 was a date of any significance. Instead, at that time, Terry stated that Gibbon would "in all probability reach the mouth of the Little Big Horn on the 25th instant,"[9] presumably the originally intended date before the day lost by the steamboat's slow progress.

Terry later tried to change this by claiming that the original had been garbled in transmission. His comments concerning what Custer should have done to coordinate an attack on any Indians found on the river are fascinating for their brass-faced nerve. What he describes as "that stream" is 138 miles long from source to mouth.

Even for the purposes of a "coordinated attack" the river ranged from 70 to 80 miles in length.

Terry did not specify how Custer was supposed to coordinate any attack with Gibbon when the Indians could have camped anywhere along that expanse (or not at all) and Gibbon was at times over 100 miles away from him. The damage was done however, as this second "confidential" report somehow, whether by accident or design, found its way into the hands of a journalist and into the public arena.

The purpose of Hughes's article, of course, was to defend Terry, but in doing so he rather overdid things. If Custer had, "arrived at the point of cooperation thirty-six hours in advance of the appointed time" where would that elapsed time have put him? As he started his attack at noon on June 25, Hughes places the cooperation at midnight of June 26. If Hughes means "arrived" at the crossing into the divide at midnight June 24 then the cooperation is at noon June 26 where a dawn attack would have been the anticipated strategy.

Custer's known rate of march was 30 miles a day from 5 a.m. to roughly 5 p.m. so the 60-plus miles from the Busby bend to the village location via the Little Bighorn would have placed him near to the actual location at mid-to-late-afternoon June 26, not exactly an ideal time for any attack, coordinated or otherwise.

In any case, when Hughes says that Terry's plan was "based on known facts" he is being liberal with the truth. Several sources corroborate that the location of the Indian village was certainly unknown when Terry formulated his plan.

Reno had communicated his findings to Gibbon after his Rosebud scout, after which the colonel, in a June 18 note to Terry, speculated: "I presume the only remaining chance of finding Indians now is in the direction of the headwaters of the Rosebud or Little Big Horn."[10] Terry's June 21 dispatch to Sheridan spells out the tentative framework of his plan and ends with, "I only hope that one of the two columns will find the Indians."[11] Brisbin's dispatch to the *New York Herald*, published June 28, also demonstrated uncertainty about the village location: "It was believed that the Indians were on the head of the Rosebud, or over on the Little Big Horn."[12]

Even Terry's June 22 letter of instructions to Custer was not specific. Custer was to follow the trail found by Reno but even if it turns toward the Little Horn, it is suggested that he nevertheless continue southward, "perhaps as far as the headwaters of the Tongue,"[13] but that between the movements of his regiment and Gibbon's command, "it is *hoped* that the Indians, *if* upon the Little Horn, *may be* so nearly inclosed [italics mine] …"[14]

Hughes too, in his partisan article, gave the lie to his assertion that, "Exactly what was found to be true, Terry had anticipated would be found to be true," when he asserted that, "The Indian encampment was believed to lie to the north of the Big Horn Mountains, east of and near the Big Horn River, in the valley of the Little Big Horn River; but it was considered possible that it was located on the Rotten Grass, which was one day's march further up the Big Horn River."[15] Perhaps Hughes did not want to admit that the actual location of the Indian village represented one of the "unforeseen conditions" he maintained did not exist.

There is nothing in any of this information to definitively establish that a coordinated attack on a given date and time at an unspecified location was achievable, given two army columns at least 60 to 100 miles apart at times, with no method of easy communication. Anyway, there are pre-battle records which show that no such cooperation was anticipated.

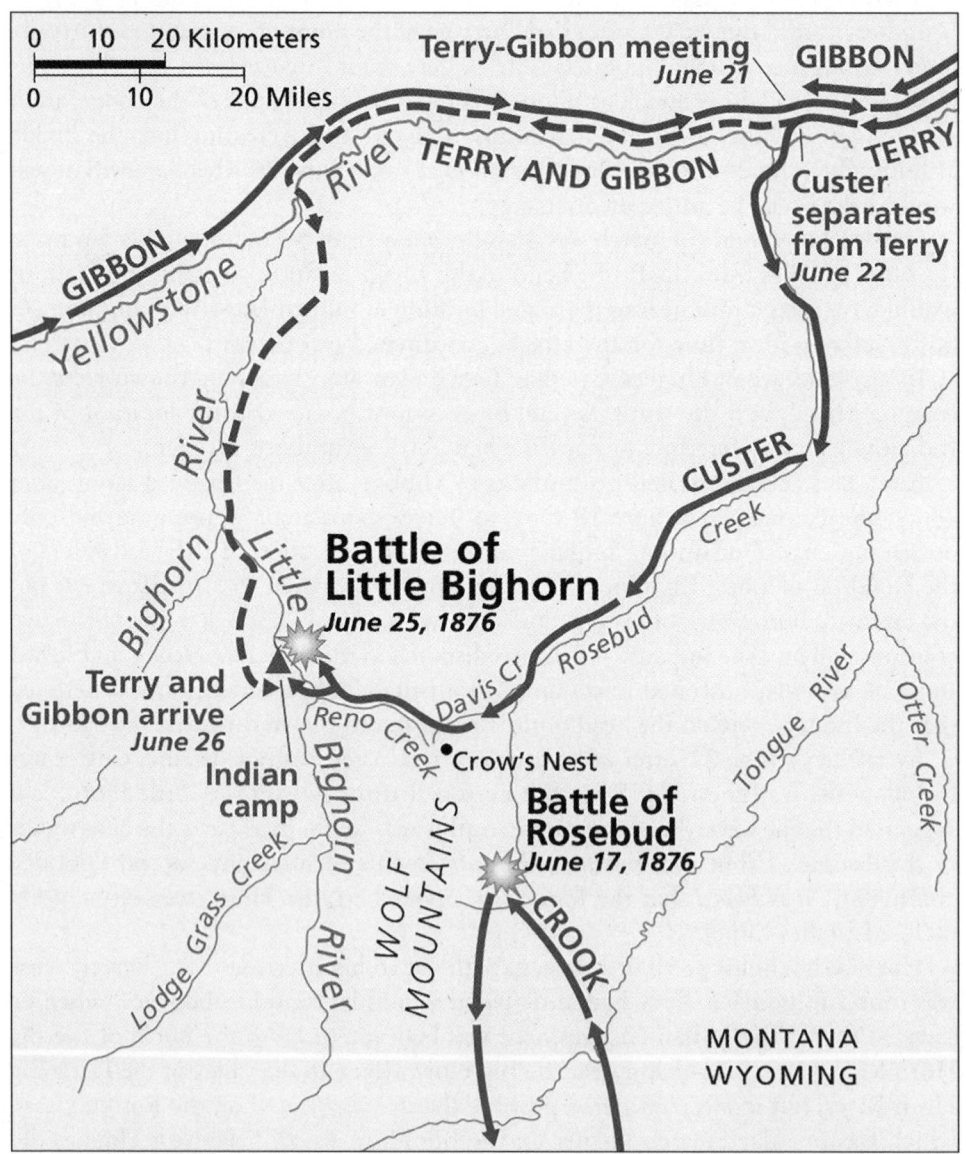

Map of Little Bighorn area showing troop movements. (U.S. National Park Service)

First Lieutenant James H. Bradley's June 21 journal references discussions about a coordinated attack but adds, "It is understood that if Custer arrives first, he is at liberty to attack at once if he deems prudent."[16] Brisbin's June 28 *New York Herald* dispatch went further saying: "It was announced by Gen. Terry that Gen. Custer's column would strike the blow and Gen. Gibbon and his men received the decision without a murmur ..."[17] Brisbin later wrote the very opposite in his letter to Godfrey.

Lastly, Terry's letter of instructions to Custer discredits both the idea of a coordinated attack and of June 26 being of special importance. Its final paragraph reads, "The supply steamer will be pushed up the Big Horn as far as the forks if the river ... and the department commander ... desires you to report to him *there* [italics mine] not later than the expiration of the time for which your troops are rationed, unless in the meantime you receive further orders."[18]

As Custer received no further orders, and as his troops were rationed for 15 days, Terry, by his own instructions, would have expected him at the confluence of the rivers no later than July 6. That final paragraph also makes it clear that Gibbon's command did not originally anticipate moving far from the confluence. These facts destroy any notion of the Montana Column joining in any attack and refute the claim that such an attack was scheduled previously for June 26.

Often in the debates that take place on these controversial matters, those who believe that it was right to blame Custer will use as evidence the implied criticisms of the lieutenant colonel contained in Terry's "confidential" report presumably based on the idea that because Terry was the commanding officer he must be both right and truthful.

The army needed someone to blame for a military disaster and Terry, good man though he was, did not want to be that someone. As dead men can tell no tales, who better to blame than the deceased Custer? The army would have its scapegoat and the public would be none the wiser.

CHAPTER 9

Who Speaks for Custer?

This article is an analysis of some of the testimony given at the Reno Curt of Inquiry by Custer's two senior officers, which, to say the least, was self-serving. Whilst it is generally accepted that much of the testimony was a concerted attempt to protect the reputation of the 7th Cavalry Regiment, it also had the effect of laying the blame for the disaster at the feet of Lieutenant Colonel Custer. I have tried to set the record straight here by laying bare the truth as the evidence reveals it.

Was Custer insane at the Battle of the Little Big Horn? A demented Custer on Last Stand Hill ranting, "Mr. President, Distinguished Visitors, Honorable Members of the Senate, taking the Indian as we find him ...." would seem to say so.

That image, however, is a fiction from the movie *Little Big Man*, yet according to some of the evidence at the Reno Court of Inquiry Custer must have been out of his mind on June 25, 1876. What other conclusion can we reach about a commander who, by the sworn testimony of his two most senior subordinates, rode into the Little Big Horn valley believing there were no Indians there, yet planned to strike a non-existent Indian village without a plan of attack and issued idiotic orders to his subordinates? This article will show that Custer, far from being mad, was a commander who knew where his target lay, had a frequently used plan to deal with it and issued his subordinates with orders commensurate with that plan.

For that to be true, parts of the testimony given by Captain Frederick W. Benteen and Major Marcus A. Reno at the inquiry must be shown to be false. The first matter then that needs to be addressed is what was believed about the presence of Indians in the valley?

Indian Presence—Inquiry Testimony

From Captain Benteen: a) "General Custer told us that he had just come down from the mountains, that he had been told by the scouts that they could see a village, ponies, tepees and smoke. He gave to us his belief that they were mistaken ...,"

b) "In General Custer's mind there was a belief that there were no Indians nor any village," and c) "He did not believe there was a village there according to my belief."[1]

Indian presence—Custer's Knowledge

The Arikara scout Red Star, who led Custer to the Crow's Nest, said:

> Charley Reynolds came up and he and Custer went ahead leaving the others behind. Charley Reynolds pointed where Custer was to look, and they looked for some time and then Gerard joined them.
>   Gerard called back to the scouts: 'Custer thinks it is no Sioux camp.' ... Charley Reynolds then pointed again, explaining Custer's mistake, then after another look Custer nodded that he had seen signs of the camp. Next Charley Reynolds pulled out his field glasses and Custer looked through them at the Dakota camp and nodded his head again."[2]

The Crow scout Hairy Moccasin, who was on the Crow's Nest, said in an interview that Custer had said, "'You go and find the village.' I went to a butte at the head of Reno Creek, from where I could see the village, I reported the camp to Custer. He asked if any were running away from the camp. I said, 'No.'"[3]

Benteen too, unwittingly contradicted himself in another part of his testimony when he said, "We knew there were eight or ten thousand Indians on the trail we were on."[4] That statement negates the idea that Custer did not believe there was a significant gathering of Indians in the valley because "we knew" must include Custer. Finally, Reno in his report stated, "24th the march was continued .... [A]t 9:25 p.m. Custer called the officers together and informed us that beyond a doubt the village was in the valley of the Little Big Horn," and on the 25th, "... by this time Indians had been seen and it was certain we could not surprise them and it was determined to move at once to the attack."[5]

Indian Presence—Analysis

We know there was a very large Indian village in the Little Big Horn valley that day but does Benteen's testimony nonetheless have any validity? Not based on the comments of First Lieutenant Edward S. Godfrey:

> I confess to considerable surprise that Reno and Benteen had testified at the Court of Inquiry, 'That Custer expressed a disbelief in the near proximity of any village whatever at that time.' ... the General soon returned and officers' call was sounded ... Benteen was beside me at the officers' call. I relate this to show that what one could hear the other could hear. I feel perfectly sure that such an expression of disbelief from the General would have made an unforgettable impression on my mind.[6]

Godfrey also said, "At all events, the General must have accepted the scouts' point of view, because he made their location of the village his objective."[7]

Was Custer himself convinced about the location of the village? He was evidently quite satisfied because on the divide early on June 25 Herendeen asked him about Tullock's Creek and Custer replied, "Yes, but there are no Indians in that direction—they are all in our front …"[8]

There can be little doubt then that in his testimony Captain Benteen was untruthful about what Custer believed concerning the presence of an Indian village. So, as we have established that Custer knew where the village was, did Benteen have a case about the lack of a battle plan?

Plan of Attack—Inquiry Testimony

From Captain Benteen: a) "There was no plan at all," and b) "If there had been any plan of battle, enough of that plan would have been communicated to me so that I would have known what to do under certain circumstances. Not having done that I do not believe there was any plan."[9]

From Major Reno: a) "There was no plan communicated to us if one existed. The subordinate commanders did not know of it," and b) "I might say there that I do not think there was any plan."[10]

Plan of Attack—Custer's Options

On June 25, 1876, Custer had been a successful cavalry commander for over 10 years and did not suddenly forget what he had learned during that time. Thus, when he stood on the Crow's Nest with Mitch Bouyer, three Crow scouts and others, he knew they were looking into a valley that was part of their homeland. Being aware of that he obtained all the information he could from them about the terrain from there to the Indian village.

Returning to the command Custer was informed that Indians, rifling a lost hard-tack box, had seen the command. Believing that the village, once warned, would scatter, he decided on an immediate attack. First Lieutenant Edward S. Godfrey confirms this, reporting Custer as saying: "At all events our presence has been discovered … that we would march at once to attack the village …"[11] Second Lieutenant Winfield S. Edgerly says the same, "… as our presence had been discovered it would be necessary to attack at once …"[12] and Courier George B. Herendeen agrees when Custer tells him: "… besides they have discovered us … The only thing to do is to push ahead and attack the camp as soon as possible."[13] Finally, the same from Reno, "… we could not surprise them and it was determined to move at once to the attack."[14]

Custer was primed to attack, and his subordinates were fully aware of that. Knowing that they probably faced a standing village the usual tactic in those circumstances was the envelopment, whereby a holding force would engage the enemy while other parts of the command swung to the left or right to hit him in the rear or on the flank. The late Jay Smith described such tactics in two articles he authored. In one, citing Von Clausewitz as his source, he says: "Custer used an envelopment while employing the principles of offense, maneuver, and surprise,"[15] and in the other, "These were some of the best professional soldiers in the world. A few words or gestures were all that were needed to provide all the information required for a complete battle. Objectives and unit tactics were understood by all. Often a complete battle plan consisted only of stating which units would go where."[16] The envelopment plan had of course been used at the Washita and Powder River fights, so it was widely known. There are corroborations that it was also to be used at the Little Big Horn from testimony and elsewhere.

Second Lieutenant Winfield S. Edgerly. (Wikimedia Commons)

At the inquiry, Sergeant Edward Davern testified that First Lieutenant William W. Cooke, George Custer's adjutant, had said to Reno: "Girard comes back and reports the Indian village three miles ahead and moving. The General directs you to take your three companies and drive everything before you."[17] In answer to the question "Was anything else said?" Davern replied, "Yes, sir: Colonel Benteen will be on your left and will have the same instructions."[18] Lieutenant Edgerly, in his papers says, "Major Reno was ordered to 'march straight to the village, attack any Indians you may meet, and you will be supported.' Captain Benteen was ordered to 'move to the left at an angle of about forty-five degrees from Reno's direction, attack any Indians he might meet, and he would be supported.'"[19] Plus we have Major Henry R. Lemly's assertion that Second Lieutenant George D. Wallace told him that when Custer separated from Reno his plan was to march to the lower end of the village, crossing at one of the lower fords, and to make his attack there. His attack was to be the signal for Reno, just as soon as the latter saw or heard him, to press forward in the reasonable expectation that the combined pressure would stampede the Indians out of their villages.[20]

Perhaps the most significant evidence in terms of Benteen's intended role, is Second Lieutenant Charles A. Varnum's letter to his parents saying: "Just then Colonel Benteen and three companies came in from a trip they had endeavored to make to the rear of the of the village …"[21] which is endorsed by part of Captain Myles Moylan's testimony where he is questioned regarding support for Reno:

> Q. But at the time you were moving down this bottom and engaged in the timber and in going back to the top of the hill, was there any belief as to where the balance of the command was? What was your opinion?
> A. My opinion was that it was on the rear of our trail and was coming to our assistance.
> Q. And Captain Benteen's command?
> A. That I do not know so much about. It passed away to the left and I thought might come in through the foothills.[22]

That the recorder, First Lieutenant Jesse M. Lee had grasped the possibility that an envelopment was intended is evidenced by further questions he put to Moylan:

> Q. State whether any attack on that village in flank by another column, or an attack lower down than from where Major Reno was would or would not have been supporting Major Reno's attack?
> A. I think it would have been supporting his attack, that is, to the extent of drawing off the number of Indians necessary to resist it.
> Q. I understand that by a support, you do not necessarily mean that a command must be immediately in rear of another command to support it in attack?
> A. I think it would be supporting an attack if Reno attacks this end and General Custer attacks that end. It draws a number of Indians from his front and consequently is supporting Major Reno.[23]

In his response to the summing up of Lyman Gilbert, Reno's Counsel, Lee made the following observations: "Captain Moylan said he thought Captain Benteen might come in on the left, in the sand hills, and he supposed General Custer would come to their support from the rear. Major Reno must have known as much as his officers about the support, in fact he knew that General Custer said he would be supported."[24]

Private Peter Thompson also understood the tactic because he says: "The plan marked out was to attack the Indians in the following manner: Major Reno was to cross the river to its left bank and proceed down until Custer had time to pass down the right bank and cross over and attack them in the rear."[25] Sergeant Daniel A. Kanipe too grasped the idea, "You could tell that the plan was to strike the Indian camp at three places."[26] If enlisted men knew the basics of what was to happen it is beyond belief that the battalion commanders did not.

In fact, Reno almost admitted as much in answer to Lee's question: "Were you in any position to have seen troops on your side of the river while you were in the bottom?" he said, "Yes, sir, to the rear or on the left,"[27] a clear indication that he was looking for Benteen coming in from his left, which is perhaps why the left of his skirmish line was the weakest point. This slip by Reno made his previous testimony that Lieutenant Cooke told him, "General Custer directs you to take as rapid a gait as you think prudent and charge the village afterwards, and you will be supported by the whole outfit,"[28] highly significant, because he had continually said that he was only expecting support from Custer's immediate command. The magnitude of the mistake Reno had made is shown by the convoluted efforts of his counsel, Lyman D. Gilbert, to cover it up when he questioned the major immediately afterwards, knowing that in his report Reno had stated, "I saw Benteen moving further to the left and as they passed, he told me he had orders to move well to the left and sweep everything before him."[29]

Gilbert opened with some innocuous questions then began his damage limitation exercise:

> Q. In your report, to which reference has been made, you said words to the effect that you were convinced that General Custer intended to support you by an attack in flank?
> A. Yes, sir.
> Q. Wasn't that a conviction after the fight was over?
> A. Yes, sir.
> Q. That was not your belief at the time you crossed to attack?
> A. No, sir.
> Q. You say that you were without support on the left bank of the river. You say you could see there was no support because you could look to your rear and to the left?
> A. To my left and my rear.
> Q. You expected the support to come from the direction that you had crossed?
> A. Yes, sir. I did not see at the time how any other support could have been rendered me.
> Q. Did you observe the character of the high land on the opposite bank of the river?
> A. I did.
> Q. And how far down that extended?
> A. Yes, sir. A rapid glance, of course.
> Q. And you felt that support, to be effective, could not come from that direction?
> A. I did not think they could get down there. I didn't think it was practicable to get down below me.
> Q. And, therefore, when you took that look from the timber, when you found you needed support, you had only your rear and your left in view, but you also had the character of the country on the right side of the river?
> A. Yes, sir.[30]

Reno might as well have been a ventriloquist's dummy because the testimony is entirely Gilbert's. It is also pertinent to observe that Gilbert refers only to support from Custer, ignoring the "whole outfit" part of Reno's orders and cunningly changes Reno's viewpoint from Lee's "while you were in the bottom" to "when you took that look from the timber." This is a definite indication that Gilbert did not want any focus on the likelihood of Benteen providing support to Reno.

So, the testimony which refutes an attack strategy is false, contradicted by the weight of evidence demonstrating that Custer had planned the envelopment, but were the orders given by Custer to his senior subordinates senseless as Benteen claimed? The only order Reno received was to attack the village and his command was supposed to be Custer's holding force. Benteen's column was ordered to the left with the ultimate task of attacking the village's western flank. By his own admission, Benteen disobeyed his orders.

Benteen's Orders—Inquiry Testimony

From Captain Benteen's testimony, he states:

> My orders were to proceed to a line of bluffs about 4 or 5 miles away, to pitch into anything I came across, and to send back word to General Custer at once if I came across anything …

I received instructions through the chief trumpeter ... if I found nothing before reaching the first line of bluffs, to go to the second line ... I had gone ... a mile further when I received orders through the sergeant-major ... that if I saw nothing from the second line of bluffs, to go on into the valley, and if there was nothing in that valley, to go to the next valley.[31]

Benteen was then asked, "Q. Go back to the time you received the order from General Custer to separate yourself from the entire command and state whether there was any order given to you to unite at any time with Major Reno's column? A. Neither with Major Reno nor anyone else."[32]

Asked further as to what his orders were, "Q. What were your orders? A. Valley hunting ad infinitum," and "Q. Was any order afterwards sent to you to join Major Reno or assist him? A. Never."[33] Then finally, "Q. In answer to a question by Major Reno as to what were your orders, you stated 'valley hunting ad infinitum.' Do you mean that was the order or the conclusion of your own mind? A. That is the way I would like to have it, that is the way I understood it. I understood it as rather a senseless order ..."[34]

In addition, Benteen took every opportunity to greatly exaggerate what his command had experienced on their move to the left, all intended to endorse his claim that his orders were "senseless."

Two examples are: a) "The ground was very rugged and we had to go through defiles and around high bluffs to get to the point to which I had been sent," also b) "I might have gone 20 miles in a straight line without finding a valley."[35]

Benteen's Orders—Custer's Requirements

When Custer sent Benteen to the left from the divide just what did he have in mind? Various authors have stated that it was Custer being faithful to Terry's admonition to constantly feel to his left. Roger Darling called it "Benteen's Scout-to-the-Left" and others have labelled it a reconnaissance in force. In my opinion it was none of those things.

Obviously, Custer would not have sent Benteen off into the unknown when on an attack mission. To do so would be to foolishly risk the elimination of one quarter of his force from the expected action and Custer was not a fool. Bearing in mind the news from Hairy Moccasin that the village was not running, Custer probably did not expect Benteen to see any action until he came up to the village itself via the Little Big Horn valley route. That is the most likely reason that Benteen did not have a doctor with his command.

Custer knew, later intelligence to the contrary, that he would use the envelopment against the village and sending Benteen to the left was a verification of that plan. I believe there is already sufficient evidence to show that the captain's command was meant to move into the Little Big Horn valley and attack the village's west flank. Reno unwittingly confirmed that this was the case in his post-battle report and at the same time gave the lie to his testimony and Benteen's that they had not discussed Benteen's orders: "I saw Benteen moving further to the left and as they passed he told me he had orders to move well to the left and sweep everything before him."[36] His testimony on this point was remarkably similar, "I don't recollect his reply exactly, but it was to the effect that he was to drive everything before him on the hill."[37] In both cases Benteen is cited as either "sweeping" or "driving" everything before him. The question is where to? The logical answer can only be back towards the village, which is where Custer expected Benteen to reach, with or without any contact with Indians. The captain of course, could not afford to acknowledge that the real order he had disobeyed was to take his command up the Little Big Horn valley, hence his distortion of the difficulties and distances his command experienced on their move to the left.

Benteen's Mission—Analysis

Whatever orders Custer gave to Benteen would be to urgently implement the attack plan and when he sent the captain to the left, the Crows had given him a reasonable understanding of what he would face. Contrary to his testimony, Benteen's post-battle report states that he had orders to get back to the main trail,[38] but First Lieutenant Francis M. Gibson wrote to his wife that they were to find the Little Big Horn valley "… after which we were to hurry and rejoin the command as quickly as possible."[39] In view of Benteen's admission of disobedience, I think Gibson was saying that they were to rejoin the command by carrying on up the Little Big Horn valley as the left wing of a proposed coordinated envelopment.

In documents both pre and post the inquiry, Benteen showed that he had omitted pertinent information from his testimony. For instance, Benteen wrote to his wife: "I was ordered with 3 Co's [sic] … to go to the left for the purpose of hunting for the valley of the river—Indian camp—or anything I could find,"[40] and, "… I was ordered with my battalion to the left, in search of the valley, which was supposed to be nearby …"[41] In his narrative, he says, "My real, Simon-pure, straight orders, were to hunt that valley …"[42]

Lieutenant Gibson confirmed the command's real purpose: "Benteen's battalion … was sent to the left about five miles to see if the Indians were trying to escape up the valley of the Little Big Horn …"[43] and, "Now as to my little scout to the left to find the Little Big Horn valley, I can state definitely that I did find and see it …"[44] also, "Benteen told him to keep going until he could see the valley of the Little Bighorn … and that he thought that he did so."[45] This was corroborated by Lieutenant Godfrey: "Lieutenant Gibson, with a detail, was sent to the ridge, where he had a view of the valley of the Little Big Horn."[46]

Initially, Benteen was probably elated that he was going on a positive assignment but having marched his command 3 miles to the west without finding either the valley or any Indians he lost faith in his task. With no trust in Custer's original or additional orders, he ignored them and decided to return to the main trail. Gibson meanwhile had gone to a ridge further west which overlooked the south fork of Reno Creek. Coming back from there, he confirmed that he had seen the river valley, but hearing that no Indians were in sight, Benteen decided to continue along the route he was on.

At the inquiry he was asked about this: "Q. State whether or not in bearing to the right to strike the main trail you complied with the instructions he had given you? A. It was scarcely a compliance. Q. Did you consider it a violation of his instructions? A. I must say I did."[47] Benteen's admission of disobedience was truthful but calculated. He was demonstrating to the court two things. First, his military acumen in abandoning a pointless mission which facilitated his timely arrival to save Reno's command and second, his unauthorized return to the main trail meant that Custer could not then know where Benteen was. There was also another effect. The court's focus would be diverted from his real mission: acting as one arm of an envelopment.

Unaware that Benteen had aborted his mission so quickly, Custer wanted the pack train to close up to be nearer to the action and via his brother Tom sent Sergeant Kanipe to hurry it forward. Assuming that Benteen was still on his mission and the first dust cloud they could see was therefore the pack train, Tom's orders to Kanipe were, "Tell McDougall to bring the pack train straight across to high ground ..."[48] plus significantly, "And if [italics mine] you see Benteen tell him to come quick,"[49] an unnecessary qualification if the Captain had to be bypassed to reach the pack train.

Benteen stated that he met Kanipe about a mile past the Lone Tepee and spoke with him concerning the pack train's whereabouts. It is unlikely that he failed to ask the sergeant what was happening up ahead. If he did not, he was not behaving like the experienced soldier he was and Kanipe[50] confirmed that some conversation took place. This is probably one reason why he was not called to testify at the inquiry, the other being the order to Captain Thomas M. McDougall to bring the pack train straight across to high ground because that order was ignored. It seems to me that the order to McDougall was not meant to indicate that the pack train should meet up with Custer as is often proposed, but that it should take a shorter route closer to where Custer supposed Reno was still fighting.

About a mile or so after the Kanipe meeting, Trumpeter John Martin reached Benteen with a message for him from Custer, the famous, "Benteen, come on, big village, be quick, *bring* [italics mine] packs etc.," which so puzzled the captain. The reason for his dilemma is plain. The sighting of a second dust cloud fooled Custer into thinking that Benteen, unable to find his way into the river valley, had been forced back to the main trail behind the pack train and the order meant that he was to bring the pack train along with him when he caught up to it. The consequences of Benteen's disobedience were now manifesting themselves.

The interpretation of the order to Benteen has usually been that Custer wanted Benteen to quickly join him and the questions asked at the inquiry indicate that this meaning was held by the court. In my opinion, the court and many historians who have held that view since, are wrong. My reasoning is that if Custer knew Reno was in trouble he could not possibly have wanted Benteen to bypass the major as it was imperative to Custer's envelopment plan for the Indians to be occupied with the attack at the south end of the village. If he did not know that Reno was in trouble then having seen the size of the village and assumed that most of the Indian force had gone to attack Reno, he would have surmised that without reinforcements the major could not hold out against the number of warriors such a village would contain. The order to Benteen was urging him to support Reno but to make sure that the packs were not left too far behind. With Custer urgently wanting to attack and keen to take advantage of what appeared to him to be little resistance at the northern end of the village, it makes no military sense for him to just deploy in defensive positions whilst waiting for Benteen, specifically if the latter was thought to be behind the pack train.

Finally, there is one piece of evidence that seems to make it clear that Custer did not expect Benteen to join him. In his testimony Martin says:

> The adjutant called me. I was right at the rear of the general. He said, "Orderly, I want you to take this dispatch to Captain Benteen and go as fast as you can." He also told me if I had time and there was no danger in coming back to do so, but if there was danger or there were any Indians in the way not to come back but to remain with my company. My company was with Captain Benteen and report to him when I came down there.[51]

Martin then, is to return on his own if he can, but to remain with Benteen's command if he can't. That can only mean that Custer was not expecting Benteen's command to come to him and makes all the theories to that effect irrelevant. Did Benteen realize what Custer really required? I am sure that he did, but it suited him for the court to think otherwise, as it fitted well with his mantra that Custer had no plan and was issuing pointless, and confusing orders.

After meeting with Martin, Benteen joined an already retreating Reno and all his expectations of participating in a successful attack evaporated. With Reno trauma-tized, and Benteen preoccupied with the possible repercussions of his disobedience, it is little wonder that no positive actions were either considered or implemented until Captain Thomas B. Weir made his unauthorized sortie. The arrival of Terry and his command with the news that Custer and all his immediate command had perished changed everything for Benteen and Reno. Now they could say what they liked with no Custer to answer to and they did so in the self-serving reports they wrote immediately after the battle.

What they did not anticipate were the public accusations brought against them, by firstly former Confederate Major General Tom Rosser and then Frederick Whittaker, author of *A Complete Life of General George Armstrong Custer*, both of which cast

Reno, in particular, in a very bad light. In response Reno requested and was granted a Court of Inquiry. I have shown that much of the testimony is replete with lies, distortions and evasions but why the need now that Custer was dead? Obviously, by claiming that Custer had no plan, it allowed Benteen and Reno to assert that without one they had no idea what Custer expected them to do. Further, Benteen could also claim that being sent to the left was a pointless mission. The whole purpose of Benteen's constant emphasis on the uselessness of his trip to the left and his violation of orders by returning to the main trail has already been explained.

His testimony was intended to impress upon the court that his disobedience of orders was merited in the circumstances and that his astute military thinking was in sharp contrast to the woolliness of his orders from Custer. This aspect was carefully emphasized by Reno's counsel, Lyman D. Gilbert, when he posed a leading question to Benteen: "A few moments ago you stated that your departure to the right was, in your judgment, a departure from the instructions you received from General Custer. I wish you, in justice to yourself, to state whether that was not the direction in which you afterwards found Major Reno?" Benteen prevaricated in his reply, "I did not find the first valley and therefore did not go to the second but returned to the trail because I thought I would be needed there. I had ascertained more about that country than General Custer and his adjutant knew."[52]

Another aspect of his disobedience that Benteen turned to his advantage was the Court's misconception that the "come on, big village" message meant that Benteen was to go to Custer quickly as the following extracts show:

> Q. The order sent to you was to join General Custer and assist him?
> A. By Trumpeter Martin was the only one I got.
> Q. From the tenor of the order you received, was it or was it not manifest that General Custer expected you would be found on the trail within communicating distance of the pack train?
> A. It was not evident to me for it was evident to me that he could not have expected any such thing from the orders I started out with. He could not have possibly known where to have found me, according to my belief, within 10 or 15 miles. My going back there was providential or accidental or whatever you may be pleased to term it.[53]

So, Custer yet again had issued an irrational order because he could not have expected Benteen to be on the main trail as unbeknown to him, the captain had disobeyed his orders.

Benteen also denied that he knew where Custer was and that he met up with Reno's battalion, believing it to be the entire command. He testified that he just told Kanipe where the pack train was and the only thing Martin had told him when he delivered the "bring packs" order was that the village was "skedaddling." In other words, he had no information regarding the whereabouts of Custer's command. Kanipe, however, had come to him from the northeast and Martin from much the same direction, so it did not take any stretch of the imagination to infer the general direction that Custer had taken. In later years, both Kanipe and Martin made statements to Walter Camp[54] which challenged Benteen's version of events.

This article has shown that much of the testimony regarding Custer's leadership given by Reno and especially by Benteen at the Court of Inquiry, is untruthful. Benteen at the inquiry and Reno in his post-battle report both acknowledged that Custer was trying to attack the village from the north. Further, the descriptions they both use are informative. In his report Reno says, "After traveling over his trail, it is evident to me that Custer intended to support me by moving further down the stream and attacking the village in the flank"[55] and Benteen in answer to the question, "Do you think that General Custer formed no plan of attack on that day, if so, what grounds have you for thinking so?" answered, "I think that after he sent Major Reno across to charge the Indians his intentions were to get to the rear of the village and attack them from the left."[56] Evidently then both the major and the captain were not unaware of the concept of the envelopment.

I have seen it proposed that anyone who suggests that some witnesses, and Benteen in particular, lied at the Court of Inquiry must have some kind of agenda. I freely admit to such an agenda. It is called seeking the truth and I am quite ready to shame the devil with it.

CHAPTER 10

Custer—Personal Bias vs Reality

Often on online specialist Little Bighorn message boards, some modern army officers are scathing about the mistakes they accuse Custer of making. When however, one of them condemned him for not training his regiment using the tactics underlying modern army acronyms which didn't exist in his day, I felt it necessary to bring to light exactly what the situation was prior to the 1876 campaign. It will help readers to gain a better understanding of what prevailed at the time.

I have often wondered why some modern army officers are so critical of Lieutenant Colonel George Armstrong Custer for the defeat of his 7th U.S. Cavalry at the Battle of the Little Bighorn in 1876, that to "prove" their case they regularly apply current military concepts, tactics, or acronyms, to that nineteenth-century conflict, whilst overlooking the realities of the attitudes that prevailed in 1876.

One retired colonel has been particularly scathing about the 7th Cavalry's lack of training prior to the expedition against the so-called hostiles. To illustrate his views this man used several army acronyms. Three will suffice by way of example. The first was that Custer did not implement TOE, a Table of Organization and Equipment. That idea was not introduced by the U.S. Army until 1943, so one can only assume that army officers in 1876 were unaware of it. Then there was

Custer Memorial at West Point. (Wikimedia Commons)

Custer's apparent non-appliance of METL, or Mission Essential Task List. METL was created in early 2004 by Special Forces veteran Greg Miller, which means Custer did not have such an idea available to him in any of the manuals of his day. Thirdly, there was no GOTWA preparation, that is, the Five Point Contingency Plan for patrol missions when the leadership is absent. The initials represent: G—where am I Going, O—Others I am taking, T—Time of my return, W—What to do if I don't return and A—Actions to take if either you or I are hit. As this relatively modern concept appears to rely on radio communication to relay rapid information, I am not sure how in 1876 the 7th Cavalry Regiment was supposed to rapidly communicate such information as, "General Custer has been hit," but that is not explained by the officer suggesting Custer did not use GOTWA. So, there we have one modern military man's view of what training was lacking in the 7th Cavalry prior to the 1876 campaign. However, how does that view compare with the realities at the time?

As it is Lieutenant Colonel Custer who is targeted for this apparent lack of training, I will focus on his situation at the time from the period September 24, 1875 when he left Fort Abraham Lincoln with his wife to begin an official leave, to May 17, 1876 when the Dakota Column left Fort Abraham Lincoln to find the "hostiles." When he went on leave, there was no hint of any action against any Indians. Although there was a prior secret meeting at the White House, it was not until December 6, 1875 that Indian agents were requested to communicate to the so-called hostile bands that they had to surrender at their designated agencies by January 31, 1876 or be forced to do so by the military. On December 14, 1875, Lieutenant General Philip H. Sheridan requested reports from Brigadier Generals Alfred H. Terry and George Crook about a possible winter campaign. Crook was ready but Terry's department was weather-bound, yet at least the plans were afoot. Terry was obviously keeping Custer informed by telegraph as in a January 1876 letter to his brother Tom, George Custer wrote, "I expect to be in the field, in the summer, with the 7th, and think there will be lively work before us. I think the 7th Cavalry may have its greatest campaign ahead."[1]

Custer's leave ended on February 15, 1876 and he reported to Terry in St. Paul on that date, quickly involving himself in the planning for the anticipated Indian campaign, for which Terry had appointed Custer in command, as evidenced by his telegraph of February 21, to Lieutenant General Philip H. Sheridan, "I think my only plan will be to give Custer a secure base well up the Yellowstone …"[2] On March 6, Custer with his wife and entourage, left St. Paul for Fort Lincoln, but his train was halted by snowdrifts and after a week's delay his party had to be rescued by his brother Tom in a sleigh, which reached Fort Lincoln on March 13. The expedition was planned to begin on April 5, but the bad winter weather caused that to be postponed until April 15, but that too was postponed. Just two days after reaching the fort, Custer was subpoenaed to testify in Washington regarding the investigation into the corrupt practices of Secretary of War William W. Belknap and left Fort Lincoln on March 21.

After being involved in some messy matters arising from his testimony against both Belknap and Orvil Grant, the President's brother, as well as testifying in an investigation into a charge of bribery against Major Lewis Merrill, a 7th Cavalry officer, Custer was released by the Board of Managers pursuing the case against Belknap and left Washington on April 20, stopping briefly at the Philadelphia Centennial and then New York. He was summoned back by the Board on April 24, probably at the instigation of President Grant. Grant was furious with Custer for naming his brother Orvil as part of Belknap's corrupt circle and within the course of one day Terry was ordered "to send someone other than Custer in charge of the expedition from Fort Lincon"[3] and was pressured into taking over that role himself. A shocked Custer was advised by General of the Army William T. Sherman to delay leaving Washington until May 1 so that he could see Grant. An angered, spiteful Grant refused to see him. Receiving permission from the Adjutant General and Inspector General to leave for his post and unable to see Sherman who was in New York, Custer left by train that evening. On May 2, Sherman wired Sheridan to stop Custer from leaving Chicago when he arrived and to tell him that he would not accompany the expedition. On reaching Chicago on May 4, Custer was detained and told that he would not be going on the expedition. His request to be detained at Fort Lincoln was authorized but first Custer went to St. Paul to beg Terry for help.

Terry knew that he needed Custer's experience in Indian fighting and did not want Major Reno commanding the 7th Cavalry, so he assisted Custer in writing a contrite and diplomatic letter to Grant, and which Terry endorsed "Custer's services would be very valuable with his regiment,"[4] which was then grudgingly also endorsed by Sheridan. Grant relented and Custer was to be allowed to go on the expedition but only in command of his regiment. The result of Grant's spiteful actions against Custer was to further delay the departure of the Dakota Column. Terry and Custer left St. Paul and reached Fort Lincoln on May 10 with Terry taking over command of the expedition on May 14. All 12 companies of the 7th Cavalry were present as well as the rest of the force that together formed the Dakota Column.

Major Marcus Reno had been in nominal command at Fort Lincoln since November 1875 with his duties including training, especially new recruits and in the Fall and Winter of 1875/76, troops performed normal garrison tasks plus some escort duty. The bitter Dakota winter allowed only limited duty outside the immediate fort area.

Prior to this time, only companies A, C, D, F and I of the 7th Cavalry were at Fort Lincoln, with three, B, G and K, in the Department of the Gulf, whilst H and M were at Fort Rice, 28.5 miles away and E and L were at Fort Totten, 16.5 miles away. When Terry and Custer arrived at the Fort on May 10 the 12 companies were already there. Adding to the five companies already stationed there, Companies E and L arrived on April 17 from Fort Totten and were quartered in camp two miles south of Fort Lincoln. Companies B, G and K arrived at that camp from the Gulf

District on May 1 whilst Companies H and M arrived there from Fort Rice on May 5 at the same time as the five companies stationed at the fort, plus Custer's staff and the band.

When the expedition eventually started its march on May 17, Custer would have had less than one week in which to train his regiment as May 16 had been washed out by heavy rain. That he made some difference is reported by one private who in a letter home wrote that Custer, "... was as happy as a boy with a new red sled. He put a lot of zip into us."[5] The reality is therefore, that Custer was only at Fort Lincoln for eight days in March, when only five companies of his regiment were there, plus six days in May when the entire regiment was there.

Common sense alone dictates that he had no chance to put the regiment through a rigorous training schedule or indeed, any type of training, except perhaps marksmanship. In any case, what was he training them for? The purpose of the expedition was to find the so-called hostiles, attack them if necessary and force them to live at their appointed agencies. The whole army command, from Sherman on down, were utterly confident that this would be achieved. These were just Indians, who when you attacked their villages, ran away.

Indeed, the belief they would flee from Custer is underpinned by Captain E. S. Godfrey in his 1892 publication where he states:

> If the advance to the attack be made in daylight it is next to impossible that a near approach can be made without discovery. In all our previous experiences, when the immediate presence of the troops was once known to them, the warriors swarmed to the attack, and resorted to all kinds of ruses to mislead the troops, to delay the advance toward their camp or village, while the squaws and children secured what personal effects they could, drove off the pony herd, and by flight put themselves beyond danger, and then scattering made successful pursuit next to impossible.[6]

What training was necessary then, against an enemy who had been fought many times before, was predictable in his reactions, was undisciplined and poorly armed? There was no manual on what tactics to use against them, but prior experience had shown that you either charged into their villages or used the envelopment to create two or more attacks from different directions, a method which was known to disconcert Indian warriors who did not like to fight on more than one front. Training, other than to follow orders in the field, could not be simulated, as an attack against a village depended on the location of that village, the number of people in it and the opportunity to execute a surprise dawn attack. Modern army thinking and jargon, does not consider the mindset of the U.S. military in the 1870s, particularly about how the Indians were viewed. If there is one modern acronym that is always applicable to a study of the Battle of the Little Bighorn, it is KISS—Keep It Simple ... Soldier!

CHAPTER 11

Custer and the Internet

Having come across totally misleading information on some Internet sites, including the specialist message boards, it seemed essential to me to reproduce some of what was being said and show why it was wrong. I also felt it prudent to try and demonstrate the realities of what happened at the battle and what led to it, to shed some light on how fate played a significant part.

What does the future hold for the continuing study of the Battle of the Little Bighorn and the part played in it by Lieutenant Colonel George Armstrong Custer? On January 22, 2017, the *New York Post* columnist Karol Markowicz wrote an article headed, "Why schools have stopped teaching American history," in which she examines the varying reasons why American history is no longer a core subject in American schools. One of the most startling pieces of information was that in North Carolina it was proposed that high schools change their curriculum so that history is taught only from 1877. It does not take a genius to realize what that would do to the study of our subject.

The trend in recent years to disregard history as a core subject is worrying generally but is of particular concern when it comes to that battle and its participants, because the main source for young people to access when it comes to seeking information about history, is of course the Internet. Whether it be via computers, tablets or the evermore sophisticated smart phones, instant answers are available at the touch of a screen. The concern is, are those instant answers accurate or misleading? In the case of Lieutenant Colonel Custer, can they be relied upon, or does the tendency for some leading authors to hold him solely responsible for the defeat of his immediate command prejudice those who post their views on the Internet?

The Internet and the Blame Game

My trawl through what is available on the internet about Custer and the battle has produced worrying results. In *Time* magazine, Zachary Karabell wrote in October 2010,

"... yet another example of the blame game that has become endemic in American life. It's always someone else's fault and government makes an easy and familiar target." Well, the blame game is alive and kicking on the Internet so far as Custer's decisions at the Little Bighorn are concerned. He is an easy target of course. He was the field commander of the 7th U.S. Cavalry Regiment, which was so unexpectedly routed by American Indian warriors on that 25th day in June, 1876 and the axiom adopted by some, that the commander is always to blame for a military defeat, is rigorously applied to him. The worst aspect of this desire to blame Custer is that the cherry-picking of matters to find him guilty of causes a plethora of opinions to appear in the public domain, which, if inaccurate, in turn misinforms those who are new to the subject and perpetuates the inaccuracy.

Internet Misinformation

Scan the internet for references to Custer's actions at Little Bighorn and what do we find? Under a heading, "What mistakes did Custer make in the Battle of Little Bighorn?" one author states, "His biggest mistakes were a failure to wait for the columns led by General Alfred Terry, General George Crook or Colonel John Gibbon which were headed to the same objective area to join him. His second mistake was a failure to conduct a proper reconnaissance of the Indians encampment." Right away there is no room for doubt—Custer made mistakes. The two alleged mistakes are then provided. Neither are fair comment. Firstly, Terry and Gibbon were the same column and Custer's letter of instructions from the expedition commander Brigadier General Alfred H. Terry makes it clear that Custer was the strike force, not expecting anyone to join him, especially General George Crook, whose Wyoming Column's whereabouts were not even known to Terry or Custer. In parts of that letter, Terry wrote:

> The column of Colonel Gibbon is now in motion for the mouth of the Big Horn. As soon as it reaches that point it will cross the Yellowstone and move up at least as far as the forks of the Big and Little Horns. Of course its future movements must be controlled by circumstances as they arise, *but it is hoped that the Indians, if upon the Little Horn, may be so nearly enclosed by the two columns that their escape will be impossible* [italics mine].
>
> The supply steamer will be pushed up the Big Horn as far as the forks if the river is found to be navigable for that distance, and the Department Commander, who will accompany the column of Colonel Gibbon, *desires you to report to him there* [italics mine] not later than the expiration of the time for which your troops are rationed, unless in the meantime you receive further orders.

These extracts clearly demonstrate that as Terry and Gibbon would remain at the forks of the Big Horn and Little Bighorn rivers and Terry hoped the Indians would be trapped between Gibbon and Custer, there is no evidence to support the idea of the two commands joining each other.

The accusation that Custer did no proper reconnaissance of the Indian village is regularly used to beat him with, but however many times I have used the specialist message boards to ask how and when he could have organized such reconnaissance (recce), I have never received a sensible answer. Even if Custer had been able to attack at dawn or about 6:00 a.m. on June 26 as he had hoped, the village was roughly fifteen miles from where the regiment was near the divide between Rosebud Creek and the Little Bighorn River and at a trot speed of around 8 mph it would have taken him between one and a half to two hours to reach the village site at say 8:00 a.m.

How then does he recce the village to plan his attack, given that his command can be spotted any minute by someone from that village? Does he do a route recce using his scouts to see what influence the Indians could have on the route chosen; an area recce to check terrain and see what the Indians are doing; or a zone recce by dispersing his subordinate leaders to obtain as much detail as they could in their designated zones, about routes, obstacles terrain and enemy strength? Details of the available routes, the terrain and the location of the village were fortunately mostly known to Custer. What is regularly overlooked in this context, is that he had with him six Crow Indian scouts and their interpreter, the frontiersman Mitch Boyer, who knew all that area very well because it was their land. Only three to four years earlier, the Crows, including White Swan, one of the scouts with Custer, had camped virtually on the same spot, so on that June day in 1876, Custer was probably conducting what is known as a reconnaissance in force, to discover the position and strength of the enemy. The charge of not conducting a proper reconnaissance is therefore unfounded.

Teachers or Misleaders?

Even those students who do study history appear to be given erroneous information about Custer. On a website called Marked by Teachers an essay on the Little Bighorn is posted in full and it contains several criticisms of Custer's actions at the battle including the already discredited one that he did not wait for the other command. Instead, he led his command to the Indian encampment as, "He needed to launch the attack and get a defeat over the Indians before the Democratic Party picked their electoral candidate two days later. He hoped, having Mark Kellogg, the journalist with him, that news would spread and he would be on his way up the presidential ladder." This question of Custer's political ambitions is one that is used to strengthen the argument that he was a glory-hunter. Author Marie Sandoz wrote about his presidential ambitions in her 1966 book, *The Battle of the Little Bighorn* but where did the idea originate? Ironically, from a misunderstood conversation that Custer had with some of his Arikara (Ree) scouts, including Bob-tailed Bull and Bloody Knife. Another of them, Red Star, was not present but later said, "Custer told him [Bob-tailed Bull] that he had been to Washington and that … no matter how small a victory he could win … it would make him President."[1] As Red Star was not at the meeting and the likelihood of misinterpretation from English to Ree is possible, or that Red Star simply misheard his fellow tribesmen, it is much more likely that Custer was repeating what he had often told his Ree scouts, namely that he would speak with the Great Father on their behalf, when he was with the Great Father in Washington. As the Democratic Convention was held from June 27–29, 1876 in St. Louis, Missouri and six candidates had already been nominated, there was little chance that Custer's name would have been added at the last minute and none that he could have been physically present.

Personality Flaws His Downfall?

Another barb aimed at Custer is that he was arrogant and overconfident. These labels are used by John Hollon in his June 25, 2015, online critique titled, "The Lessons of Custer: Five Things to Consider on 'Bad Management Day,'"[2] meaning of course, the Little Bighorn battle. Hollon begins by repeating the already discredited notion that Custer should have waited for the other command, then turns his attention to Custer's so-called personal character flaws. Apparently, because of his hubris, he "greatly underestimated the number of Indians facing him. Poo-poohed their abilities and failed to consider the many advantages his opponent had." The latest research indicates that he faced roughly 2,000 warriors at the battle, whereas he had calculated a top figure of 1,500.[3] So not such an underestimation as suggested. As the whole of the army command thought little of the Indian warriors as fighters, it is telling that it is used against Custer as if he was the sole officer who held such a view. Colonel Richard Irving Dodge once wrote that, "The first impulse of the Indian, is to scuttle away as fast as his legs will carry him." Even General Terry, who had no Indian fighting experience, wrote in his May 16, 1876 wire to General Philip Sheridan, "I have no doubt of the ability of my column to whip all the Sioux whom we can find,"[4] this about the same time that Fred Gerard, the Ree interpreter, had told him that there could be as many as 4,000 enemy warriors to face.

One of the cited advantages the Indians held is that they had several repeating rifles whilst the troops had only single shot rifles (carbines). This point is made by Hollon as if Custer knew this. He did not of course, but even if he had, as he expected the Indians not to fight but to flee as they historically did, it would not have mattered to him. This is a prime example of hindsight information being used as if it were known prior to the battle.

Apparently, according to Hollon, Custer was "outmaneuvered by an opponent [Sitting Bull] who executed a perfect plan," and, "Sitting Bull delegated well. He trusted in Crazy Horse, his able field lieutenant, who executed his battle plan perfectly."[5] It seems likely that here, Hollon has believed the rumor that emerged after the Custer defeat, that Sitting Bull was educated in military tactics at West Point. Even the most cursory research would have informed the author that the Plains Indian warriors did not fight in the way he describes. There was no overall "general" in charge of tactics as each warrior fought for personal prestige. Certain successful fighters such as Crazy Horse, Crow King or Tall Bull had their followers but did not dictate tactics, encouraging these followers by the example of their own personal bravery. Crazy Horse did not execute Sitting Bull's plan as there was no such plan. The most likely scenario is, that the greater mobility of the Indian warriors allowed them to mass rapidly at crucial points where they could inflict most damage on the soldiers, which would have swayed the battle in their favor.

In June 2019, Greg Bustin authored *How Leaders Decide: A Timeless Guide to Making Tough Choices* and an edited excerpt titled, "How Leaders Decide: Three lessons to learn from one of U.S. history's bloodiest days" inevitably found its way on to the internet. The bloodiest day is the Little Bighorn and the lessons to be learned are three things that the author claims Custer did wrong. Lesson One is headed, "Listen to the voice of experience, not your ego" and the author puts forward a scenario to justify that heading. Apparently, on June 25, 1876, the Lakota, Cheyennes and Arapaho tribes (though how only five Arapaho makes a tribe puzzles me) were not seeking trouble, though I suspect that Brigadier General George Crook would dispute that having been attacked by these Indians at the Battle of the Rosebud eight days earlier. Nevertheless, Bustin has them peacefully following the buffalo herds and gathering for the Sun Dance, even though that had happened two weeks earlier. He is another too, who has Custer aiming for the presidency on the back of a victory over the "hostile" Indians and ignoring the fact that his command was outnumbered, this time by 10 to 1. The inference is that Custer was driven by his ego, made impulsive decisions and was aiming for glory, though as usual, no evidence is produced to endorse these ideas. Perhaps Bustin had taken Hollon's work as factual.

Lesson Two in this work is headed, "Collect facts and assess conditions before making critical decisions," and immediately, Custer is vilified for having a style of battlefield leadership "unsuited for peacetime." Presumably if it is peacetime, there are no battles so quite what the author is trying to say eludes me. Returning to the day of the battle, Bustin makes a statement which is simply wrong. He says that at sun-up, Custer's scouts reported seeing large numbers of Indians, which is an exaggeration of the reality in that a few Indians had been seen by the scouts on the Crow's Nest. He goes on to say that it meant that those "large numbers of Indians" had "likely seen the 7th Cavalry too," so the element of surprise was lost. In reality, Custer was not convinced that the regiment had been spotted until apprised of some Indians seen trying to open a pack that had fallen off one of the mules.

Although he originally planned to attack at dawn the following day, we know he then made the decision to attack the Indian camp immediately as he assumed it would be warned of his regiment's approach by the Indians seen by his men. Regarding this decision, Bustin accuses Custer of making his first mistake, "pursuing his quarry against unknown odds." As the whole purpose for sending the 7th Cavalry to find the Indians was for it to act as the strike force, Custer was executing that aim and the enemy numbers were of no concern to the army as the Indians were expected to flee and scatter as they usually did in the face of an army force. Indeed, Bustin himself states that having lost the element of surprise, "Custer was afraid they would slip away and scatter," so if that was their course of action, what relevance did their numbers have? So far, there is no timescale in the article but suddenly it is noon and "Custer halted his regiment between the valleys of the Rosebud and Little Bighorn Rivers and made his second mistake: splitting his troops into three combat groups and a pack train." If it was a mistake, it could only have been regarded as such in hindsight, after the result was known. At the time, it was standard operating procedure when attacking an Indian camp which was expected to be running away. Now Bustin then provides us with two mysteries. The first is the return of a previously unmentioned advance reconnaissance party and the second is that as it returns two hours later, therefore 2 p.m., it presumably means that Custer held his command at the noon halt for two hours simply waiting for the advance unit to return, whilst abandoning his original concern that the Indians would, "slip away and scatter." It appears that the author is confusing his advance reconnaissance party with the scouting party which had gone to the Crow's Nest the evening before, because he has Mitch Boyer telling Custer, "There are more Sioux than all of your soldiers put together have bullets," when in fact, much earlier that day, what Boyer had actually said as Custer talked with his scouts, was, "General, I have been with these Indians for thirty years, and this is the largest village I have ever known of."[6] However, in Bustin's scenario, all the other scouts agree with Boyer's "bullets" remark so Custer rebukes them and orders his troops to move out.

The article's action then moves on to 3 p.m. when Custer mounts a ridge and sees what appears to be a deserted village. There is no information regarding what orders he has given to his two senior officers, Major Marcus Reno and Captain Frederick Benteen, nor indeed, is there any mention of them. Custer is credited with shouting, "We've caught them napping," before making his third and final mistake, which begins with him shouting, "After them, boys! Charge!" This brings us to Lesson Three, "Lead people in the right direction, or risk desertion," which seems to suffer from two problems, the first being historical inaccuracy and the second being that nothing in it pertains to the heading of Lesson Three. The author leads with the statement that at the war cry of Crazy Horse, warriors engaged Custer's three separate combat groups. As we know, that is inaccurate as Major Reno's command was the only one initially attacked because Custer's force headed north and Captain Benteen's was on the way back from his scout to the left. He correctly has Major Reno attacking first but losing half of his 112 men before ordering a disorderly retreat, when in fact over 30 of his men, roughly one third, were killed during the disorderly retreat. Benteen's role is summarily dealt with: He failed to comply with Custer's order to reinforce him, perhaps because he hated his commander.

Custer's role is given almost equally short shrift, although the author does try to help him by increasing his command of 209 men to 300. With his 300 men he attacks the village, though we are not told where, but he is shot in the chest crossing the river, again we are not told at what site as no one in Custer's five companies survived. I am puzzled that Bustin states that, "Witnesses recall that, as soon as Custer fell, his men lost their fighting spirit." If the cited witnesses were the Indians, I have yet to read any of their interviews which make that claim. In any event, Custer is dragged to the ridge (which ridge is not specified), where his battalion is annihilated 20 minutes after Custer had ordered the attack.

There follows a heading, "Questions for reflection" in which the author begins by stating, "Battle or no battle, modern-day leaders can learn from Custer's mistakes," or as I see it, the mistakes attributed to Custer by an author who appears to only have a superficial knowledge of what happened at the Little Bighorn. Frankly, I cannot see that anyone can learn anything from such a piece, except perhaps to research primary records before writing.

These then are some of the Internet sites which purport to present an historical account of Custer's actions at the Little Bighorn. As can be seen, they are rife with inaccuracies, generalizations, and biased opinions, yet this is the kind of history that the young, and other curious people, are finding on the World Wide Web. If they do not look any further, they are left with a distorted view of Lieutenant Colonel Custer and what he did on June 25, 1876. It is an ongoing sadness that the idea of reading books on the subject is not as appealing as using an Internet search engine.

Biased Message Boards

Perhaps we should not be surprised at this widespread "Custer bashing" by the uninformed, when it is equally to be seen on the specialist message boards dedicated to the battle. Some of the most strident Custer disparagers on those forums are modern army officers. No matter that they mostly overlay their views with modern army tactics and parlance, their very rank creates a following, which assumes that, because of that rank, they must be right. There are many examples of this, and it must make it extremely difficult for newcomers to the subject to form an unbiased view.

For example, a lieutenant colonel, a self-confirmed Custer disparager, who I will refer to as Colonel Bill, posted this:

> The Reno BN [battalion] was the regiment advanced guard. It was leading an eight-company attack in the valley. The problem is that LTC Custer changed his mind, and did not tell Reno. LTC Custer diverted the 5-company main body up the bluffs. This area was badlands, which meant much slower movement than the valley (SLOWGO terrain, in military terminology). It also put two impassable terrain features between the Custer and Reno BNS (NOGO terrain).

In another post Colonel Bill explains that the NOGO terrain features, placed between Custer and his advance guard, prevented Custer going to Reno's aid. He also states that, "MAJ Reno executed his job leading the regiment's attack in the valley. The key to understanding LBH is why LTC Custer abandoned his main effort, and did not conduct any other offensive action until killed. Why did an officer build a career on being aggressive, and become so passive and weak willed in this battle?" There appear to be two assumptions here. The first is that Reno's battalion was indeed an advance guard and the second is that Custer was originally going to follow Reno into the valley, hence the "eight-company attack," but did not do so, opting for something different without informing Reno. Colonel Bill's comments bring into focus the question of exactly what Custer planned to do and whether post-battle, both Reno and Benteen protected themselves with self-serving untruths.

Reno the Advance Guard?

Colonel Bill's statement that "the Reno BN was the regiment advanced guard" stems from Major Reno's own description of his battalion's function. In his statement of August 8, 1876, to the *New York Herald*, Reno wrote, "The only official orders I had from him [Custer] was … when Colonel Cooke, the Regimental Adjutant, gave me his orders in these words: 'Custer says to move at as rapid a gait as you think prudent, and to charge afterward, and you will be supported by the whole outfit.'"[7] There was "No mention of any plan, no thought of junction, only the usual orders to the advance guard to attack at a charge."[8] Giving testimony at his Court of Inquiry in 1879, Reno was asked, "Had you any idea where Captain Benteen was with his column?" and he replied, "Not the most remote. There was no plan communicated to us, if one existed. The subordinate commanders did not know of it."[9] Yet even though he had not the remotest idea where Benteen was he still believes he will be supported by the whole outfit. In fact, in his testimony, Captain Benteen when asked, "State whether it was any part of the plan which you were pursuing that there should be any union between yourself and Major Reno," responded, "There was no plan at all."[10] If in fact there was no plan, then Custer was indeed remiss, but it seems appropriate at this point to consider what tactics where generally used in cavalry attacks on Indian camps to try and establish if Reno's claim to be an advance guard can be justified, or if he was meant to perform another function and indeed, if Custer did have a plan.

Cavalry Tactics

Regarding cavalry tactics against Indians, retired Air Force Major Jay D. Smith explained them well in his article, "The Indian Fighting Army"[11] published in the *Research Review*, the bi-annual magazine of the Little Big Horn Associates. The first was what he called a penetration or the "classic" European charge, riding over the enemy by sheer weight of the men and horses.[12] This tactic was generally used in combination with infantry who would consolidate the ground gained, leaving the cavalry to make a further attack. Jay Smith states that this tactic did not work against Indians, who did not meet the charge but would retreat, always keeping just beyond effective range.

According to Major Smith, the more conventional tactic employed against Indians was the envelopment.[13] He writes, "This was executed using a holding force which engaged the enemy while other parts of the command swung to the right or left and hit him in the rear. This tactic was most effective in capturing villages."[14] How does this tactic fit into Reno's claim that he was the advance guard? If he was, then according to various military descriptions of that role, "it is a detachment, usually divided into, point, advance party, support and reserve, preceding a body of troops on the march to protect it and secure its uninterrupted advance," alternatively, "a military unit sent ahead of a main body to find gaps in enemy defenses, clear away minor opposition and prevent unexpected contact." Major Reno said that Colonel William W. Cooke ordered him to, "move at as rapid a gait as you think prudent, and to charge afterward, and you will be supported by the whole outfit." In those orders he has only to "charge afterward" with no reference to any of the terms used above to define an advance guard, whereas his orders appear to fit well with the role of a holding force.

Did he in fact know that he was the holding force, but, once he knew that Custer was dead, he could say he was the advance guard thus justifying his retreat by claiming that he had not been supported? That an envelopment was possible is evidenced by what he wrote in his report of July 5, 1876 in which he stated, "After traveling over his trail, it is evident to me that Custer intended to support me by moving further down the stream and attacking the village in the flank ..."[15] The pertinent point however is, was he aware as he rode towards the Indian village that Custer would not be following him? Some of the men with him certainly were. Fred Gerard the Ree interpreter was one:

> I re-joined Reno's command just as he was drawing up his men on the skirmish line. The men were almost six feet apart along the brow of a hill below which was a belt of timber. As the Indians came charging back the men used the timber for cover and the Indians rode by on the left and around to the higher ground at the rear and left. Not more than four rounds had been fired before they saw Custer's command dashing along the hills one mile to their rear. Reno then gave the order: "The Indians are taking us in the rear, mount and charge." This was then about 1:30 p.m. I was surprised at this change of position as we had excellent cover and could hold off the Indians indefinitely, but the orders were to mount and charge. Charley Reynolds was killed as he rode up the slope at the left and Isaiah a little farther out. Reno led his men in Indian file back to the ford above which he had seen Custer's command pass.[16]

Another was Private Thomas F. O'Neill of Company G who told Walter Camp, "When about half way down to where skirmish line was formed, he saw Custer and his whole command on the bluffs across the river, over to the east, at a point which he would think was about where Reno afterward fortified, or perhaps a little south of this. Custer's command was then going at a trot."[17] Further confirmation comes from Sergeant Stanislas Roy of Company A, who told Walter Camp, "After passing ford we formed in line and while forming I heard some of the men say, 'There goes Custer.' He could be seen over on hills to our right and across river."[18] Finally, another of Camp's informants was Private Henry Petring who said, "While in the bottom going toward the skirmish line, I saw Custer over across the river on the bluffs waving his hat. Some of the men said: "There goes Custer. He is up to something, for he is waving his hat."[19] If these men and presumably others, were aware of what Custer was doing, is it believable that their Commanding Officer was not? Assuming he was, can we accept without demur, Major Reno's Court of Inquiry testimony at face value when he stated, "There was no plan communicated to us, if one existed?"[20]

Major Reno was free to make such a statement because if he was being untruthful, the only man who could have proved it was Lieutenant Colonel Custer and, as Reno well knew, he was dead. It calls into question, however, just how truthful, or accurate, was the rest of Reno's testimony? At one point in that testimony, he stated that, "I could see a disposition on the part of the Indians to lead us on, and that opinion was also confirmed when a little afterwards, on advancing a little further, I could see the Indians coming out from a ravine where they evidently had hid themselves."[21] A bit later he further stated, "There were straggling parties of Indians making around to my rear. I said to myself at once that I could not successfully make an offensive charge. Their numbers had thrown me on the defensive."[22] If however, Major Reno was in fact the holding force for an envelopment, was he reading the signs correctly? Did he know what the Indians did when their villages were attacked, especially in daylight? It is true to say that he had not personally been involved in any of the 7th Cavalry actions against Indians, but there is little doubt that he was privy to the talk of those officers who had been. What Captain Edward S. Godfrey had to say about this when he wrote in 1892, has already been quoted and there is no reason to suppose that Reno did not know this, yet at Little Bighorn, the fact that the Indians had come out against him as Godfrey describes, does not seem to have struck him as their usual practice.

Of course, he may just have been afraid, which is perhaps verified by his actions in sending back two messengers to Custer to tell him that the Indians were coming out against him. The Ree interpreter Fred Gerard had also reported that the Indians were coming out of the village, as he stated in his testimony at the Reno Court of Inquiry. In answer to the question, "State whether or not you saw anyone, before crossing the river, of General Custer's column after that, and state how it occurred," he said:

> Yes, sir, I saw Colonel Cooke, and spoke to him when we got to this knoll. The scouts were to my left, and called my attention to the fact that all the Indians were coming up the valley. I called Major Reno's attention to the fact that Indians were all coming up the valley. I halted

there a little time. I thought it was of importance enough that General Custer should know it, and I rode back towards Custer's command. At this knoll I met Colonel Cooke and he asked me where I was going. I told him I had come back to report to him that the Indians were coming up the valley to meet us, and he says, "All right, I'll go back and report." And he wheeled around and went toward Major Reno's command [he meant Custer's command].[23]

Receiving this intelligence Custer would naturally have assumed that this was the usual Indian procedure, as described by Godfrey, of warriors swarming to the attack to halt the soldiers' advance while their families escaped. He surely would also have assumed that Major Reno would reach the same conclusion. He could now proceed with his role in the envelopment tactic by moving north to either attack at that end of the large village or capture some of the noncombatants as they tried to escape. The already cited passage from his report of July 5, 1876 shows that Major Reno knew that was a valid tactic.

Colonel Bill's criticisms of Custer are therefore, in my view, not merited. He has accepted Major Reno's claim to be an advance guard because it suits his purpose, which is to advocate that Custer originally intended to follow Reno into the valley and attack the village with eight companies. But as the 7th Cavalry was not accompanied by infantry, had not brought sabers with it and Captain Benteen's battalion was off on its own mission it seems highly unlikely that Custer was contemplating charging into the big village at that time using only revolvers, as the charge would have stalled after those weapons were empty, especially given the length of the village. Colonel Bill's comments regarding the NOGO terrain features are also, therefore, invalid, because if, as I suspect, Custer was in the process of trying to achieve an envelopment he would have had no need to cross the river to reinforce Major Reno. In any case, it is entirely possible that Custer, advised by his Crow scouts who knew the terrain, saw the so-called NOGO features as an asset, as if they prevented him from getting to the river, they also prevented the Indians from attacking his left flank. Colonel Bill makes the same error as so many others do, of not looking at the situation as Custer did; putting it simply, following a way north indicated to him by his Crow scouts, whose land it was.

An Officer's Thesis

There are various theses involving the battle, written by army officers, which though produced in modern times, have often been distorted on the message boards to blame Custer for not knowing or acting upon such theories which appeared over 100 years after his death. One especially was used in that way. In 2003, Major (later Lieutenant Colonel) Mark V. Hoyt published his thesis, "The Army's Sioux Campaign Of 1876: Identifying The Horse As the Center of Gravity of the Sioux."[24] The thesis focused on how the post-Civil War army considered the Indians' villages to be their center of gravity which is why catching them in their camps was the strategy of choice.

Colonel Hoyt however, believes that this was a flawed strategy, as in his view the horse gave the Indians their mobility and was therefore their center of gravity. Throughout his thesis he constantly stresses that it was the entire army command which advocated the Indian villages as the things to attack and that Custer was merely following that dictum at the Little Bighorn. In his own words on one of the message boards, he summarized his thesis, "However, my thesis wasn't on how Custer could have been successful—it was entirely on the U.S. Army not focusing on the correct Center of Gravity of the Sioux and it wasn't the village. It was the horse. Therefore, any attack at any time should be focused on taking out what counts and hurts the enemy most." Despite these clear explanations of the nub of his thesis, a trend sprang up on the message boards to blame Custer for not going after the Indian ponies at Little Bighorn because apparently, he knew they were the Indians' center of gravity. When it was pointed out that this was a hindsight view, the response was, "We know from Col. Hoyt that the horses should have been considered the Center of Gravity (COG) and would be best addressed in the valley. Focus on the COG is not a hindsight issue." A further comment on Custer targeting the horses was, "This technique was used during the civil war so it was known and not something in hindsight. Why did Custer destroy the horses at Washita?" Then this, "Guess where they took the horses to when Reno appeared. Custer could have been on the bluffs to the west shooting into the horses in the Big Village. The horses would destroy the infrastructure." Finally, "Col. Hoyt writes his paper on the horse herd being the center of gravity (COG) which Custer would know from experience, [Colonel Hoyt said no such thing]." He suggested that Custer erred in not going to the left, but, only if he had appreciated that the horses were the Indians center of gravity.

That the quoted remarks are total misrepresentations of Colonel Hoyt's thesis would appear to be of no concern to those who grasp at yet another stick with which to beat Custer. Indeed, in that thesis, the colonel spells out how Custer might have won. He states:

> Custer *could* [italics mine] have won the Battle of the Little Bighorn by striking earlier and striking at the horse herds with a consolidated force. However, Custer like all other Army commanders in accordance with Army strategy was focused on attacking and destroying or capturing the enemy village.[25]

The colonel précised the thrust of his thesis in another of his message board posts, "General Sheridan writing about the remaining hostile Sioux and Cheyenne bands in his 1876 Annual Report might have recognized the answer: 'the Sioux war will be at an end, and I think all future trouble with them, as it is intended to put most of them on foot, and a Sioux on foot is a Sioux warrior no longer.'"[26] Colonel Hoyt continued:

> No Army field commander in the Sioux Wars ever questioned whether the focus of an Army attack should not be the village. The COG of the Sioux was the horse, but developing a strategy to attack horse herds would have required a commander willing to challenge this old assumption. This challenge never happened, and the Army fought a drawn out and expensive

war against the Sioux using a strategy of exhaustion, aimed at attacking villages to wear out the enemy's will to fight. Even after Army commanders had evolved their strategy and operational maneuver in reaction to the enemy's mobility, the Army never changed its focus to attack the enemy's COG—the horse.[27]

In another post he addressed the matter of Custer's tactics:

> ... the very classic flank attack was the method almost any officer would probably have used (or some variant) ... Custer would have had to know that he was taking the village nearly completely by surprise [I don't think he knew that—in fact I think he felt they had been alerted]. He would have had to understood that forcing the Lakota to fight dismounted would have allowed him to dominate the battle—as their lack of mobility and lack of a unified command structure would have been great barriers [not to mention the panic ... etc.].

In all his comments about targeting the horses, the colonel makes it plain that he is dealing in what ifs and is not stating that Custer knew that was a valid tactic but chose to ignore it, yet those who are determined to heap blame on Custer use the colonel's thesis as if it were not written in 2003 in hindsight, but represents a blunder by Custer because he should have thought of it in 1876.

The fact is, that though Colonel Hoyt's thesis has logic going for it, even if the army of 1876 had focused on the idea that the Indians' horses were their center of gravity, it seems unlikely to me that the 7th Cavalry would have been able to make use of that intelligence. On March 17 that year, Colonel J. J. Reynolds had attacked a Cheyenne village on the Powder River after it had been reconnoitered and ordered one of his companies to capture the horse herd. In the event, 700 ponies were captured though about 500 were later recaptured by the Cheyennes. The point here is that Colonel Reynolds had about 380 men and one company, say 40 men, was assigned to capture the ponies. With about 100 more men than Colonel Reynolds, and knowing only that there was a large horse herd on the benchlands to the southwest of the Indian village, Custer would have had to try to get to it whilst defending against warrior attacks, then being faced with the task of running off that herd as he would not have been left free to shoot them as he did at the Washita. That southern herd would have numbered at least 5,000 ponies, which, with all the firing, would have been wild with fright and accordingly uncontrollable. Furthermore, that southern herd was not the only one. According to the Cheyenne warrior Wooden Leg, "The Cheyenne horses were put out to graze on the valley below our camp. Horses belonging to other tribes were placed at other feeding areas on the valley and on the bench hills ... The tribal herds were kept separate from each other."[28] This is where so many theories fail, by not considering facts which render them untenable.

A Simple Cause for Failure?

That then is a litany of the many fingers of blame pointed at Lieutenant Colonel Custer for being the cause of the disaster at Little Bighorn in June 1876. Most of the anti-Custer brigade focus their arguments on what he did or didn't do during the fighting or what led to it. What, however, if there is a much simpler reason for the disaster that befell him? To consider such a possibility it is necessary to repeat what Captain Edward S. Godfrey wrote in 1892:

> If the advance to the attack be made in daylight it is next to impossible that a near approach can be made without discovery. In all our previous experiences, when the immediate presence of the troops was once known to them, the warriors swarmed to the attack, and resorted to all kinds of ruses to mislead the troops, to delay the advance toward their camp or village, while the squaws and children secured what personal effects they could, drove off the pony herd, and by flight put themselves beyond danger, and then scattering made successful pursuit next to impossible.

In those few lines I believe, lie the root cause of why Custer was defeated and that cause is encapsulated in these words, "… to delay the advance toward their camp or village, while the squaws and children secured what personal effects they could, drove off the pony herd, and by flight put themselves beyond danger …" Captain Godfrey's description is of course, true of attacks on villages or camps which were considerably smaller than the one at the Little Bighorn, so that the Indian ponies were readily available for swift flight.

On June 25, 1876, the information provided by Wooden Leg that, "The Cheyenne horses were put out to graze on the valley below our camp. Horses belonging to other tribes were placed at other feeding areas on the valley and on the bench hills … The tribal herds were kept separate from each other" indicates that the huge horse herds were not readily available for swift flight, which meant that the noncombatants could not escape quickly or in fact, at all. Thus, the warriors knew they needed to be protected and were prepared to fight fiercely to do just that.

The remoteness of the horse herds had another important effect in that most of the warriors were late in getting their horses and were not, as Custer anticipated, engaging Reno at the southern end of the village. They were, in fact, at the northern end of the village, ready to engage him when he approached the northern fords. So fate had worked against Custer landing him in the midst of an aggressive enemy who were further bolstered by Sitting Bull's vision of defeating these soldiers, the warriors' belief that they had defeated Brigadier General George Crook's command at the Rosebud Battle on June 17, 1876, Major Reno's retreat and the knowledge that their way of life was under threat and you have all the ingredients for a complete reversal of the usual Indian tactic of flight. Custer did not know this and indeed, could not have known this, so naturally proceeded on the usual assumption. By overlooking the fact that the Little Bighorn was a unique event, that nothing like it had happened before, or occurred after, and ignoring the simplicity of army thinking in 1876, is where many theories and criticisms founder, but it will not stop some from blaming Custer, the eternal scapegoat.

CHAPTER 12

How Many Warriors Did Custer Face?

As this is a question that has exercised minds since 1876, I investigated the various records and individual views to try and make some sense of the wildly differing opinions. The result was a figure which is now widely accepted as most likely and will help readers to make more sense of what Custer faced.

At Major Marcus A. Reno's Court of Enquiry in early February 1879, Captain Frederick W. Benteen was questioned about what he saw from Weir Point, "Q. Give your estimate of the number of Indians that pursued or engaged that command on its return, within engaging distance. A. I thought at that time there were about 2,500 warriors surrounding us. I think now there were between eight or nine thousand."

Whether or not Benteen was being his usual awkward self, or truly believed the need to inflate his original figure, is not relevant but his answer does highlight the problem that has plagued authors and buffs to this day; namely, what figures for the number of Indians in the Little Bighorn valley on June 25, 1876, are reliable? My research has discovered nine Indian sources and over 20 white sources that have offered estimates of how many Indians were along the Little Bighorn River that day.

Cheyenne warrior Wooden Leg told Dr. Thomas B. Marquis that the Cheyennes had 300 lodges[1] in the Indian village, stating that, "The Blackfoot Sioux had about the same number, or a few less, The Arrows All Gone (Sans Arc) had more. The Miniconjou and the Oglalas each had more than the Arrows All Gone. The Uncpapas had, I believe, twice as many as had the Cheyennes."[2] From this information, Dr. Marquis estimated that the Cheyennes numbered 1,600 people and the entire camp about 12,000.[3]

Colonel Rodney G. Thomas, U.S. Army (Ret.) demonstrated that the figures—and therefore Dr. Marquis' estimates—were inflated in his 2004 Custer Battlefield Historical and Museum Association (CBHMA) Symposium talk, "Maps, Myths, Miscalculations and Monesetah," where he referred to the work of Harry Anderson who, in 1960, working from 1877 reservation surrender rolls, showed the Northern Cheyenne population to have been close to 1,200, or 175 lodges. As 600 Cheyenne did not leave the Red Cloud Agency and thus were not at Little Bighorn, that leaves about 600 possibly at Little Bighorn, or 70-plus lodges with two warriors per lodge.[4]

As Marquis's estimate for the entire camp was 12,000 people and the Cheyennes' numbers are now 600 not 1,600, the Lakota population per Marquis would be 11,400. But given Anderson's work on the Cheyennes' numbers, a similar analysis for the Lakota would no doubt produce a comparable reduction in their numbers. Some of the Lakota accounts are not helpful in this respect. The Miniconjou Feather Earring, told General Hugh L. Scott in 1919 that by giving the men willow sticks as a tally device, they had counted over 5,000 and that was not the entire population.[5] The Oglala He Dog interviewed by Scott, in 1920, stated that there were 2,000 lodges in the village.[6]

Cheyenne head man Flat Iron[7] estimated a total population of 14,000 with 8,000 warriors; George Bird Grinnell, the historian and authority on the Cheyennes, was told by Young Two Moon that there were 200 Cheyenne lodges there, whilst others told him there were more than 1,500 lodges in all with as many as three or four fighting men per lodge totaling to between 4,500 and 6,000 warriors in the camps.[8]

While these wide discrepancies are puzzling, two things must be considered when dealing with the data in Indian accounts. First, at the time of the battle, the Indians had a base-10 or decimal system, using the number of fingers on two hands and anything above 100 was generally referred to by the Lakota as "ota" or many, so the exact number of lodges in the village and the number of fighting men, was beyond most of them. Secondly, in the main they were interviewed between 30 to 50 years after the battle, so total recall was unlikely.

The main military source for Indian numbers were naturally the letters and testimonies at the Reno Court of Inquiry, from officers and men who survived the battle, Benteen, in a July 4, 1876 letter to his wife, wrote of 3,000 warriors being present.[9] At the Court of Inquiry however, at one point, questioned about the return from Weir Point, he answered that there may have been between eight or nine thousand,[10] so the number of warriors had increased threefold since the 1876 letter.

Sampling other estimates we have: First Lieutenant Carlo DeRudio who thought there were 3,000–4,000 warriors, but believed at the time of the battle the number was higher.[11] First Lieutenant Edward Settle Godfrey's estimate of the number of warriors was at least 3,000 to cover the ground he saw.[12] Second Lieutenant Luther Hare, who said he counted where 40 teepees had stood and from that estimated there were about 1,500 lodges plus 500 wickiups. Based on that, a low estimate of the Indian fighting force would be around 4,000.[13] Captain Myles Moylan thought 3,500–4,000 warriors,[14] while Reno stated, "The lowest computation puts the Indian strength at about 2,500, and some think there were 5,000 warriors present."[15] First Lieutenant Winfield S. Edgerly stated that there were no less than 3,000 warriors.[16] Private Theodore W. Goldin estimated the warrior strength as about 4,000 to

5,000 men.[17] Private Charles A. Windolph estimated that "altogether there may have been as many as one third of all the Sioux tribesmen here, possibly close to 10,000 out of 30,000. That would figure out somewhere between 2,000 to 3,000 warriors."[18]

Finally, there were the observations of the plainsman/scout George Herendeen, someone with a more experienced eye when it came to dealing with Indians. Quite soon after the battle he estimated that there were about 6,000 people in the village with half being warriors.[19] Three years later when giving testimony at the Court of Inquiry he had revised his opinion to a total of 1,800 lodges in the village with 3,500 warriors.[20]

Harry Anderson's work on providing a more accurate figure for Cheyennes at the battle, by working from the 1877 surrender rolls, points to a similar exercise being needed for the Lakota. Author Kingsley M. Bray, in an essay "Teton Sioux: Population History," published in the *Nebraska State Historical Society* magazine, compiled data on that subject for the year 1870 from the individual tribal divisions, to arrive at a total Lakota population of 14,370.[21] Calculating a six-year growth to 1876, Lakota numbers can be extrapolated to be 15,000 to 16,000 which I have seen proposed as reasonably accurate. As about half of this number stayed at the agencies or at least did not join the Little Bighorn village, it is likely that the total numbers on June 25 were in the region of 7,500 to 8,000 giving us a range of 1,500 to 1,600 warriors and a lodge count in the region of 1,200.

Bray and others have gone into complicated mathematical computations to reach their conclusions. Without attempting to emulate them, the above figures seem to me to be close enough to my own view of what numbers Custer faced. I know that some people believe they have the numbers pinpointed right down to an exact figure, but in my experience with this subject there are too many imponderables to make such a claim. Perhaps Benteen summed it up in his first unpublished narrative: "I state but the facts when I say that we had a fairly warm time with those red men as long as sufficient light was left for them to draw a bead on us, and the same I'm free to maintain, in the language of Harte. I don't know how many of the miscreants there were—probably we shall never know—but there were enough."

CHAPTER 13

Three Indian Leaders—Three Controversies

Was Touch The Clouds at the Little Bighorn?

Having read most, if not all, of the Indian participant interviews, plus other writings concerning the better-known leaders, I was astonished when one author insisted that Touch The Clouds was at the battle. I wrote this article using Indian participant accounts, to show that his presence there was unlikely and why.

Various sources today cannot even agree on the name of a tribal leader of one band of the Miniconjou Lakota who may have been at the Little Bighorn. Was it Touch The Clouds or Touch The Cloud? It shouldn't therefore, come as a surprise that multiple sources, again, can't even say with certainty whether he did participate in that battle in June 1876.

The name disparity still causes friction among his various descendants in their reliance on differing oral traditions. In Lakota the name is rendered as Mahpiya Icahtagya. A Lakota–English dictionary[1] shows that the Lakota word *mahpiya* means "the clouds" as that word is plural of itself. The literal translation of his name is therefore Clouds Touching. If he was Touch the Cloud the Lakota would be Mahpiya Ayaskapa Icahtagya, as I understand it. I will therefore refer to him as Touch The Clouds throughout as I examine whether he was at the Battle of the Little Bighorn.

The information for his presence at the Little Bighorn is largely contained in tribal oral histories and in some cases authors who appear to want him to be there. For example, in the first edition of his book *Participants in the Battle of the Little Bighorn*, author Frederic C. Wagner III has this entry for Touch The Clouds:

Touch The Clouds [aka Tall Sioux—Miniconjou Lakota—Teuton Sioux, d.1905.] Fairly tall, as his name may indicate. One of the four sons of Lone Horn [d.1875]. Listed as a Dakota chief in the LBH [Little Bighorn] Summer 2001 Research Review. [See Crazy Horse]. Donovan says he remained at the Cheyenne River Agency and was not at the LBH [*A Terrible Glory*, 185]—as do several well-respected historians—but Myers and very strong Sioux oral tradition confirm his presence at the battle. A moderate leader [which might support his being at the agency rather than the Little Bighorn]. His three brothers, however, were at the battle: Frog, Spotted Elk, and Roman Nose and his tribal importance cannot be understated. Unless definitive proof arises, Touch The Clouds must be carried as "at the battle."[2]

Oral History

In the ebook appendices to his book, *Fights on the Little Horn*, Gordon Harper has an item headed, "The Miniconjou Lakota People, Their Involvement in the Fights on the Little Horn, as Transcribed from their Oral History by their Historians on the Cheyenne River Reservation and Reproduced with their Permission."

The authenticity of this is debatable, as there are no signatories to the document or no sworn affidavits by Miniconjou historians to verify it as their oral history. I do know however, that this item was passed to Harper by someone of impeccable character who regularly visited the Miniconjou reservation. In any event it has been entered into the annals of the Little Bighorn and can therefore be used as a source.[3]

Oral history is heavy with references to Touch The Clouds's involvement preceding and in the battle. It mentions him as being part of the family camp of Waglula (Worm), the father of Crazy Horse, as the combined tribes moved along the Rosebud valley, then as part of a Miniconjou camp circle at the Deer Medicine Rock gathering. Early morning at Little Bighorn on June 25, he is said to have been officiating at a sweat lodge ceremony for some of the Suicide Boys. When the fighting started, he was apparently with a contingent of Spotted Elk, the Cheyennes, some 40 to 50 Suicide Boys and additional experienced warriors riding up Deep Ravine to engage E Company. It is also claimed that he was with Crazy Horse in the final rush that overwhelmed the last of Custer's command.

Is there any corroborating evidence for this? On July 27, 1912, at the Standing Rock Indian Reservation, the researcher Walter Mason Camp interviewed the Miniconjou warrior, Flying By,[4] who said that at the Little Bighorn, the Miniconjou Lakota chiefs were Lame Deer, Make Room, Lone Horn and Black Shield. The original Lone Horn, who had died in 1875, was the father of four sons, one of whom was Touch The Clouds, who later in his life had adopted his father's name. As the interview was in 1912, and Touch The Clouds died in 1905, it would have been customary for his fellow tribesmen to use his adopted name. In an earlier interview with Camp in May 1907,[5] Flying By is cited as being 57 years old, so it is puzzling that author Frederic C. Wagner III has him as killed at the Little Bighorn Battle.[6] It is an example of just how risky it is to rely on secondary sources and the memories of participants 31 years after the battle.

Evidence pointing to his absence from the Little Bighorn fights seems to rely on several documents from the Cheyenne River Agency "letters received file" that show him in councils at the agency during the summer of 1876.[7] There is also a source showing that in the fall of 1877, a reporter met the delegation of Indian headmen heading to Washington, D.C. and learned from them that He Dog, Little Big Man, Iron Crow, Red Bear and Big Road had all been at the battle but gleaned from the man himself, that Touch The Clouds had not been there. This brings into focus his July 29, 1876, comment at the Cheyenne River Agency to army negotiators,

"Have compassion on us. Don't punish us all because some of us fought when we had to."[8] Now this phrase can be interpreted in two ways. In saying "some of us fought when we had to" it can be assumed that "some of us" included himself. It is more likely however, that as he was pleading for leniency for his band of moderates, he was referring to those at the battle, not including himself or his people, when he said, "some of us fought."

Nobody Mentioned Him

Despite the claims made in the Miniconjou Lakota Histories, the most telling factor in demonstrating that Touch The Clouds was not at the battle, is that he, a warrior of great renown, is not mentioned in any of the participant Indian accounts, save that of Flying By and even then, without mention of any of his deeds if he had been in the fighting. It has been argued that individual warriors only talk about their own deeds and not those of their leader.[9] A cursory look at some of the warrior accounts reveals that to be incorrect, also that there is no mention of Touch The Clouds.

In 1919, fellow tribesman Feather Earring was asked by General H. L. Scott, "Who got a good reputation in that fight?" The warrior replied, "All—Crazy Horse, Sitting Bull and all that I heard of." It would seem churlish, if Touch The Clouds was there, for another Miniconjou warrior to ignore mentioning his famous tribal leader having a "good reputation."

The Brule warrior Two Eagles told Walter Camp in 1908 that "Lame Deer was the chief of the Miniconjou Lakota." Again, there was no mention of Touch The Clouds, a prominent leader of his tribe. The Blackfeet Lakota leader, Kill Eagle, told Captain R. E. Johnston in September 1876, that the principal chiefs aside from Sitting Bull were, "Crazy Horse of the Oglala Sioux; Big Man of the Oglala Sioux; High Elk of the Sans Arc." Would someone as well-known as Touch The Clouds have escaped his notice?

Another Miniconjou Lakota participant, Lights, told Camp in 1909 that, "He fought under several chiefs: but Spotted Elk was his main chief." Later he states, "… Lame Deer and Spotted Eagle led the Miniconjou Lakotas." This man mentions three of the Miniconjou Lakota leaders but not the impressive Touch The Clouds, who could hardly have gone unnoticed.

There are numerous other accounts which mention prominent Indians, so Brock's idea that individual warriors only mention their own deeds is incorrect as already mentioned. Since they do also mention the names of their leaders, the belief that someone as well-known as Touch The Clouds, a man with a well-earned reputation as a fighting man, would not be noticed, particularly by his own tribespeople, if he was present, is simply unbelievable. The logical conclusion can only be that he was not at the Little Bighorn battle, unless of course, rather like Achilles, he was sulking in his teepee.

Sitting Bull at the Little Bighorn

The famous Hunkpapa was undoubtedly at the battle, but the unanswered question was—did he fight in it? By using Indian participant accounts I was able to establish that it was doubtful if he was involved in the fighting but was a powerful influence there. His Sun Dance vision had a huge effect on the mood of the warriors. This article was requested by The Custer Association of Great Britain.

One of the most often asked questions about the Battle of the Little Bighorn is, "Was Sitting Bull involved in the fighting?" There are numerous references to him in the interviews given years later by warriors who participated in the battle, and it is fascinating to analyze what they had to say in the light of the honesty or otherwise of their comments.

Of the 17 opinions given, eight state that he was not in the fighting and nine say he was. Of these 17, two clearly have personal agendas. One of these was Kill Eagle, the *Sihasapa* (Blackfeet) headman, who clearly wanted to distance himself from any possible retribution by the soldiers. Worried about both the government embargo on ammunition and the possible lack of rations to feed his people, he illegally took 26 lodges from Standing Rock in May 1876 to go on a buffalo hunt. Successful in that endeavor, they nevertheless attended the annual sun dance held at Deer Medicine Rocks along the Rosebud River but allegedly were made to join those gathering around Sitting Bull. Kill Eagle apparently refused to join in the fighting at Little Bighorn and said he was publicly abused for his stance. After the battle, he took his people back to Standing Rock where he surrendered.

Interviewed on September 15, 1876, his story was essentially that his people had been forced to join the "hostiles" but had not fought against the soldiers. When asked by Captain R. E. Johnston "Was Sitting Bull in command at the fight?" Kill Eagle stated that the Hunkpapa medicine man had started out with them (the warriors) in command and that Sitting Bull had told him that, "After crossing the creek with his warriors he met the troops [Custer] about 600 yards east of the river. He drove the soldiers back up the hill. He then made a circuit to the right around the hill and drove off and captured most of the horses." How likely is it however, that someone who had refused to join in the fighting and had been publicly punished because of it, would be confided in by the man who had no doubt authorized that punishment? I think we need to take Kill Eagle's whole story with a large pinch of salt.

Another who undoubtedly had an agenda was Gall, the one-time friend and tribal ally of Sitting Bull. Having gone to Canada together after the Little Bighorn, Gall fell out with his former friend and took his own followers and others back to the United States and surrendered at Fort Buford on May 26, 1881. Sitting Bull and his people followed two months later. The two never reconciled and in his narrative of July 18, 1886, Gall's antipathy is plainly evident. He stated that Sitting Bull had little or nothing to do with the fight and that he was in his lodge at the time making medicine for the destruction of the whites and the success of the reds.

Rubbing salt into the wounds he also said that:

> His prowess as a fighter is simply a creation of the white man's brain and nothing else. When the warriors sallied out to attack the troops, he was really left behind to make medicine and to look after the women and children. If he has any latent fighting qualities, or abilities as a great leader, his kinsmen don't know it, nor does anybody else.

Of course, a lot of this venom may have been instigated by the Indian Agent at Standing Rock, Major James McLaughlin, who mentored Gall because he could not get Sitting Bull to cooperate with him.

So far then, one says Sitting Bull did fight and one says he did not. I believe that if Kill Eagle was, rather like Achilles, sulking in his teepee, then he would not have known who was or was not fighting and it is not feasible that Sitting Bull would have said anything to someone in disgrace, so I think we can discount this pro-fighting version. I am also quite sure that Gall's version is heavily tainted but that he was accurate in his description of Sitting Bull looking after the women and children.

Turning to other evidence that he was not in the fighting, Crow King, a Hunkpapa himself, stated at Fort Yates in July 1881 that, "Sitting Bull did not fight himself, but he gave orders." Another Hunkpapa, Little Knife told the *Billings Gazette* in 1926 that, "Sitting Bull had very little to do with the big battle. He was on the butte on the flank of the Indian camp. Towards the close of the fight, he was in the camp keeping it in order and looking after the women and children." Young Eagle, another from the same tribe, told Walter Campbell in September 1929, "Sitting Bull was not in the battle but was on the warpath against the Crows. I don't think Sitting Bull took part in the fight with Custer. I don't think Sitting Bull took part even with Reno."

One Bull, a Hunkpapa, Sitting Bull's nephew and adopted son, told Walter Campbell in September 1929, that he was fighting against Reno's command when his adoptive father arrived near the river and told him to quit, then went from Reno's field to the west side of the Cheyenne village, looking north on the flat west of that camp. He was about two miles from the fighting with Custer at that time.

One Bull, Hunkpapa. (Wikimedia Commons)

Another of his nephews, the Miniconjou warrior White Bull, interviewed by Walter Campbell in June 1932, stated, "When I got to Sitting Bull's camp his wife, child and everyone ran away, and every man who could fight got on a horse and stood his ground. Sitting Bull was with the latter and had a gun. Doesn't know if Sitting Bull shot his gun. Sitting Bull near river with White Bull, then they move around and White Bull loses track of Sitting Bull." He also said, "Never did see Sitting Bull in whole fight. Sitting Bull never told White Bull about his part in fight. When soldiers first came, Sitting Bull take one twin and ride away? Must be so as Sitting Bull and I were there; then I left and did not see Sitting Bull again." Question: "Ever know Sitting Bull to be a coward?" Answer: "No." Question: "Was Sitting Bull on hill making medicine during battle?" Answer: "No. Just talk. Sitting Bull shot through foot and was not healing right, so Sitting Bull could not run. One reason Sitting Bull not in fight, if not, was taking women and children back, then went to fight."

Another Miniconjou warrior, Feather Earring, in answer to the question, "Who got a good reputation in that fight?" told Hugh L. Scott in September 1919, "All—Crazy Horse, Sitting Bull and all that I heard of. We heard Sitting Bull had run away and was not in the fight. I heard him giving orders."

In September 1929, Walter Campbell also interviewed the Yanktonai warrior, Gray Whirlwind, who told him that, "when Reno deployed his men, Sitting Bull's horse was shot in two places and Sitting Bull said, "Now my best horse is shot, it is like they have shot me; attack them. When the warriors cross the river, they wait up a coulee for Sitting Bull. When Sitting Bull arrived, he did not go into battle, but told them to go on and fight."

Turning now to those who suggested that Sitting Bull was in the fighting, the Miniconjou, Hump, in his narrative at Fort Yates in July 1881, stated that "I know that Sitting Bull was in the fight, but on account of my wound I did not know anything he did. Every able-bodied Indian there took part in the fight, as far as I could tell."

The Hunkpapa Iron Hawk, fourteen years old at the time of the battle, told Eli Ricker in 1907, "They all made a rush and got across the river. At one end of the attacking Indians was Sitting Bull, and at the other end was Crazy Horse. [He is not sure about Sitting Bull, but thinks he was in the fight.

Flying Hawk, Oglala. (Wikimedia Commons)

Says there were so many Indians that there was no telling about many things.]" Flying Hawk, an Oglala, in his 1928 narrative, stated, "There was more than one chief in the fight, but Crazy Horse was leader and did most to win the fight, along with Kicking Bear. Sitting Bull was right with us. His part in the fight was all good."

Another Oglala, White Cow Walking, told Walter Campbell in September 1929, "Sitting Bull took part in the fight with Custer and Reno. Sitting Bull and some women fought Reno and then Custer." He then said that he doubts Sitting Bull's presence at the fighting. He doubts the part Sitting Bull took in it," but finishes off with, "He thinks Sitting Bull counted coup."

The Hunkpapas Turning Hawk and White Hair on Face, were both interviewed by Walter Campbell in June 1930. Turning Hawk told him that, "Sitting Bull was not in battle at '9,' but was with others who confronted Custer [Reno?]." Sitting Bull just got back from Crow Reservation when Custer massacre took place. White Hair on Face said, "Sitting Bull was there also with due to all the excitement. Sitting Bull was in front of the warriors and White Hair was initially on foot behind."

In December 1908, the Brule Two Eagles, was interviewed on behalf of Walter Camp and in response to the question, "What chief or chiefs or what tribes went to this Reno fight?" he said, "Sitting Bull mounted." In June 1878, Lieutenant Oscar F. Long took down the combined narrative of three Cheyenne warriors, White Bull, Brave Wolf and Hump who stated that, "Sitting Bull and Crazy Horse were the greatest chiefs among the Sioux. Sitting Bull had one pony shot under him and Crazy Horse two."

In my view, none of those statements are indisputable and some are downright vague. It seems to me that Hump, the Miniconjou, was guessing, Iron Hawk was unsure, Flying Hawk was noncommittal, White Cow Walking could not make up his mind, Turning Hawk was vague and so was White Hair On Face. Two Eagles was unclear, "Sitting Bull mounted" could have meant watching the fighting or participating and the three Cheyennes do not add anything helpful though the inference is that shot horses mean fighting.

In his own story of the battle given at Fort Walsh, Canada, in October 1877, Sitting Bull strongly implies that he was not in the fighting where he states:

> I started down to tell the squaws to strike the lodges. I was then on my way up to the right end of the camp, where the first attack was made on us. But before I reached that end of the camp where the Miniconjou and Uncpapa squaws and children were and where some of the other squaws—Cheyennes and Oglalas—had gone, I was overtaken by one of the young warriors, who had just come down from the fight. He called out to me. He said, "No use to leave the camp; every white man is killed." So, I stopped and went no further. I turned back, and by and by I met the warriors returning.

It must also be noted that by Lakota tradition, he was beyond fighting age and furthermore, that he was in any case represented in the fighting by his nephews One Bull and White Bull. Finally, whilst the combat deeds of prominent warriors such as Crazy Horse, Crow King and White Bull were remarked on by participants in their interviews with Walter Camp and others, it is notable that none of them mention any such involvement by Sitting Bull.

In summary therefore, I think it is safe to say that he did not take part in the fighting, but that the vision he had on June 6 of "soldiers falling upside down into camp" convinced the warriors that they could beat Custer's soldiers, especially as they believed they had already defeated Crook's command because he had retreated. Sitting Bull may not have fought at the Little Bighorn, but his influence on the outcome must never be underestimated.

Gall at the Little Bighorn

Another request from the Custer Association of Great Britain, this article was prompted by Gall's claims at the 10th anniversary gathering in 1886 that he had been a prominent participant in the fighting. Once again, Indian participant accounts disproved his claims, and I was also able to stress just how much influence Gall's Indian agent had over him and what he said.

On July 3, 1886, the *Army and Navy Journal* published a report of the account of the Battle of the Little Bighorn as told by the Hunkpapa warrior Gall on June, 25 1886, at the gathering to recognize the 10th anniversary of that event. The account was controversial in that Gall both demeaned his former mentor, Sitting Bull: "His prowess as a fighter is simply a creation of the white man's brain and nothing else,"[10] whilst giving a detailed rendering of what he claimed was his own participation in the fighting: "and Gall was unquestionably the leader who executed the details and led the young bucks on."[11] By the time of the 10th anniversary proceedings to commemorate the battle, Gall had already been made a chief of the Hunkpapa tribe by the Indian agent, James McLaughlin, at the Standing Rock Agency on the

Gall, Hunkpapa Lakota, photographed in 1881 by D. F. Barry at Fort Buford, Dakota Territory. (Wikimedia Commons)

Great Sioux Reservation. If taken at face value, his claims would have made him a prominent leader at the battle. To seek an accurate picture of his status in that context, however, requires a close look at his status prior to the battle and what therefore, that status represented in the pecking order of leaders in the Indian village on June, 25 1876.

Early Years

Born in 1840, near the Moreau River in what became South Dakota,[12] Gall had other names as a young boy, Little Bear Cub, or Bear Shedding His Hair, but became known as Pizi, the Lakota word for Gall, because he unwittingly ate the gall bladder of a slaughtered animal. As a young boy, he lost his father, a man of little recognition and was raised by his mother and her relatives. Growing into a fine physical specimen, he excelled at sports and once defeated at wrestling a young Roman Nose, who would go on to be a famed Cheyenne warrior.[13] Yet, because of his father's near anonymity, little was expected of him in leadership terms.

As he got older, Gall fought against traditional enemies such as the Crow and Assiniboine and, recognizing in him "an unusual physical prowess and fearlessness for a youngster"[14] Sitting Bull took him under his wing, making him a member of the Strong Heart Society, then a new, even more elite group, the Midnight Strong Heart Society.[15] By the age of 24, Gall was known for his skill as a warrior, often in the company of Sitting Bull, and for attacks on army units. There is no record, however, of him leading any large group of followers during that period.

In 1864, with a small group of followers—probably part of his extended family, he was with Sitting Bull at Killdeer Mountain when the Hunkpapas were forced to flee from the forces of Brigadier General Alfred Sully.[16] From 1866–68 he was involved in Red Cloud's War. And between 1868 and 1872, as he reached the age when Lakota men would start to show their leadership qualities, he had several skirmishes with U.S. Army troops. In 1873, he was in the fights against Custer's 7th Cavalry during the regiment's Yellowstone expedition. At that time, he was better known as The Man Who Goes In The Middle.[17]

During the winter months he would take his small band into the Grand River Agency (later the Standing Rock Agency), the part of the Great Sioux Reservation serving the Hunkpapas among other Lakota groups, where they could be fed by the government. In December 1875, he led his now growing band of followers out of the reservation to be near Sitting Bull who was camped on the Yellowstone River.[18] Faced with the federal government's ultimatum that all the free-roaming Indians must settle on the designated Indian agencies by 31 January 31, 1876, the stage was set for the confrontation at the Little Bighorn on 25/26 June.[19] There is still no evidence that he led a large group of followers at this stage.

Gall's Status at the Little Bighorn

Although he was 36 years old at the time of the Battle of the Little Bighorn, and by now a prominent and respected warrior, Gall could not be described as a "chief." That word is in fact a white man's concept. In the early days of negotiating with the Indians, white officials wanted to deal with someone in charge, as was the habit of the white race. They therefore dubbed any—preferably cooperative—Indian headman or leader as "chief" and so the likes of Chief Red Cloud or Chief Crazy Horse came into being. (Although these two were not particularly cooperative from the point of view of the U.S. government.)

These leaders were usually men who were followed by others because they were good fighters, successful hunters, and displayed wisdom. The head of a family was known as *tiwahe*, whilst a leader of warriors in battle was a *blotahunka*, neither of which translates as "chief." Gall is most likely to have fallen into the latter Lakota category and in his 1934 pamphlet, *Sitting Bull and Gall, The Warrior*, author Thomas B. Marquis stated:

> Now there were six tribes at the Little Bighorn camp. Among those six tribes were about 25 warrior societies. Each society had one leading chief and about nine minor chiefs. So, there were in the battle about 25 leading warrior chiefs and 225 minor warrior chiefs. Gall was one of those warrior chiefs, perhaps a leading warrior chief. But, if so, whatever fighting he did was as an individual, the same as in the case of every other Indian warrior there. He may have had great influence as an advisor or as an exemplar, but he had no authority.

This view is upheld by the lack of any reference to Gall leading any large group at the battle in any of the post-battle Indian interviews.

There is however, evidence that both Crazy Horse and Crow King were followed by substantial bodies of warriors. In the book *The Sixth Grandfather, Black Elk's Teachings Given to John G. Neihardt*, Black Elk recalls: "Close after the crying about courage we heard that Crazy Horse was coming. He was riding a white-faced horse. Everyone hollered: 'Crazy Horse is coming!' Just then I heard the bunch on the hillside to the west crying: 'Hokahey!' and making the tremolo. We heard also the eagle bone whistles. I knew from this shouting that the Indians were coming for I could hear the thunder of the ponies charging."[20]

In his July 30, 1881 story given at Fort Yates, Dakota Territory, to a reporter from the *Leavenworth Weekly Times*, which appeared in that newspaper on August 18, 1881, Crow King, in referring to the first contact with Custer's command, recalled that, "The party commenced firing at long range (indicating nearly a mile). We had then all our warriors and horses. There were eighty warriors in my band."[21] It is interesting to note that the same reporter tried to interview Gall, who refused to speak with him, denying that he was in the fight and claiming that "he was helping the women catch the horses and took no other part."[22]

Gall's denial may have been attributable to a fear of punishment for his actions in the battle which had occurred a mere five years before. Five years later, however, ten years after the battle, he was claiming a significant role in the fight. Before turning to that though, it is necessary to examine the aftermath of the battle for Gall.

Post Battle and Canada

After departing the battlefield, the Indians broke up into smaller groups and the summer roamers mainly returned to their agencies. The winter roamers found themselves being chased by many more soldiers and eventually, some bands surrendered. Sitting Bull refused to do that and in May 1877 he took his band, including Gall, into Canada's northwest territories.

After three years in that country with food scarce and many pining for their homeland, some were discontented enough to begin pleading to go back to the United States. Sitting Bull refused and some acrimony crept in, with Gall falling out with his old mentor over the matter. What then occurred sowed the seeds for Gall's 10th anniversary diatribe.

Late in December 1880, Gall took more than half of the Hunkpapas back to the United States, surrendering on January 3, 1881, at Fort Buford, Dakota Territory. On May 26, 1881, those who had surrendered were taken to the Standing Rock Agency (the Grand River Agency having relocated to that location in 1875), where three months later the Indian agent would be one James McLaughlin. On July 19, 1881, hungry and desperate, Sitting Bull surrendered himself and the rest of the Hunkpapa people. Confined as a prisoner of war at Fort Randall, Dakota Territory until 1883, when he was sent to Standing Rock, where Gall was already highly favored by McLaughlin.

Standing Rock Agency

At this time, Standing Rock was home to several Sioux divisions, not just the Hunkpapas. There were Oglalas, Brules, Miniconjous, Sans Arcs, Blackfeet, and Yanktonais, many of whom had been at the Little Bighorn. McLaughlin would have gleaned from them much of what had happened at the battle. He would also have realized that if Gall was rarely mentioned as a presence at the important phases of the fighting, having already made Gall a chief and his Indian right-hand man, he would need to set about building up Gall's role at the Little Bighorn. This was especially important as a battle of wills developed between McLaughlin and Sitting Bull.

McLaughlin's memoir, *My Friend the Indian*, has many references to Gall as a principal mover in organizing the Indians' defense of their camp against Custer's force. For example: "It was the generalship of Gall that kept the strength of the Indians concealed from the white soldiers …"[23] Bearing in mind that Indian warriors fought as individuals and were not organized by a "general" as in the white man's army, the agent's comments are pure rhetoric and have no basis in fact.

Compare also the description of Gall's position as given by Thomas B. Marquis, and it is easy to see why Gall would have been seduced by the upgrade given to him by McLaughlin. The agent also did everything he could to diminish Sitting Bull's influence and reputation. He denounced the Hunkpapa leader as a coward more than once, and has him running away when Reno attacked, telling his readers that, "… when the firing began … His ponies were close at hand and … he made straight for the hills to the southwest."[24] Indian participant interviews post-battle, make it clear that the agent was being untruthful. Indeed, it is hard to know what is believable in his book where Gall and Sitting Bull are concerned.

Tenth Anniversary—Gall's Claims

On June 25, 1886, preparations had been completed to mark the 10th anniversary of the Battle of the Little Bighorn. Many military survivors returned to the battlefield including Captain Benteen, Dr. Porter, Captains McDougal and Godfrey, but notable among the dignitaries was Gall, the Hunkpapa leader who apparently returned to the scene of his greatest victory to provide details of the battle.

Interviewed during the commemoration, Gall's account of the battle appeared in several periodicals, including the *Bismarck Daily Tribune* for June 25, 1886, as well as the July 3 issue of the *Army and Navy Journal*. It should be noted that the description of Gall and his greatest victory was undoubtedly the result of McLaughlin's promotion of the Hunkpapa warrior.

Gall's account of the Little Bighorn Battle given at the 10th anniversary commemorations has been called into question by author Greg Michno in both his book, *Lakota Noon*, and his article, "The Fall of Gall" that appeared in the Little Big Horn Associates *Research Review* for June 1996. The author uses his own timeline to pinpoint Gall's movements at the battle and thus disprove the leadership claims made by that Hunkpapa warrior in his 1886 account. Both the book and the article make a good case, and I have no issue with the author's findings, but I believe that the Standing Rock Reservation politics were at the root of the claims made by or on behalf of Gall, and go a long way to explaining why he exaggerated his role in the battle.

His account began with a misrepresentation: "We saw soldiers early in the morning crossing the divide." If that had been the case, the noncombatants would have been sent to safety, and the warriors would have sallied out to confront Custer much as they did when attacking Brigadier General Crook's command eight days earlier. That did not happen, and the absence of what would have been standard Sioux and Cheyenne tactics in Gall's comments persuades me that his account was largely coached by McLaughlin who would have had no idea of how the Indians behaved in given combat circumstances.

However, rather than try to analyze the many disputed claims made by Gall, which has been exhaustively covered by Michno, in this article I have chosen to examine the views of his fellow warriors at the battle. There were various interviews with Indian participants post-battle, most many years later, but in the majority, the exploits of Crazy Horse are mentioned. The claims made by Gall about his participation would appear to place him in the same category as Crazy Horse. I have in my library, most, if not all, of the books which contain the participant interviews, and the relevant information is revealing. Of the 72 interviews consulted, 58 make no mention of Gall at all, which is odd if what he claimed was the truth.

Gall at the Little Bighorn as Seen by other Lakotas, Dakotas and Cheyennes

The following are the 14 different Indian interviews in which Gall is mentioned or alluded to in the context of the Battle of the Little Bighorn.

In an interview conducted by Eli S. Ricker with Nicholas Ruleau at Pine Ridge on November 20, 1906, Ruleau being a latter-day fur trader and an interpreter, of mixed Dakota and French heritage, conveyed to Ricker what he had heard from Austin Red Hawk, Shot in the Face, Big Road (all Oglalas), and Iron Bull (a Yanktonais). Ruleau first mentions Gall when he says that he had been told that at the hill now known as Weir Point, "Crazy Horse, Gall and Knife Chief were haranguing the Indians to get together so they could make another charge on the soldiers."[25]

Ruleau added that "Sitting Bull took no part in the battle. Gall, Crazy Horse and Knife Chief were the leading chiefs in command." In the transcript of this interview edited by Richard Hardorff, the editor adds a footnote saying: "Although only a minor chief among the Hunkpapas, Gall's reputation and status among the whites received a considerable boost from his frank interview given on the tenth anniversary of the Custer battle."[26]

He went on to say that "the chiefs in this battle ranked as follows—Crazy Horse had command of all the Indians; Gall was next in precedence, and Knife Chief third."[27]

It is worth bearing in mind that Ruleau was not present at the Little Bighorn and gained his information secondhand, albeit from eyewitnesses.

Ricker interviewed Iron Hawk, a Hunkpapa veteran of the battle, at Chadron, Nebraska, on May 13, 1907. Although only 14 at the time of the Custer Fight, Iron Hawk recalled that, "Custer [probably a reference to the troops, rather than Custer individually] did not get anywhere near the river; his nearest approach was about a mile off." Hardorff adds a footnote commenting that: "Although this statement is supported by others, notably the Hunkpapa Gall, there is opposing and more convincing evidence that some of Custer's men came close enough to the river to fire into and over the tepees on the other side ..."[28] Although not mentioning Gall, Iron Hawk provides some corroboration for at least one of the claims made by him.

In the early twentieth century, Sewell B. Weston, an amateur researcher with an interest in Native American history, carried out interviews on behalf of Walter M. Camp. He interviewed Two Eagles (Brule) in December 1908;[29] Lone Bear (Oglala) at Cody, Wyoming, on January 5, 1909;[30] and Lights (Miniconjou) in spring 1909.[31] Camp had submitted a pro forma questionnaire to Weston for use in the interviews. It included questions about which chiefs fought Reno's men, and the course of the battle generally. None of the three mentioned Gall's participation in the battle—perhaps something that is telling in itself. In relation to a single specific question about "any quarrelling between Sitting Bull and Gall" in the aftermath of the battle, all three answered that they had not heard of any acrimony between them.

Thunder Bear, a Yanktonai, interviewed by the photographer and historian Edward S. Curtis at a Sioux Reservation about 1907, recalled that, "Sitting Bull, Tatanka Iyotaka, was chief of the Sioux. His chiefs were Shunka Hanska, Long Dog, I-to-ma-gho-zhi, Rain In The Face, Pizi, Gall, [and others]."[32] Significantly, this interview was long after the event and may not have reflected the reality of events over thirty years before.

On September 2, 1929, historian Walter Stanley Campbell (Stanley Vestal) interviewed Young Eagle

Two Moons, a Cheyenne veteran of the Battle of the Little Bighorn, photographed by Edward S. Curtis, c. 1910. (Northwestern University, Digital Library Collections/Wikimedia Commons)

(Hunkpapa) at Fort Yates, North Dakota. He noted that, "Gall, [who was] Young Eagle's half-brother, [was the] leader of the fight [against Custer's command]."[33]

In summer 1930, Campbell recorded that White Hair On Face, a Hunkpapa whom he interviewed at Fort Yates, told him that, "Gall [was] there on horseback." The context suggests that Gall was in the midst of the action. He also commented that Sitting Bull was leading the fighting from the front, which contradicts most accounts of the battle.[34]

Two years later, in June 1932, Campbell interviewed the famous Miniconjou warrior White Bull and a nephew of Sitting Bull, at the Cheyenne River Reservation, South Dakota. White Bull recalled going to Sitting Bull's camp on the day of the Battle of the Little Bighorn, after learning of the attack by Custer's troops. He recalled that, "Pizi [Gall was] in camp, but I didn't see him at that time."[35]

Author Hamlin Garland interviewed Two Moons, a Cheyenne, at the Northern Cheyenne Indian Reservation, Montana, in 1898. The account is somewhat unclear, presumably because of the manner in which it was obtained and recorded, but seems to say that, regarding the Reno fight, "Chief Gall was there fighting. Crazy Horse also."[36]

Cheyenne chief Two Moons was interviewed several times, including a 1901 interview conducted by J. M. Thralls at the Custer Battlefield, Montana, in 1901. Speaking at this time, he attributed a central role in the fight to Gall. Regarding the fighting against the forces of Captain Myles W. Keogh and Lieutenant James Calhoun, he said that "this was followed by the complete annihilation of those two companies by the Sioux warriors commanded by Chiefs Gall and Rain In The Face."[37]

Two Moons was also interviewed on behalf of *The Harness Gazette* at the Custer Battlefield, Montana, in 1901, or 1907. Quoting Two Moons, the *Gazette*'s article said in part, that "the Indians consisted of Sioux and Cheyenne under such leaders as Gall, Crazy Horse, Rain In The Face and Two Moons."[38] Unfortunately, the circumstances in which this information was obtained are not known, and Two Moons would have had to have been interviewed through an interpreter.

Cree photographer Richard Throssel worked for the Bureau of Indian Affairs in Montana, and interviewed Two Moons in 1907, passing on the details obtained to Walter Camp. The information is therefore secondhand, but Camp recorded that Two Moons had told Throssel, regarding the Reno fight at the commencement of the battle, "He [Two Moons] ... started in the direction of [the] fighting which had already began between Gall and Reno."[39]

Young Two Moons, a Cheyenne, was a nephew of Two Moons, and also participated in the Custer battle. Walter Stanley Campbell interviewed him at the Custer Battlefield, Montana, in 1929. For the purposes of this article, his comments were not particularly helpful, however. Regarding the fighting against C Company along Custer Ridge, he said that "[Lt. Henry M.] Harrington [escaped] one mile toward [the southeast]. I don't know where Gall was."[40] How Young Two Moons identified the officer who attempted to escape as Harrington is not clear. Perhaps Campbell tailored the note to suit his own theories.

In 1956, seventy years after the battle, Don Rickey Jr. interviewed Northern Cheyenne tribal historian John Stands In Timber at the Custer Battlefield, Montana. John Stands In Timber told Rickey that, "The chiefs in the fight were all equal. The leading warrior was Crazy Horse—also Gall, Iron Thunder, Two Moons ... [and others]."[41] John Stands In Timber's comments were, however, hearsay. He was not born until eight years after the battle.

One Bull, a Miniconjou Lakota, was 23 when he participated in the Battle of the Little Bighorn. Over 50 years later, he gave his account of the battle to John P. Everett, and it was published in *Sunshine Magazine* in September 1930. Speaking of being in Sitting Bull's camp at the Little Bighorn: "... Cheyenne. They were a different tribe, not Lakota. They were friends of Lakota. Pizi [Gall] had another band. All the different bands camped together."[42] He thus confirms the presence of Gall and his band at the great extended village on the Little Bighorn River but gives no information concerning his participation in the battle.

It must be noted that some of these interviews should be assessed critically, as they would have been obtained through an interpreter, generally without any record of the questions asked of the interviewee, or his precise reply. Added to this, the earliest interview took place over 20 years after the battle, and many took place at much later dates, by which time memories must have been fading, or contaminated by accounts given by others. Further, not only are the accounts contradictory, but they should be taken with a pinch of salt as, for example, despite some assertions in the interviews, we know that Gall was not in the fighting against Reno.

Conclusion

It seems to me that for the 10th anniversary commemoration, McLaughlin had seen the ideal opportunity to demonstrate that Gall, not Sitting Bull, was the leader of the Hunkpapas both in the present and at the Little Bighorn. Gall did not speak English, and his 1886 account was presented via an interpreter and by pantomiming the scenarios he was describing. It was easy therefore, for the result to be as McLaughlin required. It has already been pointed out that Gall's account started with a lie and here is another one. The claim that, "Reno swept down so rapidly on the upper end that the Indians were forced to fight. Sitting Bull and I were at the point where Reno attacked."[43] We know from his own admission that Gall had left the Hunkpapa camp to go north after his horses before Reno attacked. There are several other examples but to a degree, repeating them would only parallel author Michno's conclusions.

Another example of McLaughlin's coaching of Gall for political points scoring can be seen in the latter's comments about Sitting Bull in a later narrative given at Fort Custer, Montana on July 18, 1886:

The new points brought out were that Sitting Bull personally had little or nothing to do with the fight. He was a medicine man of the Sioux and was in his lodge at the time making medicine for the destruction of the whites and the success of the Indians. As the battle (or massacre, whichever, you please) turned out favorably for the Indians and to the confusion of their enemies, Sitting Bull at once became the great medicine man of all the tribes, and was from that time forth a leading spirit among them. His prowess as a fighter is simply a creation of the white man's brain and nothing else. When the warriors sallied out to attack the troops, he was really left behind to make medicine and to look after the women and children. If he has any latent fighting qualities, or abilities as a great leader, his kinsmen don't know it, nor does anybody else.[44]

Although they had quarreled in Canada and not reconciled, to say those things about a man who had mentored him and beside whom he had fought many times, not to mention Sitting Bull's esteemed position in Lakota society, calls Gall's whole narrative into question.

Whilst it is possible to say that the evidence suggests that Gall was not in the Reno fight, or that he was not one of the leaders during the fighting at Ford B, and thus did not meet Custer at that point or chase him, nor did he head up "hundreds of warriors" in Deep Coulee, the reality of Gall's participation is evidenced in the post-battle interviews of his fellow warriors. That 52 of them do not mention him at all, and the 14 that do, do not describe him involved in any of the actions he says he was in, indicates at the very least that author Marquis was accurate in his description of Gall's standing at the Little Bighorn. The almost total lack of any reference to Gall as a leader in the fighting belies the totally opposite view found in McLaughlin's book.

By the time of the 10th anniversary, Gall was so friendly with that Indian agent, that he likely believed everything that McLaughlin said. Coupled with that, the agent's manipulation of Sitting Bull to a minor role and the scene was set for what Gall said on June 25, 1886. Not exactly a day of infamy, but a sad commentary on what following the white man's path had done to a once feared fighting man.

CHAPTER 14

A Slip of the Tongue?

Reading what transpired between the commands of Major Reno and Colonel Gibbon on June 18, 1876, I was puzzled by the discrepancy between the lodge count at the first Rosebud Indian camp as apparently depicted by Major Reno's scouts and the description of that camp given by the Cheyenne warrior Wooden Leg. Further research made me believe that an error had been made in the information understood by Colonel Gibbon, hence the article, which will serve to demonstrate how difficult communication was between the various commands.

In our modern world of instant electronic communications, misunderstandings can still occur. Imagine, therefore, just how much confusion could arise between parties using older and cruder methods. I believe some such confusion occurred within the U.S. Army forces in the field, during the Sioux War of 1876, that has embedded erroneous information into the history of that military campaign and thus remained unchallenged for nearly 150 years.

It concerns what took place between Colonel John Gibbon's command and Major Marcus Reno's 7th Cavalry scouting detachment on June 18, 1876. Lieutenant James H. Bradley set the scene in his journal for that day, "This afternoon" he recorded, "Major Reno, with six companies of the 7th Cavalry, appeared at the mouth of the Rosebud and went into camp. General Gibbon went up opposite the camp and held a conversation with him by means of signal flags and afterwards communicated with him by letter through two Crows, who swam the river for that purpose."[1] Gibbon himself, stated that, "being curious to know who was in the party, one of our officers tied a handkerchief to a stick, and commenced waving it from side to side as a signal. It was soon answered in the same way …"[2] So, not exactly an infallible means of communication.

The letter Bradley mentioned was the note Gibbon sent to Brigadier General Alfred H. Terry via Reno, which said in part, "[Colonel] Reno made an appearance at the mouth of the Rosebud today and I have communicated with him by signal and scouts swimming the river. He had seen no Indians, but I gather from the conversations which the scouts had with Mitch Bouyer that they found signs of camps on Tongue and Rosebud."[3] Bradley, who had previously located those two camps, confidently wrote in his June 18 journal entry:

> Reno's command had scouted up Powder River, then crossed to the Rosebud, and scouted down the latter stream, meeting with no Sioux but finding recent traces of a large village at the place I discovered it on twenty-seventh of May. Mitch Bouyer, our guide, who had been detached to accompany Reno, counted 360 lodge fires, and estimated that there were enough beside to make the number of lodges about 400 hundred.[4]

His entry can only have been made following conversations with the Crow scouts who had swum the river and spoken to Boyer, so the information thus obtained was secondhand. Yet ever since, any reference to the number of lodges at the Rosebud site quotes the figure of 400, the number attributed by Bradley to Boyer. There are, however, some interesting pieces of evidence concerning the two men and their observations. In connection with the camp smoke seen by Bradley and the Crows on the Tongue on May 16, Bradley states that the Crows estimated 200–300 lodges, going solely by the smoke.

Regarding Reno at the Tongue site, John S. Gray wrote:

> At this moment Reno was only 33 miles from completing his mission and by pushing ahead could report to Terry at the mouth of the Tongue that evening. Instead, he decided to violate his orders drastically by moving to the Rosebud. The reason could only have been Mitch Boyer's report that the month-old Sioux campsite … numbered about four hundred lodges, representing the majority of winter roamers.[5]

Yet later on the same page he refers to the Rosebud site as being where Boyer counted the lodge circles taking the Bradley journal entry as his source.

Gray also mentioned that Bradley had sighted the Rosebud campsite but that the lieutenant had not specified the number of lodges, merely calling it immense. Yet on that same page he also noted that a letter under the penname "Long Horse" published in the Helena *Daily Herald*, on May 28 stated, "Yesterday Lt. Bradley … discovered a camp of 500 lodges of Sioux on the Rosebud …" Whoever Long Horse was, his information could only have come from the estimate of the lodge count by Bradley, who had been unable to obtain more than a partial glimpse of the camp and thus judged by the smoke and horses observed. His Crow scouts had likely upped their lodge estimate from those seen on the Tongue. Bradley had no opportunity to verify anything with Boyer because early on the morning of June 19, Reno, with Boyer in tow, had broken camp, moving east to join Terry and the rest of the 7th Cavalry. On June 21, as Captain Edward Ball led Gibbon's 2nd Cavalry battalion, together with Bradley, towards Fort Pease, Bradley noted in his journal that, "… the entire 7th Cavalry [including Boyer] … appeared in view on the table-land across the river …"[6]

Gray quoted an anonymous letter published in the July 4 edition of the Helena *Daily Herald* that referred to Boyer:

On Tongue River he came to the old Indian camp he had seen when out on a similar scout with Lt. Bradley ... He counted the lodge fires that had been there; they numbered 800 lodges [400 lodges and 800 warriors, according to Gray]. He followed their trail ... to Rosebud River. He next saw their old camp only twenty miles from where the three men were shot [on Little Porcupine Creek on, May 23].[7]

The relevant point here is that there is no mention of counting lodge fires at the Rosebud site, so (as suggested) I believe that Bradley misunderstood the information brought back by the Crow scouts who had communicated with Reno and Boyer at the mouth of the Rosebud. Unfortunately, he further muddied the water. Having assumed that the lodge count referred to the Rosebud camp, he added to his journal entry, "A well-defined trail led from the site of the village across the plain toward the Little Big Horn, and it is now thought that the Indians will be found upon that stream."[8] Those comments have contributed to the erroneous view that the 400 lodges were at the Rosebud site.

The lodge numbers at the Tongue site had, in fact, increased considerably by the time the Indians had reached the Rosebud site. The Cheyenne Wooden Leg verified this conclusion in three ways. First, he stated that the camps stayed "six or seven sleeps"[9] at the site, hunting buffalo "on the hills west of the Rosebud."[10] Second, he told Dr. Thomas B. Marquis that "Charcoal Bear, chief medicine man of the Northern Cheyennes, came to us at the first Rosebud camp. Lots of people were with him. About ten lodges were with Charcoal Bear."[11] Wooden Leg, however, only recorded Cheyenne arrivals. The arrival of only 10 Cheyenne lodges during the several days stayed at one site would not have been likely or logical in view of the constant stream of arrivals from the agencies to the combined camps.

Wooden Leg's third piece of information underscores this assumption:

After one sleep at the second Rosebud camp we traveled on up the valley another twelve or fifteen miles. This time the Uncpapas occupied land now on both sides of the highway road and to the west and south of a painted peak the white people now call Teat butte. The other camps were scattered irregularly on up the valley, all yet on the east side of the creek. It was about a mile and a half from the lower or last Uncapa site to the upper or advanced Cheyenne site.[12]

As Greg Michno in his book *Lakota Noon* has estimated that the entire village at the Little Big Horn covered no more than a mile and a half, we can safely state that Wooden Leg is describing many more than 400 lodges, thus making Bradley's "500" lodges a conservative estimate.

Verification of Wooden Leg's description appears in the journals and narratives of some 7th Cavalry officers. The reminiscences of Second Lieutenant Charles A. Varnum, for example, stated: "On the 23rd we made a long march. We struck not only the trail of the Indians but the entire valley of the Rosebud appeared to have been a camp, where they had moved along as the grass was grazed off."[13] In his diary entry for June 23, First Lieutenant Edward S. Godfrey recorded that "after marching about 8 miles we came across a very large village grounds and during the day we passed two more camps, all indicating a very large number of Indians."[14] Captain Frederick W. Benteen described the relevant Rosebud village site as "immense" in his February 4, 1879 *Chicago Times* interview.

Bearing in mind Wooden Leg's description of the Rosebud camps, Boyer did provide information confirming that he had counted the lodges at the Tongue site. That information also appears in Bradley's Journal entry for June 18. After detailing the misconstrued lodge count as that pertaining to the Rosebud camp, he wrote of Boyer's report: "The lodges had been arranged in nine circles within supporting distance of each other, within which the Indians evidently secured their horses at night, showing they considered an attack not unlikely and were prepared for it." This statement simply does not accord with the picture provided by Wooden Leg, that there was a one-and-a-half-mile sprawl from the Hunkpapa to the Cheyenne camp circle, nor a description he gave of the previous camp on the Rosebud that the Cheyenne Crazy Dog warriors had held a war dance to prepare to fight some Crows who had apparently been seen nearby.

With evidence that the Indian numbers were constantly increasing at the Tongue and subsequent sites, it is puzzling that the Rosebud site would contain as few as 400 lodges. I believe I have demonstrated why that misconception arose and that for once, the meticulous Lieutenant Bradley was misled by his Crow scouts. They may not have spoken with forked tongue, but with a slip of the Tongue. Something appears to have been lost in the translation.

CHAPTER 15

The Horses' Tale

Custer's regiment was a cavalry unit, totally reliant on its horses to get it to its destination. Much has been written about how these horses reacted during the fighting and having read about the various favorite horses of the 7th Cavalry personnel, it seemed fitting to dedicate an article solely to them. The information will hopefully show just how important they were.

On May 17, 1876, a column of about 1,200 men, mostly soldiers, marched out of Fort Abraham Lincoln in Dakota Territory for what for some, would be their last mission. The greater part of the column was comprised of the 7th U.S. Cavalry Regiment under Field Commander Lieutenant Colonel George Armstrong Custer.

A cavalcade of over 500 excited cavalry mounts—chestnuts, bays, roans, blood bays and grays—trotted along, heads tossing, with the sun gleaming off their glossy coats, as the 7th Cavalry moved westward on its mission to force so-called "hostile" Lakota and Cheyenne Indians onto permanent reservations. Despite regulations forbidding it, many riders had named their horses. Custer was mounted on Dandy, one of the two horses he used in the field. His other horse was Vic, or Victory, back in the remuda.

Of the other officers, Captain Miles W. Keogh rode Paddy, with his favorite mount Comanche also with the remuda. Captain Frederick Benteen was on Dick; Captain George Yates on Badger; Captain E. M. Mathey on Blueskin and Captain Thomas Weir on N****r Jim.

Among the enlisted men, Sergeant Jeremiah Finley rode Carlo, Private Charles Windolph had Roman Nose, Sergeant Joseph McCurry was mounted on Tip and Private William O. Taylor's horse was Steamboat. A few other horses' names are known: Spot, Blackie, Nap [short for Napoleon], Old Dutch and Sweetcheeks. There were, no doubt, many more names that are not now known to us, but all the horses in the regiment were precious to their riders because not only were they the only means of transport but they held spare ammunition in their saddlebags.

None of the horses had been trained to remain calm in the heat of a pitched battle with its cacophony of noise and gunfire, yet 39 days later, June 25, they and

Dandy and Vic (Victory), General Custer's mounts. (Wikimedia Commons)

the 7th Cavalry troopers were engaged in a ferocious battle with the Indians they had been sent to chastise.

The first to engage were three companies with Custer's second in command, Major Marcus Reno, who confronted the Indians near the southern end of their village. Thirty men and their horses were lost when they made a desperate retreat across the Little Bighorn River. More men were lost as they tried to make the climb. Steamboat, Private Taylor's mount, had refused to climb the bluffs and Taylor recalled that after climbing further on foot, a mounted trooper gave him a horse called Old Dutch, to complete the climb.[1]

Captain Benteen with his three companies and Captain E. M. Mathey with B Company and the pack train later joined Reno on the bluffs. Blueskin, Dick and N****r Jim were safe for now, as were Private Windolph's Roman Nose and Sergeant McCurry's Tip.

Meanwhile, Custer and his five companies were gradually overwhelmed and killed by superior numbers of Indians. What happened to their horses can be found in accounts of the victorious Indians. Oglala Sioux warrior White Cow Bull recalled that "the soldiers' horses were so frightened by all the noise we made that they began to bolt in all directions."[2] Oglala headman Horned Horse said, "If the troops had not been encumbered by their horses, which plunged, reared and kicked under the appalling fire of the Sioux, they might have done better."[3] Miniconjou Sioux brave, Lights, answering Walter Camp's questionnaire said, "The soldiers who were afoot either had their horses shot or were stampeded."[4] Hunkpapa Sioux warrior Little Soldier stated that "Indians scared [the] horses ... [and the] horses got away and ran to the river."[5] Low Dog, a Hunkpapa, recalled, "... the white warriors dismounted to fire, but they did very poor shooting. They held their horses' reins on one arm while they were shooting, but their horses were so frightened that they pulled the men all around ..."[6] And finally, a female Hunkpapa, Moving Robe Woman, said: "We crossed the Greasy Grass ... and came upon many horses. One soldier was holding the reins of eight or 10 horses. An Indian waved his blanket and scared all he horses. They got away from the men [troopers.]"[7]

What fate befell the various mounts with Custer's command which have been named? Custer had been riding Vic, who was either killed near him or captured by a warrior. Yates's Badger was also either killed or captured and Keogh's Comanche was found badly wounded but survived to become famous as being the sole survivor of Custer's battalions. Dandy and Paddy were back with the pack train and remained unharmed. Sergeant Finley's Carlo perished with his rider near Keogh's I Company. The fate of Spot, Blackie and Sweetcheeks is not recorded. Nap (Napoleon), a gray, suffering from wounds, followed the remnants of the 7th Cavalry when it left the battlefield on June 29.

Many theories have been advanced for the 7th Cavalry's defeat, but simplicity suggests that the loss of their horses is as good a reason as any.

CHAPTER 16

A Warning Flag?

I was intrigued by the provenance supplied for the 7th Cavalry Guidon sold at auction in 2010 for $2.2 million, as it did not ring true with research I had done on the individuals mentioned. By going into the matter in more depth I was able to show that the evidence provided by those 7th Cavalry troopers concerned could not be verified. It will help readers to understand just how dangerous it is to take the words of participants at face value.

If I had $2.2 million to spend on a historical artifact I would certainly need indisputable provenance to show that I was buying a genuine article. The so-called Culbertson Guidon, purportedly one carried by the 7th U.S. Cavalry at the Battle of the Little Bighorn, was sold in 2010 for the sum mentioned above, but to me, the provenance provided with it does not stand up to scrutiny.

In the paperwork attached to the Sotheby's catalog[1] covering the sale, recently made available by the Custer Battlefield Historical and Museum Association (CBHMA), the first page, under the title "Custer's Last Flag" has a sidebar stating, "The traditional story of the recovery of the flag is now confirmed by recently discovered letters and documents written by troopers of the 7th Cavalry."[2] The troopers in question are Sergeant Samuel Alcott and Corporal, later Sergeant, Stanislaus Roy, both of Company A, as was Sergeant Ferdinand A. Culbertson who claimed to have discovered the guidon. Do their letters and documents bear out Culbertson's claim? Let us see what they say, as cited in Appendix 1 to the catalog, an article by George F. Kush titled, "There Lies Foley of C!"

The sole source for the guidon's discovery was Culbertson who later claimed to have found it on the body of Corporal John Foley of Company C. The discovery, according to Kush's article, took place early on June 28, 1876, when the first thorough search of Custer's battlefield was undertaken. The only early mention of the discovery is however in Walter Camp's notes—made over 25 years later in which Camp states under Culbertson's name, "Found a bloodstained guidon torn from its staff beneath a soldier's body on Custer's battlefield *says himself* [italics mine]."[3] The meticulous Camp makes no mention of Foley or indeed a corporal, just "a soldier" so it is apparent that Culbertson did not convey either of those details to him. It is equally apparent that at that point, nobody else was making any claims about seeing Culbertson discover the guidon. There is also a glaring error in the Kush article where Culbertson is said to have "dismounted to examine the body" whereas the records indicate that the search for bodies was made by dismounted skirmish lines.

That brings us to Stanislaus Roy. In the entry under his name Camp[4] makes no mention of any links with either Alcott or Culbertson. In Kenneth Hammer's *Custer in '76* covering many of Camp's interviews, there is one conducted with Roy at the Battlefield in August 1909 in which Roy relates the finding of the first dead body, that of Corporal John Foley of Company C, but makes no mention of a guidon being found on his body, which if it had been was hardly something trivial and certainly worthy of mention to Camp.[5] Nor is there any recall in Roy's interview of Culbertson's presence when Foley's body was found, again a rather mystifying omission given Roy's later endorsement of Culbertson's claim. Even earlier, in a letter from Roy dated March 4, 1909 in response to questions by Camp, the finding of Foley's body is mentioned but there is nothing about the guidon, although Roy does confirm that "There was a skirmish line formed, dismounted, and as we came to a dead body it was covered up quickly with sod and earth."[6]

Having not relayed any information to Camp about the guidon in March and August 1909, especially at the Battlefield, it is surprising to note that in June 1909—so Mr. Kush tells us—Roy apparently wrote to Alcott stating that he, Roy, "remembered that he [Foley] was the guidon bearer of Company C." That letter is apparently in a private collection and unpublished, so we have no knowledge of what the remainder of the contents disclose.

What we do know however, is that Sergeant Samuel Alcott now comes very much into the picture regarding the finding of the guidon. In his article "There Lies Foley of 'C'!," George Kush makes some interesting observations about Alcott. Apparently, he was "an eyewitness" to the discovery and identification of Corporal Foley, yet Roy never mentions either him or the remarkable find of the guidon to Camp. Kush also says that Alcott was serving as the expedition quartermaster sergeant on board the steamboat *Far West* and goes on to say that when Curley arrived at the *Far West*, Alcott "volunteered to accompany his 'boss' First Lieutenant Henry Nowlan, who was determined to accompany General Alfred H. Terry's strike force and eventually rejoin his regiment in the field." Kush apparently obtained this information from Alcott's diary, "After a hard ride through difficult country, Lieutenant Nowlan and Sergeant Alcott joined General Alfred H. Terry's command on June 27th." This would, of course, fit in with him being on time to witness the discovery of the guidon the following morning.

This is where things start to unravel. The rosters show that position of Assistant to Nowlan on the steamer, was held by Sergeant George Gaffney of Company I, not Alcott. Under Gaffney's name Camp has him (Gaffney) stating that he was on the *Far West* with Lieutenant Henry J. Nowlan, Terry's Quartermaster, from June 22 to 24, when Terry's staff disembarked to rejoin the rest of the Montana Column at the camp on Tullock's Creek.[7] Sergeant Michael Caddle confirms that Gaffney was with Nowlan.[8]

Then, of course, there is the question of irreconcilable time frames. Sergeant James E. Wilson the Engineering Officer, who remained on board when the *Far West* sailed from near Fort Pease up the Big Horn, wrote in his report of January 3, 1877, that on June 28, the *Far West*, "remained at the mouth of the Little Big Horn all day. An Indian scout named 'Curley' (known to have been with General Custer) arrived about noon with information of a battle, but there being no interpreter on board very little reliable information was obtained. He wore an exceedingly dejected countenance, but his appetite proved to be in first-rate order."[9]

In his interview with Curley, Thomas B. Marquis has the Crow[10] arriving later than noon at the steamboat, which would mean that if Alcott did ride to the battlefield some 15 miles away, he would have taken about 3 hours to get there, so sometime around early evening on June 28 at the earliest. This in any event conflicts with Alcott's diary, which apparently has him meeting Curley and setting off on June 27, a whole day before such a meeting could have occurred. Clearly however, there are other questionable issues with the information provided by Mr. Kush via the correspondence and Diary of Sergeant Alcott.

As Quartermaster, Nowlan was an integral member of Terry's staff which left the *Far West* on June 24. He had responsibility for the pack mules and the civilian packers who had been employed by him. There is no way that Terry would have let him remain on the boat and let someone else take up his duties. Then we have Gaffney's confirmation that he was with Nowlan on the boat until June 24, the day all Terry's staff disembarked. Nowlan was certainly at the Battlefield on June 27 as confirmed by Colonel Robert P. Hughes in his 1896 article, where he says about Terry's first report, "The dispatch was written late in the day, June 27th, when all the horrors of the disaster had fully appeared to him. Before sending it, Terry read it to a group of his staff officers by the light of a candle. It is within the knowledge of Captain (now Major) H. J. Nowlan, 7th Cavalry, and myself, as two of the members who made up that group ..."[11] But Nowlan had not ridden there from the mouth of the Little Bighorn because Curley did not arrive at the boat moored there until June 28 as stated in Wilson's report. Alcott then could not have "volunteered to accompany his boss" as Nowlan was not aboard but already at the battlefield and Alcott could not have made a lone ride on June 27, because Curley did not make contact with those on the *Far West* until noon or later on June 28.

That brings us to Alcott's claims about what he saw whilst involved with the burial details on June 28. In a letter dated July 28, 1910 to Camp, Roy writes, "One particular thing that Alcott told me, that I now remember was common talk in Co. for years after, was that Pat Sullivan's body was found midway in the bottom in a wash entering the river and was not mutilated and was recognized by the no. of carbine and pistol …"[12] The fact that Alcott relayed the information to Roy in no way places Alcott at the battlefield on June 28. Roy states that the information was common knowledge in his company, so Alcott was most likely passing on hearsay but in such a way as to make it look as if he had personally seen the body of Sullivan. What is more, Camp states for Alcott, "[Member of burial details 6/28 says Nugent.] [Not so; was] D.S. (Detached Service) Powder River since 6/15. (Ditto says Taylor.) (Was Acting Company QM Sergeant at Powder River says Roy.)"[13] So if Roy has him at Powder River how could he have got to the battlefield on June 28 to take part in the burials and then how can Roy later verify anything about the guidon with Alcott if that soldier was never at the battlefield?

In his letter of February 28, 1927, Private William Nugent of Company A stated that Alcott was a member of a burial detail with Nugent and others. If that was verified by anyone else, other than Alcott, it would at least strong evidence that Alcott was at least at the battlefield on June 28 but there is no corroborating evidence for this assertion. Indeed, Roy himself says otherwise as does Private William O. Taylor also of Company A. Taylor obviously did have some correspondence with Camp, one response to that researcher being dated December 12, 1909, for example, but I cannot locate anything more from Taylor to Camp in any of the published works. Camp's comment (ditto says Taylor) regarding Alcott being at Powder River is in all likelihood a response from that soldier to a question from the researcher as he tried to compile his 7th Cavalry Rosters.

I am satisfied that Alcott's fiction about riding from the *Far West* on June 27 with Nowlan after hearing Curley's story is evidence enough to confirm that he was on detached service at the Powder River Depot, was not on the *Far West*, was not the quartermaster sergeant aboard the *Far West* (because Gaffney was), did not accompany Nowlan, on June 27 or any other day, as the lieutenant had disembarked on June 24, and was not at the battlefield in any of the burial details. Having established that Alcott's story of his so-called ride to the battlefield is a fabrication, given no evidence to the contrary, it is necessary to closely examine all the other claims made by him as well as those made by both Roy and Culbertson.

As Alcott was at Powder River or at least not at the battlefield on June 28, he could not have been an eyewitness to the discovery and identification of Corporal Foley or by inference, be in any position to endorse the claim of Culbertson as to the finding of the guidon as Kush relates, "In his correspondence with Camp, Sergeant Alcott, then living in Canada, confirmed the fact that a 'corporal of C Troop … was found about 300 yards from the river,'" and added that, "Fred Culbertson found a company guidon underneath the dead body which he kept as a memento for many years." According to the endnotes against these two quotations, the letter to Camp is apparently dated "4/3/1918" and is—once more—in an unidentified private collection. Oddly enough, there is no mention of it in any of the published Camp works and as it's a very significant matter it would hardly be something that Camp would ignore. Yet Camp's only mention of the matter is his reference to Culbertson's self-proclaimed finding of the guidon in *Little Bighorn Rosters*.

There is another puzzle here too, that Alcott's letter to Camp of April 3, 1918 is apparently in a private collection. This is surprising given Kenneth Hammer's account in *Custer in '76* of what happened to the material collected by Camp when he died.

> [It was all] held by his widow Emeline for some years and was acquired from her by Brigadier General William Carey Brown of Denver, Colorado, in June 1933. He classified the books, papers, photographs, letters, and Camp's notes, then transferred them to Robert Spurrier Ellison, formerly chairman of the Historical Landmark Commission of Wyoming and an intense collector of Western Americana. Ellison died on August 16, 1945, and the following year most of his large collection was presented to the Lilly Library at Indiana University, including some of Walter Camp's notes. Additional material was given to the Lilly Library on March 13, 1967, including part of Walter Camp's notes, as a gift from the estate of Mrs. Robert Ellison. The Denver Public Library also acquired a small but valuable part of Camp's notes. Other material from Walter Camp's collection, including the bulk of his notes, was acquired by the Harold B. Lee Library at Brigham Young University in 1972.[14]

There is also a collection of Camp's work held by the Little Bighorn Battlefield National Monument, so it seems unlikely that a letter containing such important information would have found its way into private hands and even if it did, that the information in it would not have been referred to by Camp under the names of Alcott and Culbertson in *Little Bighorn Rosters*. It is also unlikely that such significant information would have been overlooked by Kenneth Hammer and Richard G. Hardorff as they combed through the Camp collections.

All of Alcott's other claims regarding his "observations" at the battlefield must therefore be considered as suspect, perhaps stemming from listening to those who were actually there. Roy's input on the guidon must also be called into question. Again, according to Kush, Roy wrote to Alcott, in a letter for which no date is given and which is once more in the ubiquitous private collection, "Do you remember that was while he [Culbertson] was examining the body that he found the guidon. Poor Foley, he died trying to save the colors." Seemingly Camp wrote to Alcott (again, no date given), and Alcott wrote back on "11/10/11" (again, private collection), "'Fred' Culbertson discovered a blood-stained company guidon under the body which he [Culbertson] kept as a relic of that famous massacre for many years." This is odd because it virtually duplicates what Alcott purported to say in his apparent later letter to Camp of April 3, 1918, some six and a half years later. The question that arises is why would Camp need to write to Alcott about the same matter so long apart and why would yet another letter to Camp from Alcott on this important matter have been lost to a private collector?

So, using the published versions of Camp's notes as a guideline we have the following:

Walter M. Camp's *Little Bighorn Rosters*—Alcott: no mention of guidon; Culbertson: mentions the guidon; Roy: no mention of guidon.[15]

Custer in '76—Alcott: no mention of the guidon; Roy: lengthy interview of August 1909 at the battlefield in which he mentions finding Foley, but there is no mention of the guidon, Alcott or Culbertson and there is no mention of Culbertson at all in this work.[16]

On the Little Bighorn with Walter Camp—Alcott: no correspondence; Roy: letter of March 4, 1909 to Camp—no mention of the guidon, Alcott or Culbertson; No correspondence with Culbertson.[17]

Camp, Custer and the Little Bighorn—Alcott mentioned in Roy's letter to Camp of July 28, 1910 in connection with Sullivan's body. Roy has four mentions. Firstly, in connection with his visit to the battlefield in August 1909 with Camp and others as published in *Custer in '76*. Secondly, he is mentioned by Heyn in his interview with Camp. Thirdly his interview of September 16, 1910 with Camp, in which he again mentions Foley, but not the guidon, Alcott or Culbertson. Fourthly, a repetition of the previously mentioned letter of July 28, 1910 regarding Alcott and Sullivan's body.[18]

What is strange is that Roy had visited the battlefield with Camp in August 1909 and shown him the Foley kill site and had later corresponded with Camp in 1909 through 1912, all without revealing any information about Culbertson and the guidon. Yet in 1911 he is asking Alcott to remember that Culbertson had found the guidon on Foley. Camp did correspond with Alcott, mainly about the Yellowstone Expedition but also the Little Bighorn as that information is shown to be in the Camp Papers, though I cannot locate whereabouts. The point is that if something as important as the guidon matter had arisen in that correspondence, it would not have been kept out of Camp's wider-ranging work which includes all other such relevant matters. It also seems unlikely that it would not have come to public notice before the recent sale of the guidon.

The Culbertson Guidon may well be one of those used by the 7th Cavalry at the Little Bighorn and it may well be the one that belonged to Company C, but I believe that the evidence to show it was found on the body of Corporal John Foley is seriously flawed.

One final thought: Alcott intrudes on yet another of the Little Bighorn controversies, that of the Frank Finkel/August Finckle saga. Author George F. Kush penned an article in the CBHMA quarterly publication, *The Battlefield Dispatch* of spring 2013 in which he quotes Alcott as saying, "I still possess a photo of Sergt. Finckle who I saw buried on that barren plain." Those are stirring words from a man who does not appear to have been present at the battlefield to see that burial. Fortunately, Sergeant Daniel A. Kanipe did witness the finding of August Finckle's body, so we don't have to rely on Alcott for evidence.

Endnotes

Chapter 1

1. Letter to Annette Humphrey, October 9, 1863, in *The Custer Story: The Life and Intimate Letters of General George A. Custer and His Wife Elizabeth*, ed. Marguerite Merington (Lincoln, NB: University of Nebraska Press, 1987), 65.
2. Ronald H. Nichols, ed., *Reno Court of Inquiry. Proceedings of a Court of Inquiry in the Case of Major Marcus A. Reno Concerning His Conduct at the Battle of the Little Big Horn River on June 25–26, 1876* (Hardin, MT: Custer Battlefield Historical & Museum Association, 1996), 421, 427.
3. Ibid., 563, 580.
4. Colonel W. A. Graham, *The Custer Myth: A Source Book of Custeriana* (Lincoln, NB: University of Nebraska Press, 1986), 138.
5. George M. Clark, ed., *Scalp Dance: The Edgerly Papers on the Battle of the Little Big Horn* (Oswego, NY: Heritage Press, 1985), 16.
6. Barry C. Johnson, "George Herendeen: The Life of a Montana Scout," in *More Sidelights of the Sioux Wars*, eds. Barry C. Johnson and Francis B. Taunton (London: Westerners Publications Ltd., 2004), 18.
7. John M. Carroll, ed., *General Custer and the Battle of the Little Big Horn: The Federal View* (New Brunswick, NJ: Gary Owen Press, 1976), 102.
8. *The Teepee Book: Custer Battle Number*, June 1916.
9. Jay Smith, "What Did Not Happen at The Battle of the Little Big Horn," *Research Review: The Journal of the Little Big Horn Associates* 6, no. 2 (1992): 10.
10. Jay Smith, "The Indian Fighting Army," *Research Review: The Journal of the Little Big Horn Associates* 3, no. 1 (1989): 8.
11. Nichols, *Reno Court*, 332.
12. Ibid.
13. Clark, *Scalp*, 16–17.
14. John D. MacKintosh, *Custer's Southern Officer: Captain George D. Wallace 7th U.S. Cavalry* (Lexington, SC: Cloud Creek Press, 2002), 110–11.
15. Charles Varnum, "A Letter of July 4, 1876, to his parents," *Lowell Weekly Journal*, August 1876.
16. Nichols, *Reno Court*, 235.
17. Carroll, *Fed View*, 105.
18. Captain E. S. Godfrey, 7th Cavalry, *Custer's Last Battle 1876* (Olympic Valley, CA: Outbooks, 1976. Reprinted from *Century Magazine*, January 1892), 19.
19. Nichols, *Reno Court*, 388.
20. Edward Settle Godfrey, *The Field Diary* (Portland, OR: The Champoeg Press, 1957), 20.
21. O. G. Libby, *The Arikara Narrative of the Campaign Against the Hostile Dakotas June, 1876* (New York: Sol Lewis, 1973), 159.
22. Herbert A. Coffeen, *The Custer Battle Book* (New York: Carlton Press, 1964), 48–49.

23. Ibid., 49.
24. Fred Dustin, *The Custer Tragedy* (El Segundo, CA: Upton and Sons, Publishers, 1987), xiv.
25. Kenneth Hammer, ed., *Custer in '76: Walter Camp's Notes on the Custer Fight* (Provo, UT: Brigham Young University Press, 1976), 175.
26. Ibid., 174–75.
27. Graham, *Myth*, 17–18.
28. James H. Bradley, *The March of the Montana Column* (Norman, OK: University of Oklahoma Press, 1961), 152, 153.
29. Thomas B. Marquis, *Rain-in-the-Face/Curly, The Crow* (Scottsdale, AZ: Cactus Pony, 1934), 6.
30. Ibid., 7.
31. Ibid.
32. Libby, *Narrative*, 119–20.
33. Hammer, *Custer in '76*, 214.
34. Daniel Knipe, "A New Story of Custer's Last Battle," in *Montana Historical Society Contributions*, Volume 4 (Helena, MT: Independent Publishing Company, 1903), 277–83.
35. Nichols, *Reno Court*, 16.
36. Hammer, *Custer in '76*, 101.
37. Thomas B. Marquis, *Wooden Leg: A Warrior who Fought Custer* (Lincoln and London: University of Nebraska Press, 1971), 206.
38. Richard G. Hardorff, *Lakota Recollections of the Custer Fight* (Spokane, WA: The Arthur H. Clark Company, 1991), 75.
39. Hammer, *Custer in '76*, 206.
40. Richard G. Hardorff, *Cheyenne Memories of the Custer Fight* (Spokane, WA: The Arthur H. Clark Company, 1995), 90.
41. Marquis, *Wooden Leg*, 229.
42. Joseph K. Dixon, *The Vanishing Race: The Last Great Indian Council* (Amsterdam: Fredonia Books, 2004), 181.
43. John Stands In Timber and Margot Liberty, *Cheyenne Memories* (Lincoln and London: University of Nebraska Press, 1972), 198.
44. Ibid.
45. Ibid., 199.
46. Ibid.
47. Peter J. Powell, *People of the Sacred Mountain: A History of the Northern Cheyenne Chiefs and Warrior Societies, 1830–1879* (HarperCollins, 1981).
48. George Bird Grinnell, *The Fighting Cheyennes* (Norman, OK: University of Oklahoma Press, 1983), 350.
49. Hardorff, *Cheyenne*, 29.
50. Ibid., 35, 36.
51. Ibid., 39, 40.
52. Ibid., 43.
53. Ibid., 47.
54. Ibid., 51.
55. Ibid., 52.
56. Ibid., 53.
57. Ibid., 169.
58. John Gibbon, *Gibbon on the Sioux Campaign of 1876: Hunting Sitting Bull* (Bellevue, NE: The Old Army Press, 1970. Reprinted from *The American Catholic Quarterly Review*, October 1877), 39.
59. Bruce A. Trinque, "The Fight in Fishing Woman Ravine," in *Custer and His Times: Book Four*, ed. John P. Hart (Dexter, MI: Thomson-Shore, Inc., Little Big Horn Associates, Inc., 2002), 214.

60. Ibid.
61. Ibid.
62. Michael N. Donahue, *Drawing Battle Lines: The Map Testimony of Custer's Last Fight* (El Segundo, CA: Upton and Sons, Publishers, 2008), 97, 139.
63. Trinque, "The Fight in Fishing Woman Ravine," 216.
64. Ibid., 217.
65. Ibid.
66. Marquis, *Wooden Leg*, 204.
67. Ibid., 214.
68. Hammer, *Custer in '76*, 198.
69. Hardorff, *Lakota Recollections*, 137.
70. Ibid., 104.
71. Ibid., 68.
72. Ibid., 181.
73. Hammer, *Custer in '76*, 212, 213.
74. Ibid., 116.
75. Richard G. Hardorff, *The Custer Battle Casualties: Burials, Exhumations and Reinterments* (El Segundo, CA: Upton and Sons, Publishers, 1991), 114.
76. Hammer, *Custer in '76*, 202.
77. Ibid., 207.
78. Hardorff, *Lakota Recollections*, 86.
79. Marquis, *Wooden Leg*, 232.
80. Hammer, *Custer in '76*, 254.
81. Richard G. Hardorff, *Walter M. Camp's Little Bighorn Rosters* (Spokane, WA: The Arthur H. Clark Company, 2002), 61.
82. Richard G. Hardorff, *On the Little Bighorn with Walter Camp: A Collection of W. M. Camp's Letters, Notes and Opinions on Custer's Last Fight* (El Segundo, CA: Upton and Sons, Publishers, 2002), 41.
83. Hardorff, *Lakota Recollections*, 31.
84. Ibid., 43
85. David Humphreys Miller, *Custer's Fall: The Indian Side of the Story* (Lincoln and London: University of Nebraska Press, 1985), 139.
86. Richard Allan Fox Jr., *Archaeology, History, and Custer's Last Battle* (Norman and London: University of Oklahoma Press, 1993), 245.
87. Trinque, "The Fight in Fishing Woman Ravine," 219.
88. Nichols, *Reno Court*, 322.
89. Hardorff, *Cheyenne Memories*, 53.
90. Yellow Nose, "Yellow Nose Tells of Custer's Last Stand," *Bighorn Yellowstone Journal* 1, no. 3 (1992): 16.
91. Unpublished Mnicoujou oral history in the possession of the late Gordon Harper.
92. Douglas D. Scott, Richard A. Fox Jr., Melissa A. Connor and Dick Harmon, *Archaeological Perspectives on the Battle of the Little Bighorn* (Norman and London: University of Oklahoma Press, 1989), 121.
93. Hardorff, *Cheyenne Memories*, 52, 53.
94. D. H. Miller, "Echoes of the Little Bighorn," *American Heritage* 22, no. 4 (1971): 28–39.
95. Dixon, *The Vanishing Race*, 181.
96. Miller, "Echoes of the Little Bighorn," 34.
97. Hardorff, *Cheyenne Memories*, 170.
98. Hardorff, *Lakota Recollections*, 59.
99. Marquis, *Wooden Leg*, 230.

100. Dixon, *The Vanishing Race*, 175.

101. Graham, *The Custer Myth*, 103.

102. Hardorff, *Cheyenne Memories*, 170.

103. Ibid., 52.

104. Miller, "Echoes of the Little Bighorn," 34.

105. Ibid.

106. M. I. McCreight, *Firewater and Forked Tongues: A Sioux Chief Interprets U.S. History* (Pasadena, CA: Trails End Publishing, 1947), 112–113.

107. James McLaughlin, *My Friend the Indian* (Boston and New York: Houghton Mifflin Company, 1910), 174.

108. Stanley Vestal, *Warpath: The True Story of the Fighting Sioux: Told in a Biography of Chief White Bull* (Lincoln and London: University of Nebraska Press, 1984), 195.

109. Hammer, *Custer in '76*, 198, 199.

110. Marquis, *Wooden Leg*, 230, 231.

111. Ibid., 231.

112. Hardorff, *Cheyenne Memories*, 66, 67.

113. Stanley Vestal, *Interview with White Bull (Mnicoujou) in 1932*, in the personal papers of Walter Stanley Campbell at The University of Oklahoma Libraries.

114. Nichols, *Reno Court*, 236.

115. Hardorff, *Lakota Recollections*, 104.

116. McLaughlin, *My Friend the Indian*, 173.

117. Hardorff, *Lakota Recollections*, 95.

118. John M. Carroll, ed., *A Seventh Cavalry Scrapbook #11* (Bryan, TX: privately published), 9–10; Major Marcus A. Reno, interview in *The Philadelphia Press*, reported in the *Army & Navy Journal* (November 26, 1887).

119. Miller, "Echoes of the Little Bighorn," 35.

120. McCreight, *Firewater*, 113.

121. Marquis, *Wooden Leg*, 231.

122. Ibid.

123. John Stands In Timber and Margot Liberty, *Cheyenne Memories*, 200, 201.

124. Ibid.

125. Ibid.

126. Graham, *The Custer Myth*, 110.

127. Yellow Nose, *Yellow Nose Tells of Custer's Last Stand*. Yellow Nose misidentifies Reily as Custer, but the only officer fitting the description of Yellow Nose is Reily.

128. Marquis, *Wooden Leg*, 268.

129. Ibid., 234.

130. Raymond J. DeMallie, *The Sixth Grandfather: Black Elk's Teachings Given to John G. Neihardt* (Lincoln and London: University of Nebraska Press, 1984), 186.

131. Graham, *The Custer Myth*, 111.

132. Richard G. Hardorff, *The Custer Battle Casualties: Burials, Exhumations and Reinterments* (El Segundo, CA: Upton and Sons, Publishers, 1991), 108.

133. Hardorff, *Lakota Recollections*, 43.

134. Graham, *The Custer Myth*, 60.

135. Hardorff, *Lakota Recollections*, 44.

136. McCreight, *Firewater*, 113.

137. Dr. Charles Eastman, "The Story of the Little Bighorn," *Chautauquan Magazine* 31, no. 4, (1900).

138. Godfrey, *Custer's Last Battle*, 35.

139. McCreight, *Firewater*, 113.

140. Hardorff, *Lakota Recollections*, 87, 88.
141. Ibid., 75.
142. Hammer, *Custer in '76*, 207.
143. Ibid., 95.
144. McCreight, *Firewater*, 113.
145. Graham, *The Custer Myth*, 78.
146. Hardorff, *Lakota Recollections*, 88.
147. Graham, *The Custer Myth*, 60.
148. Hammer, *Custer in '76*, 199.
149. Ibid., 201.
150. Hardorff, *Lakota Recollections*, 66.
151. Dixon, *The Vanishing Race*, 175.
152. Usher L. Burdick, *David F. Barry's Indian Notes on "The Custer Battle"* (Baltimore, MD: Wirth Brothers, 1949), 27.
153. Thomas B. Marquis, *Custer on the Little Bighorn: She Watched Custer's Last Battle* (Lodi, CA: End-Kian Publishing Company, 1967), 39.
154. Leslie Tillett, *Wind on the Buffalo Grass: The Indians' Own Account of the Battle at the Little Big Horn River, & the Death of their life on the Plains* (New York: Thomas Y. Crowell Company, 1976), 54.
155. Marquis, *Wooden Leg*, 236.
156. Hammer, *Custer in '76*, 201, 202.
157. Hardorff, *Lakota Recollections*, 44.
158. Graham, *The Custer Myth*, 110.
159. Miller, "Echoes of the Little Bighorn," 38.
160. Graham, *The Custer Myth*, 110.
161. Hardorff, *Lakota Recollections*, 157.
162. Ibid., 32.
163. Ralph Heinz, "Bigelow Neal and Dr. Porter," in *Custer and His Times: Book Four*, ed. John B. Hart (Dexter, MI: Thomson-Shore, Inc., Little Big Horn Associates, Inc., 2002), 228. Porter thought that George Armstrong Custer had shot himself. As the wound was in his left temple and he was right-handed, I believe otherwise.
164. Hammer, *Custer in '76*, 237.
165. Marquis, *Wooden Leg*, 240.
166. Hardorff, *Lakota Recollections*, 44.
167. Tillett, *Wind on the Buffalo Grass*, 81, 82.

Chapter 2

1. Custer's Orders dated July 2, 1876.
2. Dispatch of June 21, 1876, Terry to General Sheridan.
3. Custer's Orders.
4. Custer to the *New York Herald*, June 21, 1876.
5. Kellogg to the *New York Herald*, June 21, 1876, in Colonel W. A. Graham, *The Custer Myth: A Source Book of Custeriana* (Lincoln, NB: University of Nebraska Press, 1986), 233, 234.
6. John S. Gray, *Centennial Campaign: The Sioux War of 1876* (Norman, OK and London: University of Oklahoma Press, 1976), 161.
7. Charles F. Roe, *Custer's Last Battle on the Little Big Horn, Montana Territory, June 25, 1876, March Of The Montana Column down the Yellowstone River and through the Big Horn Region* (New York: Robert Bruce, 1927), 4.

8. Barry C. Johnson, "George Herendeen: The Life of a Montana Scout," in *More Sidelights of the Sioux Wars*, eds. Barry C. Johnson and Francis B. Taunton (London: Westerners Publications Ltd., 2004), Herendeen's interview with Walter Camp in 1909.
9. Attributed.

Chapter 3

1. "Henry Porter's Story of the Battle: A 7th Cavalry survivor's account of the Battle of the Little Bighorn," The Astonisher, accessed August 11, 2025, https://www.astonisher.com/archives/museum/hr_porter_little_big_horn.html.
2. Cong. Globe, 42nd Cong., 3d Sess. Report in House Executive Documents, No. 1, Part 2, (1872).
3. John S. Gray, *Centennial Campaign: The Sioux War of 1876* (Norman, OK and London: University of Oklahoma Press, 1976) 75–76.
4. Ibid., 90.
5. Report in House Executive Documents, No. 1, Part 2.

Chapter 4

1. "Report of Lt. George D. Wallace, January 1877" in *General Custer and the Battle of the Little Big Horn: The Federal View*, ed. John M. Carroll (New Brunswick, NJ: The Garry Owen Press, 1976), 65.
2. George B. Herendeen, "Letter of January 4, 1878 to the New York Herald" in Gordon Harper, *The Fights on the Little Horn: 50 Years of Research into Custer's Last Stand* (Havertown, PA and Oxford: Casemate Publishers, 2014), ebook.
3. Hairy Moccasin, "The Teepee Book Narrative June 1916," in Gordon Harper, *The Fights on the Little Horn: 50 Years of Research into Custer's Last Stand* (Havertown, PA and Oxford: Casemate Publishers, 2014), ebook.
4. Second Lieutenant Charles A. Varnum, "Undated Second (Unfinished) Narrative," in Gordon Harper, *The Fights on the Little Horn: 50 Years of Research into Custer's Last Stand* (Havertown, PA and Oxford: Casemate Publishers, 2014), ebook.
5. Trumpeter John Martin, "Interview given to the *Cavalry Journal*, in July 1923" in Gordon Harper, *The Fights on the Little Horn: 50 Years of Research into Custer's Last Stand* (Havertown, PA and Oxford: Casemate Publishers, 2014), ebook.
6. Hairy Moccasin, "The Teepee Book Narrative June 1916," in Gordon Harper, *The Fights on the Little Horn: 50 Years of Research into Custer's Last Stand* (Havertown, PA and Oxford: Casemate Publishers, 2014), ebook.
7. White Man Runs Him, "Interview with General Hugh L. Scott in 1919," in Gordon Harper, *The Fights on the Little Horn: 50 Years of Research into Custer's Last Stand* (Havertown, PA and Oxford: Casemate Publishers, 2014), ebook.

Chapter 5

1. Franklin D. Roosevelt, Radio Address to the *New York Herald Tribune* Forum. Online by Gerhard Peters and John T. Woolley, The American Presidency Project, accessed August 12, 2025, https://www.presidency.ucsb.edu/node/210184.
2. Colonel Robert P. Hughes, "The Campaign Against the Sioux in 1876," Journal of the Military Service Institute of the United States in W. A. Graham, *The Story of the Little Big Horn: Custer's Last Fight* (Harrisburg, PA: The Stackpole Company, 1959).

3. Ibid., 28.
4. Brigadier General Alfred H. Terry, "July 2 Report" in Roger Darling, *A Sad and Terrible Blunder* (Vienna, VA: Potomac Western Press, 1990), 255.
5. Hughes in Graham, *The Story of the Little Big Horn*, 35.
6. Darling, *Blunder*, 73.
7. Ibid., 67.
8. Hughes in Graham, *The Story of the Little Big Horn*, 36.
9. John S. Gray, *Centennial Campaign: The Sioux War of 1876* (Norman, OK and London: University of Oklahoma Press, 1976), 146.
10. Francis B. Taunton, *"Sufficient Reason?": An Examination of Terry's Celebrated Order to Custer* (London: The English Westerners' Society, 1977), 24.
11. Gray, *Centennial Campaign*, 145.
12. Lieutenant James H. Bradley, *The March of the Montana Column* (Norman, OK: University of Oklahoma Press, 1961), 143.
13. Lieutenant Edward J. McClernand, March of the "Montana Column" in Charles F. Bates, Charles F. Roe, Edward J. McClernand, George D. Wallace, Charles King, et al. *Custer Engages the Hostiles* (Fort Collins, CO: The Old Army Press, n.d.), 25.
14. Bradley, *March*, 145.
15. Lieutenant Edward S. Godfrey, *Diary of the Little Big Horn*, 8.
16. Bradley, *March*, 141.
17. Darling, *Blunder*, 67.
18. Colonel John Gibbon, *Gibbon on the Sioux Campaign of 1876* (Bellevue, NE: The Old Army Press, 1970), 22.
19. James Willert, *Little Big Horn Diary: Chronicle of the 1876 Indian War* (La Miranda, CA, 1977), 221.
20. Ibid., 232.
21. The Field Diary of General A. H. Terry—June 23rd, 1876, 23.
22. Ibid.
23. Willert, *Diary*, 247.
24. Brisbin to Godfrey, 1892, in *Two Battles of the Little Big Horn*, ed. John M. Carroll (New York: Liveright, 1974), 147.
25. Terry, *Diary*, 23.
26. Ibid., 23, 24.
27. Darling, *Blunder*, 160.
28. Lieutenant Edward J. McClernand, *On Time for Disaster* (University of Nebraska Press, 1989), 47.
29. Darling, *Blunder*, 147.
30. Hughes in Graham, *The Story of the Little Big Horn*, 32.
31. Darling, *Blunder*, 73.
32. Hughes in Graham, *The Story of the Little Big Horn*, 28.
33. Barry C. Johnson, "Dr. Paulding and his Remarkable Diary," in *Sidelights of the Sioux Wars*, ed. Francis B. Taunton (The English Westerners' Society, 1967), 60.
34. Darling, *Blunder*, 252, 253.
35. Darling, *Blunder*, 260.
36. C. Lee Noyes, *An Officer's Perception of The Little Big Horn* (The English Westerners' Society, 1993), 4–7.
37. John M. Carroll, ed., *General Custer and the Battle of the Little Big Horn: The Federal View* (New Brunswick, NJ: Gary Owen Press, 1976), 27.
38. John M. Carroll, ed., *Two Battles of the Little Big Horn* (New York: Liveright, 1974), 147.

39. Ronald H. Nichols, ed., *Reno Court of Inquiry. Proceedings of a Court of Inquiry in the Case of Major Marcus A. Reno Concerning His Conduct at the Battle of the Little Big Horn River on June 25–26, 1876* (Hardin, MT: Custer Battlefield Historical & Museum Association, 1996), 181.

40. Colonel John Gibbon, *Gibbon on the Sioux Campaign of 1876* (Bellevue, NE: The Old Army Press, 1970), 22.

41. William Shakespeare, *Julius Caesar*, Act 3, Scene 2, line 76. The original says, "the good is oft interred with their bones."

Chapter 6

1. Colonel Robert P. Hughes, "The Campaign Against the Sioux in 1876" in Colonel W. A. Graham, *The Story of the Little Big Horn: Custer's Last Fight* (Harrisburg, PA: The Stackpole Company, 1959), 178ff (1).

2. Frederic C. Wagner III, *The Strategy of Defeat at the Little Big Horn* (Jefferson, NC: McFarland & Company, Inc., Publishers, 2014).

3. Loyd J. Overfield II, *The Little Big Horn, 1876* (Lincoln, NB: University of Nebraska Press, 1990), 24.

4. Hughes in Graham, *The Story of the Little Bighorn*, 178ff (3).

5. Overfield II, *The Little*, 23.

6. General Hugh L. Scott, interview on the battlefield in 1919, interpreted by Russell White Bear.

7. Wagner III, *Strategy of Defeat*, 193–94.

8. Hughes in Graham, *The Story of the Little Bighorn*, 178ff (29).

9. Overfield II, *The Little*, 24.

10. Wagner III, *Strategy of Defeat*, 193.

11. Department of Dakota, Letters Received, 1876, RG 98, NARA.

12. Wagner III, *Strategy of Defeat*, 191.

13. Brigadier General Alfred H. Terry, "July 2 Report" in Roger Darling, *A Sad and Terrible Blunder* (Vienna, VA: Potomac Western Press, 1990), 255.

14. Overfield II, *The Little*, 23.

15. Overfield II, *The Little*, 24.

16. Francis B. Taunton, *"Sufficient Reason?": An Examination of Terry's Celebrated Order to Custer* (London: The English Westerners' Society, 1977), 24.

17. Wagner III, *Strategy of Defeat*, 169.

Chapter 7

1. Loyd J. Overfield II, *The Little Big Horn, 1876* (Lincoln, NB: University of Nebraska Press, 1990), 36–38.

2. Lawrence A. Frost, *Custer Legends* (Madison, WI: Popular Press, 1981) 192.

3. E. C. Watkins, "Extract from Report of November 9, 1875" in John S. Gray, *Centennial Campaign: The Sioux War of 1876* (Norman, OK: University of Oklahoma Press, 1988), 29.

4. Zacharia Chandler to Secretary of War W. W. Belknap, December 3, 1875, in John S. Gray, *Centennial Campaign: The Sioux War of 1876* (Norman, OK: University of Oklahoma Press, 1988), 31.

5. Lieutenant General Philip H. Sheridan to the New York Herald, February 26, 1876 in John S. Gray, *Centennial Campaign: The Sioux War of 1876* (Norman, OK: University of Oklahoma Press, 1988), 44.

6. Colonel John Gibbon to General Terry, April 21, 1876, in John S. Gray, *Centennial Campaign: The Sioux War of 1876* (Norman, OK: University of Oklahoma Press, 1988), 74.

7. Brigadier General Alfred H. Terry to Lieutenant General Sheridan, Telegram of May 16, 1876, in John S. Gray, *Centennial Campaign: The Sioux War of 1876* (Norman, OK: University of Oklahoma Press, 1988), 90.

8. Sheridan, *Centennial*, 90.

9. Sheridan, *Centennial*, 94–95

10. First Lieutenant Edward S. Godfrey, *Century Magazine* article of 1892 reprinted in Konrad F. Schreier Jr., *Custer's Last Campaign* (Santa Monica, CA: Quail Ranch Books, 1981), 18.

11. Sheridan, *Centennial*, 90.

12. Terry, *Centennial*, 140.

13. Overfield II, *The Little*, 23–24.

14. Overfield II, *The Little*, 24.

15. Colonel Robert P. Hughes, "The Campaign Against the Sioux in 1876" in Colonel W. A. Graham, *The Story of the Little Big Horn: Custer's Last Fight* (Harrisburg, PA: The Stackpole Company, 1959), 178ff (1).

16. Hughes in Graham, *The Story of the Little Bighorn*, 178ff (28).

17. Frederic C. Wagner III, *The Strategy of Defeat at the Little Big Horn* (Jefferson, NC: McFarland & Company, Inc., Publishers, 2014), 40.

18. Captain E. S. Godfrey, 7th Cavalry, *Custer's Last Battle 1876* (Olympic Valley, CA: Outbooks, 1976. Reprinted from *Century Magazine*, January 1892), 17.

19. First Lieutenant Edward S. Godfrey in Cyrus T. Brady, *Indian Fights and Fighters* (Lincoln, NB: University of Nebraska Press, Bison Books, 1971), 379.

20. Joseph K. Dixon, *The Vanishing Race: The Last Great Indian Council* (New York: Dover Publications Inc., 2015), 162.

21. Major James S. Brisbin to Captain E. S. Godfrey, 1892 in John M. Carroll, *The Two Battles of the Little Big Horn* (New York: J. M. Carroll & Company, Bryan and Mattituck, 1974), 142.

22. George Herendeen to the *New York Herald*, January 4, 1878 in *More Sidelights of the Sioux Wars*, eds. Barry C. Johnson and Francis B. Taunton (London: Westerners Publications Ltd., 2004), 17.

23. First Lieutenant James H. Bradley, *The March of the Montana Column* (Norman, OK: University of Oklahoma Press, 1961), 149.

24. Bradley, *The March*, 149.

25. Gray, *Centennial Campaign*, 140.

26. Herendeen to the *New York Herald*, 1878 in *More Sidelights of the Sioux Wars*, eds. Barry C. Johnson and Francis B. Taunton (London: Westerners Publications Ltd., 2004),16.

27. Overfield II, *The Little*, 23.

28. Graham, *Little Big Horn*, 178ff (30).

29. Wagner III, *Strategy of Defeat*, 15.

30. Graham, *Little Big Horn*, 178ff.

31. Winfield S. Edgerly, *The Fights on the Little Horn: Unveiling the Mysteries of Custer's Last Stand* (Philadelphia, PA: Casemate Publishers, 2014), CN 2.10, ebook.

32. Second Lieutenant George D. Wallace, "Report of January 27, 1877" in *General Custer and the Battle of the Little Big Horn: The Federal View*, ed. John M. Carroll (New Brunswick, NJ: The Garry Owen Press, 1976), 65.

33. O. G. Libby, ed., *The Arikara Narrative of the Campaign Against the Hostile Dakotas June, 1876* (New York: Sol Lewis, 1973), 91–92.

34. Overfield II, *The Little*, 23.

35. Graham, *Little Big Horn*, 178ff (39).

36. Wagner III, *Strategy of Defeat*, 14.

37. Graham, *Little Big Horn*, 178ff (26).

38. Graham, *Little Big Horn*, 178ff (22).

39. Francis C. Holley, *Once Their Home, or, Our Legacy from the Dahkatahs: Historical, Biographical, and Incidental, From Far-off Days, Down to the Present* (Chicago, IL: Donahue & Henneberry, 1891), 262.

40. John S. Manion, *General Terry's Last Statement to Custer* (El Segundo, CA: Upton and Sons, Publishers, 2000), 61–62.

Chapter 8

1. "Obfuscate," Dictionary.com, accessed August 14, 2025, https://www.dictionary.com/browse/obfuscate.

2. Colonel W. A. Graham, comp., *The Custer Myth* (Harrisburg, PA: The Stackpole Company, 1953), 305.

3. Ibid., 308.

4. Ibid., 308.

5. Loyd J. Overfield II, comp., *The Little Big Horn 1876, The Official Communications etc.* (Lincoln, NB and London: University of Nebraska Press, 1971), 23.

6. Colonel W. A. Graham, *The Story of the Little Big Horn, Inc. The Campaign Against the Sioux* (Harrisburg, PA: The Stackpole Company, 1952), 32.

7. Colonel John Gibbon, *Gibbon on the Sioux Campaign of 1876* (Bellevue, NE: The Old Army Press, 1970), 22.

8. John M. Carroll, ed., *The Two Battles of the Little Big Horn* (Bryan & Mattituck, NY: J. M. Carroll & Company, 1974), 141.

9. Overfield II, *The Little*, 28.

10. John S. Gray, *Centennial Campaign: The Sioux War of 1876* (Norman, OK and London: University of Oklahoma Press, 1976), 135–36.

11. Ibid., 140.

12. Gordon Harper, *The Fights on the Little Horn: 50 Years of Research into Custer's Last Stand* (Havertown, PA and Oxford: Casemate Publishers, 2014), ebook.

13. Overfield II, *The Little*, 23.

14. Ibid., 24.

15. Colonel W. A. Graham, *The Story of the Little Big Horn, Inc. The Campaign Against the Sioux* (Harrisburg, PA: The Stackpole Company, 1952), 22.

16. Lieutenant James H. Bradley, *The March of the Montana Column* (Norman, OK: University of Oklahoma Press, 1961), 143.

17. Harper, *The Fights on the Little Horn*, ebook.

18. Overfield II, *The Little*, 24.

Chapter 9

1. Ronald H. Nichols, ed., *Reno Court of Inquiry. Proceedings of a Court of Inquiry in the Case of Major Marcus A. Reno Concerning His Conduct at the Battle of the Little Big Horn River on June 25–26, 1876* (Hardin, MT: Custer Battlefield Historical & Museum Association, 1996), 402, 427, 430.

2. O. G. Libby, ed., *The Arikara Narrative of the Campaign Against the Hostile Dakotas June, 1876* (New York: Sol Lewis, 1973), 90–91.

3. Colonel W. A. Graham, *The Custer Myth: A Source Book of Custeriana* (Lincoln, NB: University of Nebraska Press, 1986), 24–25.

4. Nichols, *Reno Court*, 431.

5. John M. Carroll, ed., *General Custer and the Battle of the Little Big Horn: The Federal View* (New Brunswick, NJ: Gary Owen Press, 1976), 102.

6. Graham, *Myth*, 295.

7. Ibid.

8. Barry C. Johnson, "George Herendeen: The Life of a Montana Scout," in *More Sidelights of the Sioux Wars*, eds. Barry C. Johnson and Francis B. Taunton (London: Westerners Publications Ltd., 2004), 18.

9. Nichols, *Reno Court*, 421, 427.

10. Ibid., 563, 580.

11. Graham, *Myth*, 138.

12. George M. Clark, ed., *Scalp Dance: The Edgerly Papers on the Battle of the Little Big Horn* (Oswego, NY: Heritage Press, 1985), 16.

13. Barry C. Johnson, "George Herendeen: The Life of a Montana Scout," in *More Sidelights of the Sioux Wars*, eds. Barry C. Johnson and Francis B. Taunton (London: Westerners Publications Ltd., 2004), 18.

14. Carroll, *Fed View*, 102.

15. Jay Smith, "What Did Not Happen at The Battle of the Little Big Horn," *Research Review: The Journal of the Little Big Horn* Associates 6, no. 2 (1992): 10.

16. Jay Smith, "The Indian Fighting Army," *Research Review: The Journal of the Little Big Horn* Associates 3, no. 1 (1989): 8.

17. Nichols, *Reno Court*, 332.

18. Ibid.

19. Clark, *Scalp*, 16–17.

20. John D. MacKintosh, *Custer's Southern Officer: Captain George D. Wallace 7th U.S. Cavalry* (Lexington, SC: Cloud Creek Press, 2002), 110–11.

21. *Lowell Weekly Journal*, August 1876.

22. Nichols, *Reno Court*, 235.

23. Ibid.

24. Ibid., 621.

25. Peter Thompson, annotated by Walt Cross, *Thompson's Narrative of the Little Big Horn* (Dire Wolf Books, 2008), 30–31.

26. Graham, *Myth*, 248.

27. Nichols, *Reno Court*, 591.

28. Ibid., 561.

29. Carroll, *Fed View*, 102.

30. Nichols, *Reno Court*, 592–93.

31. Nichols, *Reno Court*, 403.

32. Nichols, *Reno Court*, 421.

33. Nichols, *Reno Court*, 421, 422.

34. Nichols, *Reno Court*, 431.

35. Ibid., 404, 431.

36. Carroll, *Fed View*, 102.

37. Nichols, *Reno Court*, 560.

38. Carroll, *Fed View*, 105.

39. Lieutenant Gibson to his wife, July 4, 1876, in Katherine Gibson Fougera, *With Custer's Cavalry* (Caldwell, ID: The Caxton Printers, Ltd., 1940), 268.

40. Captain Benteen to his wife, July 2, 1876, in *The Benteen-Goldin Letters on Custer and His Last Battle*, ed. John M. Carroll (Bison Books, 1991), 147.

41. Captain Benteen to his wife, July 4, 1876, in *The Benteen-Goldin Letters on Custer and His Last Battle*, ed. John M. Carroll (Bison Books, 1991), 154.

42. E. A. Brininstool, *Troopers with Custer: Historic Incidents of the Battle of the Little Bighorn* (Big Byte Books, 2016), 77.

43. Fougera, *Cavalry*, 268.

44. Lieutenant Gibson to General Godfrey, August 8, 1908, in W. A. Graham, *The Story of the Little Big Horn: Custer's Last Fight* (Harrisburg, PA: The Stackpole Company, 1959), 131.

45. Hammer, *Custer in '76*, 80.

46. Graham, *Myth*, 295.

47. Nichols, *Reno Court*, 432.

48. Graham, *Myth*, 249.

49. Hammer, *Custer in '76*, 93n7.

50. Hammer, *Custer in '76*, 93n11.

51. Nichols, *Reno Court*, 390.

52. Ibid., 435.

53. Ibid., 430.

54. Hammer, *Custer in '76*, 93n11, 101.

55. Carroll, *Fed View*, 105.

56. Nichols, *Reno Court*, 433.

Chapter 10

1. Marguerite Merington, ed., *The Custer Story: The Life and Intimate Letters of General George A. Custer and His Wife Elizabeth* (Lincoln, NB: University of Nebraska Press, 1987), 277.

2. John S. Gray, *Centennial Campaign: The Sioux War of 1876* (University of Oklahoma Press, 1976), 41.

3. Ibid., 68.

4. Ibid., 69.

5. Jeffry D. Wert, *Custer: The Controversial Life of George Armstrong Custer* (Simon & Schuster, 1996), 327.

6. Captain E. S. Godfrey, *Custer's Last Battle 1876* (Olympic Valley, CA: Outbooks, 1976, reprinted from *The Century Magazine*, January 1892), 19.

Chapter 11

1. O. G. Libby, ed., *The Arikara Narrative of the Campaign Against the Hostile Dakotas June, 1876* (New York: Sol Lewis, 1973), 58.

2. John Hollon, "The Lessons of Custer: Five Things to Consider on 'Bad Management Day,'" ERE online, June 25, 2015, accessed August 15, 2025, https://www.ere.net/articles/the-lessons-of-custer-5-things-to-consider-on-bad-management-day.

3. Gray, *Centennial Campaign*, 154.

4. Gray, *Centennial Campaign*, 90.

5. Hollon, "Lessons."

6. Kenneth Hammer, ed., *Custer in '76: Walter Camp's Notes on the Custer Fight* (Provo, UT: Brigham Young University Press, 1976), 64.

7. Major Marcus A. Reno, statement to the *New York Herald*, August 8, 1876.

8. Reno, *New York Herald*.

9. Ronald H. Nichols, ed., *Reno Court of Inquiry. Proceedings of a Court of Inquiry in the Case of Major Marcus A. Reno Concerning His Conduct at the Battle of the Little Big Horn River on*

June 25–26, 1876 (Hardin, MT: Custer Battlefield Historical & Museum Association Inc., 1996), 561.

10. Nichols, *Reno Court*, 421.
11. Jay Smith, "The Indian Fighting Army," *Research Review: The Journal of the Little Big Horn Associates* 3, no. 1 (1989): 2.
12. Smith, "Indian Fighting," 16.
13. Ibid.
14. Ibid.
15. Major Marcus A. Reno, Report of July 5, 1876, Camp on the Yellowstone.
16. Libby, *The Arikara Narrative*, 173.
17. Hammer, *Custer in '76*, 106.
18. Hammer, *Custer in '76*, 112.
19. Hammer, *Custer in '76*, 133.
20. Nichols, *Reno Court*, 563.
21. Nichols, *Reno Court*, 561–62.
22. Nichols, *Reno Court*, 562.
23. Nichols, *Reno Court*, 87.
24. Mark V. Hoyt, "The U.S. Army's Sioux Campaign of 1876: Identifying the Horse as the Center of Gravity of the Sioux," Master's Thesis (Fort Leavenworth, KS: Army Command and General Staff College, 2003), https://apps.dtic.mil/sti/citations/ADA416928.
25. Hoyt, "Sioux Campaign."
26. Lieutenant General P. H. Sheridan, "Annual Report 1876," in *General Custer and the Battle of the Little Big Horn: The Federal View*, ed. John M. Carroll (New Brunswick, NJ: The Garry Owen Press, 1976), 78–79.
27. Hoyt, "Sioux Campaign."
28. Thomas B. Marquis, interpreter, *Wooden Leg, A Warrior Who Fought Custer* (Lincoln, NB: University of Nebraska Press, 1931), 214.

Chapter 12

1. Thomas B. Marquis, interpreter, *Wooden Leg: A Warrior who fought Custer* (Lincoln, NB: University of Nebraska Press, 1971), 210.
2. Ibid.
3. Ibid.
4. Custer Battlefield Historical and Museum Association, June 25, 2004 Symposium booklet (Hardin, MT: Custer Battlefield Historical & Museum Association, 2005), 10–11.
5. W. A. Graham, *The Custer Myth* (Harrisburg, PA: The Stackpole Company, 1953), 98.
6. Richard G. Hardorff, ed., *Lakota Recollections of the Custer Fight* (Spokane, WA: The Arthur H. Clark Company, 1991), 79.
7. *Helena Independent*, October 15, 1915.
8. George Bird Grinnell, *The Fighting Cheyenne* (Norman, OK: University of Oklahoma Press, 1983), 356.
9. Graham, *Myth*, 300.
10. Ronald H. Nichols, ed., *Reno Court of Inquiry. Proceedings of a Court of Inquiry in the Case of Major Marcus A. Reno Concerning His Conduct at the Battle of the Little Big Horn River on June 25–26, 1876* (Hardin, MT: Custer Battlefield Historical & Museum Association, 1996), 411.
11. Nichols, *Reno Court*, 321.
12. Nichols, *Reno Court*, 494.
13. Nichols, *Reno Court*, 297.

14. Nichols, *Reno Court*, 238.

15. Graham, *Myth*, 229, quoting from Reno's statement to the *New York Herald*.

16. George M. Clark, ed., *Scalp Dance: The Edgerly Papers on the Battle of the Little Big Horn* (Oswego, NY: Heritage Press, 1985), 70.

17. Graham, *Myth*, 271.

18. Frazier Hunt and Robert Hunt, *I Fought With Custer* (New York: Charles Scribner's Sons, 1953) 91–92.

19. Graham, *Myth*, 260.

20. Nichols, *Reno Court*, 262.

21. Kinglsey M. Bray, "Teton Sioux: Population History, 1655–1881," *Nebraska History* 75 (1994): 165–188.

Chapter 13

1. Eugene Buechel and Paul Manhart, *Lakota Dictionary* (Lincoln, NB: University of Nebraska Press, 2002), 193.

2. Frederick C. Wagner III, *Participants in the Battle of the Little Bighorn* (Jefferson, NC: McFarland & Company, 2011), 186.

3. Gordon Harper, *Fights on the Little Horn* (Havertown, PA: Casemate Publishers, 2014), ebook appendices.

4. Richard G. Hardorff, ed., *Camp, Custer, and the Little Bighorn* (El Segundo, CA: Upton and Sons, Publishers, 1997), 89.

5. Kenneth Hammer, ed., *Custer in '76* (Provo, UT: Brigham Young University Press, 1976), 209.

6. Wagner III, *Participants*, 144.

7. Ephriam D. Dickson III, Miniconjou/Mnikojou Message Board, Touch The Clouds sub-thread, 2009, accessed August 15, 2025, https://amertribes.proboards.com/thread/776/touch-cloud.

8. Ephriam D. Dickson III, Touch The Clouds Miniconjou Lakota feature thread, www.American-Tribes.com.

9. Brock, Miniconjou/Mnikojou Message Board, Touch The Clouds sub-thread, 2009, accessed August 15, 2025, https://amertribes.proboards.com/thread/776/touch-cloud.

10. Harper, *Fights on the Little Horn*, ebook appendices.

11. Ibid.

12. ladonna Expert!, Gall thread, www.American-Tribes.com.

13. Robert W. Larson, "The Warrior Gall" *Greasy Grass* 23 (May 2007): 18.

14. Ibid.

15. Ibid.

16. Robert W. Larson, "A Victor in Defeat, Chief Gall's Life on the Standing Rock Reservation," *Prologue Magazine* 40, no. 3 (Fall 2008): 1.

17. Larson, "Warrior Gall," 21.

18. Ibid.

19. Ibid.

20. Raymond J. De Mallie, ed., *The Sixth Grandfather: Black Elk's Teachings Given to John G. Neihardt*, (Lincoln, NB: University of Nebraska Press, 1985), 182.

21. "Crow King's Story, given on 30 July 1881 at Fort Yates, Dakota Territory," *Leavenworth Weekly Times*, August 18, 1881.

22. Ibid.

23. James McLaughlin, *My Friend the Indian* (Boston and New York: Houghton Mifflin Company, 1910), 121.

24. Ibid., 141.

25. Richard G. Hardorff, ed., *Lakota Recollections of the Custer Fight* (Spokane, WA: The Arthur H. Clark Company, 1991), 39.
26. Ibid., 47.
27. Ibid., 48.
28. Ibid., 68, 69.
29. Ibid., 151.
30. Ibid., 161.
31. Ibid., 172.
32. Richard G. Hardorff, ed., *Indian Views of the Custer Fight* (Spokane, WA: The Arthur H. Clark Company, 2004), 90.
33. Ibid., 130.
34. Ibid., 148.
35. Ibid., 153.
36. Richard G. Hardorff, ed., *Cheyenne Memories of the Custer Fight*, (Spokane, WA: The Arthur H. Clark Company, 1995), 102.
37. Ibid., 110.
38. Ibid., 118–19.
39. Ibid., 125.
40. Ibid., 156.
41. Ibid., 167.
42. Jerome A. Greene, ed., *Lakota and Cheyenne* (Norman, OK: University of Oklahoma Press, 1994), 54.
43. Gall's account at the 10th anniversary of the Little Bighorn Battle, 1886.
44. Colonel W. A. Graham, *The Custer Myth: The Story of Chief Gall* (Harrisburg, PA: The Stackpole Company, 1953), 90.

Chapter 14

1. Lieutenant James H. Bradley, *The March of the Montana Column* (Norman, OK: University of Oklahoma Press, 1961), 141.
2. Colonel John Gibbon, *Gibbon on the Sioux Campaign of 1876* (Bellevue, NE: The Old Army Press, 1970), 21.
3. John S. Gray, *Centennial Campaign: The Sioux War of 1876* (Norman, OK: University of Oklahoma Press, 1976) 135–36.
4. Bradley, *March*, 142.
5. John S. Gray, *Custer's Last Campaign* (Lincoln, NB: University of Nebraska Press, 1991), 189.
6. Bradley, *March*, 143.
7. Gray, *Centennial*, 135.
8. Bradley, *March*, 142.
9. Thomas B. Marquis, interpreter, *Wooden Leg Warrior Who Fought Custer* (Lincoln, NB: University of Nebraska Press, 1967), 188.
10. Ibid., 188.
11. Ibid., 187.
12. Ibid., 189.
13. Second Lieutenant Charles A. Varnum, "Second Narrative (Unfinished)," in Gordon Harper, *The Fights on the Little Horn: 50 Years of Research into Custer's Last Stand* (Havertown, PA and Oxford: Casemate Publishers, 2014), ebook.
14. First Lieutenant Edward S. Godfrey, *Field Diary* (Portland, OR: The Champoeg Press, 1957), 9.

Chapter 15

1. From a 1917 manuscript published by Viking in 1996. Reproduced on the Astonisher website, https://astonisher.com/.
2. From a battlefield interview with David Humphreys Miller in 1937. Reproduced on the Astonisher website, https://astonisher.com/.
3. John F. Finerty, *War Path and Bivouac* (Norman, OK: University of Oklahoma Press, 1961), 138.
4. Richard G. Hardorff, ed., *Lakota Recollections of the Custer Fight* (Spokane, WA: The Arthur H. Clark Company, 1991), 167.
5. Michael N. Donahue, *Drawing Battle Lines, The Map Testimony of Custer's Last Fight* (El Segundo, CA: Upton and Sons, Publishers, 2008), 236.
6. W. A. Graham, *The Custer Myth* (Harrisburg, PA: The Stackpole Company, 1953), 75.
7. Richard G. Hardorff, ed., *Lakota Recollections*, 95.

Chapter 16

1. "Custer's Last Flag: The Culbertson Guidon from The Battle of The Little Bighorn/Lot 5001," Sotheby's Catalog, accessed September 8, 2025, https://www.sothebys.com/en/auctions/ecatalogue/2010/custer39s-last-flag-the-culbertson-guidon-from-the-battle-of-the-little-big-horn-n08705/lot.5001.html
2. George F. Kush, "There Lies Foley of C!," unpublished article, 2010.
3. Richard G. Hardorff (annotator), *Walter M. Camp's Little Bighorn Rosters* (Spokane, WA: The Arthur H. Clark Company, 2002), 61.
4. Hardorff, *Rosters*, 63.
5. Kenneth Hammer, ed., *Custer in '76: Walter Camp's Notes on the Custer Fight* (Provo, UT: Brigham Young University Press, 1976), 111.
6. Kush, "There Lies Foley of C!," 2010.
7. Hardorff, *Rosters*, 93.
8. "Walter Mason Camp interview with Michael C. Caddle," MSS 57, Walter Mason Camp papers, L. Tom Perry Special Collections, Harold B. Lee Library; Brigham Young University; Provo, UT, accessed September 29, 2025, https://contentdm.lib.byu.edu/digital/collection/p15999coll31/id/48770.
9. John M. Carroll, ed., *General Custer and the Battle of the Little Big Horn: The Federal View* (New Brunswick, NJ: Gary Owen Press, 1976), 67.
10. Thomas B. Marquis, *Rain-in-the-Face and Curly, the Crow* pamphlet (Scottsdale, AZ: Cactus Pony, Box 973, 1934), 4.
11. W. A. Graham, *The Story of the Little Big Horn: Custer's Last Fight* (Harrisburg, PA: The Stackpole Company, 1959), section 2, 18.
12. Richard G. Hardorff, ed., *Camp, Custer, and the Little Bighorn* (El Segundo, CA: Upton and Sons, Publishers, 1997), 107.
13. Hardorff, *Rosters*, 61.
14. Hammer, *Custer in '76*, xi–xii.
15. Hardorff, *Rosters*, 61, 63.
16. Hammer, *Custer in '76*, 111–17.
17. Richard G. Hardorff, *On the Little Bighorn with Walter Camp: A Collection of W. M. Camp's Letters, Notes and Opinions on Custer's Last Fight* (El Segundo, CA: Upton and Sons, Publishers, 2002), 40.
18. Hardorff, *On the Little Bighorn*, 15, 61, 66–69, 107.

List of Articles

Further Reading

Bradley, James H. *The March of The Montana Column: A Prelude to the Custer Disaster*, Edited by Edgar I. Stewart. University of Oklahoma Press, 1961.

Carroll, John M., ed. *The Two Battles of the Little Big Horn*. J. M. Carroll & Company, Bryan and Mattituck, 1974.

Darling, Roger. *A Sad and Terrible Blunder, Generals Terry and Custer at the Little Big Horn: New Discoveries*. Potomac-Western Press, 1990.

Gibbon, John. *Gibbon on the Sioux Campaign of 1876*. The Old Army Press, 1970.

Godfrey, Edward S., ed. *Custer's Last Battle with Comments by General James B. Fry*. Vista Books, Viking Press, 1965.

Graham, W. A., ed. *The Custer Myth: A Source Book of Custeriana*. The Stackpole Company, 1953.

Gray, John S. *Centennial Campaign: The Sioux War of 1876*. University of Oklahoma Press, 1976.

Hardorff, Richard G., ed. *Cheyenne Memories of the Custer Fight*. The Arthur H. Clark Company, 1995.

Hardorff, Richard G., ed. *Indian Views of the Custer Fight*. The Arthur H. Clark Company, 2004.

Hardorff, Richard G., ed. *Lakota Recollections of the Custer Fight*. The Arthur H. Clark Company, 1991.

Marquis, Thomas B., interpreter. *Wooden Leg: A Warrior Who Fought Custer*. University of Nebraska Press, 2003.

Nichols, Ronald H., ed. *Reno Court of Inquiry, Proceedings of a Court of Inquiry in the case of Major Marcus A. Reno. Concerning His Conduct at the Battle of the Little Big Horn River on June 25–26, 1876*. Custer Battlefield Historical & Museum Association, Inc., 1996.

Overfield II, Lloyd J., ed. *The Little Big Horn 1876, The Official Communications, Documents and Reports with Rosters of the Officers and Troops of the Campaign*. University of Nebraska Press, 1971.

Terry, Alfred H. *The Field Diary of General Alfred H. Terry. The Yellowstone Expedition—1876*, 2nd ed. The Old Army Press, 1970.